Photoshop Elements 2024

Beginner's Guide

Complete Beginner to Expert Guide to Mastering the Latest Tools and Techniques & Creating Stunning Visuals

Quentin Fox

Copyright © 2024 **Quentin Fox**

This book or parts thereof may not be reproduced in any form, stored in any retrieval system, or transmitted in any form by any means—electronic, mechanical, photocopy, recording, or otherwise—without prior written permission of the publisher, except as provided by United States of America copyright law and fair use.

Disclaimer and Terms of Use

The author and publisher of this book and the accompanying materials have used their best efforts in preparing this book. The author and publisher make no representation or warranties with respect to the accuracy, applicability, fitness, or completeness of the contents of this book. The information contained in this book is strictly for informational purposes. Therefore, if you wish to apply the ideas contained in this book, you are taking full responsibility for your actions.

Printed in the United States of America

TABLE OF CONTENTS

- TABLE OF CONTENTS III
- INTRODUCTION 1
- CHAPTER ONE 2
- NEW FEATURES IN ADOBE PHOTOSHOP ELEMENTS 2024 2
  - How much does it cost to get Photoshop Elements? 3
  - Photoshop Elements: What's New in the Version? 3
  - The Start Window and Organizer App 4
  - Adjusting Photos 7
    - Moving Pictures 9
    - Photo Reels 11
  - AI Artistic Style Transfer Effects 12
  - Advanced Tools 12
  - System requirements for Adobe Photoshop Elements 2024 on Windows and Mac 14
  - Window 14
    - Basic Requirement 14
  - Mac 14
    - Basic Requirement 14
  - How to Download and Install Adobe Photoshop Element 2024 15
  - Getting the Adobe Photoshop Elements 2023 15
  - Setting up Adobe Photoshop Element 2024 16
- CHAPTER TWO 18
- GETTING STARTED WITH IMAGE EDITING 18
  - Exploring the Home Screen 18
  - Opening the Photo Editor 21
    - Opening the Photo Editor in Photoshop Elements 2024 21
  - Carrying our Basic Edits in Elements' Quick Mode 22
    - Editing and making changes in Quick Edit Mode 23
  - Sharing a Photo 23
  - Photo Sharing Providers on Photoshop Elements 24
  - Sharing Photos on Photoshop Elements 25
    - Sharing photo files with the organizer 25
    - Sharing Photos with the Photo Editor 25
  - Revisiting Your Actions 26
  - Exploring the History panel 27
  - Reverting To a Previous State of an Image 27
    - Reverting to the Last Save 28
  - Erasing and Deleting States from The History panel 29
  - Getting a Helping Hand 30
    - The Help Menu 30
    - Tooltips 31

The Dialog Box Links *31*
Saving Files with Purpose *31*
The Save Command *32*
The Save As Command *32*
FILE FORMAT OPTIONS FOR SAVING FILES 33
How to Save a File in JPEG Format *34*
How to Save a File in Photoshop as a PDF *36*
How to Save a File in PNG Format *36*
Saving File in GIF format *37*
How to Save a File in TIFF Format *37*
How to Save a File in BMP Format *38*
FILE FORMAT COMPRESSION 39
WEB FILE SAVING 39

CHAPTER THREE 41

BASIC IMAGE EDITING CONCEPTS 41

MASTERING THE ART OF PIXELS 41
UNDERSTANDING RESOLUTION 41
Understanding Image Dimension *41*
Display the Image Resolution and Dimensions *42*
RESAMPLING TECHNIQUES 43
How to Resample an Image *43*
CHOOSING BETWEEN PRINT AND ON SCREEN RESOLUTIONS 44
GETTING FAMILIAR AND PROFICIENT WITH THE USE OF COLOR 44
CALIBRATING YOUR MONITOR 45
CHOOSING THE RIGHT COLOR SCHEME FOR YOUR WORKSPACE 46
UNDERSTANDING THE FUNCTIONS OF A PROFILE 47

CHAPTER FOUR 48

EXPLORING THE PHOTO EDITOR 48

DELVING FURTHER INTO PHOTO EDITOR WITH THE ADVANCED EDIT MODE 48
HOW TO OPEN THE IMAGE WINDOW 51
IDENTIFYING CONTEXTUAL MENUS 52
Choosing the right tools *53*
Using the Toolbox in the Quick Mode *53*
The Toolbox in the Advanced Mode *53*
Tool located in the View group of the Advanced Mode toolbox *54*
Tools in the Select Group of the Advanced Mode *54*
Tools within the Enhanced Group of the Advanced Mode Toolbox *56*
Tools located in the Draw group of the Advanced Mode *58*
Tools found in the Modify group of the Advanced Mode Toolbox *60*
CHOOSING FROM THE TOOL OPTIONS 61
USING THE PANELS 62
ADDITIONAL INFORMATION 63

- Working with the Photo Bin 63
  - Showing Different Views of the Same Image 63
- Getting Very Familiar with the Photo Bin Actions 64
- Exploring the Guided Mode 65
- Mastering the Editing Environment 66
  - Launching and navigating preferences in the photo editor 66
- Exploring all the Preference Panes thoroughly 66

CHAPTER FIVE 68

MOVING ALONG WITH THE ORGANIZER 68

- Sorting Images and Media on the Hard Drive 68
  - Adding pictures to the organizer 68
- Using the Element Downloader to Download Images from a Camera 69
- Working with the Media Browser 70
- Using the Scanner in the Organizer 70
  - Image Requirements for Scanning in Photoshop Elements 70
  - Importing Images Through the Use of the Scanner 71
- Exporting Images with your Mobile Devices 72
- Setting the Organizer Preferences 72

CHAPTER SIX 73

ORGANIZING YOUR PICTURES WITH ORGANIZER 73

- The Views Tabs in the Organizer 75
- Using Tags to Sort Images into Groups 76
- Creating and Viewing Tag 77
- Adding Icons to Tags 78
  - Custom Tags and their Uses 78
- Auto Curating Images 80
  - Auto Creation at Work 80
  - Adding New Events 81
  - Using Stars to Rate Images 81
  - Using Photo Albums 81
  - Creating an Album 81
- Creating an Album Category 82
- Browsing Through an Album of Photos 83
  - Deleting an Album 84
  - Removing an Image from an Album 85
  - Sorting Photos in an Album 85

CHAPTER SEVEN 87

VIEWING AND LOCATING YOUR IMAGES 87

- Cataloging a File 87
  - Creating a Catalog 87
  - Opening a Catalog 88

Using the Catalog	89
Backing up Your Catalog	90
Restoring a Catalog	91
BACKING UP YOUR PHOTOS AND FILES	92
Switching from one view to another	92
USING A SLIDE SHOW (MEMORIES) TO BROWSE THROUGH PAT	93
SEARCHING FOR PHOTOS	94
Using the Search Icon	94
Showing Recent Searches	95
LOOKING FOR UNTAGGED ITEMS	95
SEARCHING FOR CAPTIONS AND NOTES	96
Searching by History	97
Searching by Metadata	97
Searching Media Type	98
Searching by File Name	99
Searching for all missing files	99
Searching by All Version Set	99
Searching by All Stacks	99
Searching by Using Visual Searches	99
Searching for an Item with an Unspecified Date or Time	99

CHAPTER EIGHT 100

EDITING CAMERA IMAGES USING THE CAMERA EDITOR 100

WHAT IS THE CAMERA RAW EDITOR?	100
EXPLORING THE ATTRIBUTES OF RAW FILE FORMATS	101
Exploring the Camera Raw Editor Window	101
THE PANELS	103
ADJUST SHARPNESS IN-CAMERA RAW FILES	105
Minimizing Noise in Camera Raw Images	105
Adobe Camera Raw Profile	105
APPLYING PROFILE TO YOUR IMAGE	106
ADDING PROFILES TO FAVORITES	106
Creative Profiles for Raw and Non-Raw Photos	107
Creating Profiles for Raw Images	107

CHAPTER NINE 108

CREATING AND ADJUSTING SELECTIONS 108

DEFINING SELECTIONS	108
CRAFTING RECTANGULAR AND ELLIPTICAL SELECTIONS	108
MASTER THE ELLIPTICAL MARQUEE TOOL	109
USING THE MARQUEE TOOL	110
Mastering Selections Using the Lasso Tools	110
Mastering the Lasso Tool	111
Using the Polygonal Lasso Tool	112

Using the Magnetic Lasso Tool *112*
MASTERING THE MAGIC WAND 112
MASTERING THE SELECTION BRUSH TOOL 114
MASTERING THE QUICK SELECTION TOOL FOR PAINTING 115
MASTERING THE AUTO SELECTION TOOL 116
   Mastering the Refine Selection Brush Tool *116*
MASTERING THE COOKIE CUTTER TOOLS 118
   Mastering Eraser Tools *119*
ERASER TOOL 119
   Background Eraser Tool *119*
   Using the Magic Eraser Tool *120*
USING THE SELECT MENU 121
   Choosing to Select All or Deselect All *121*
   Reselecting a Selection *121*
   Reversing the Selection *121*
   Feathering a Selection *122*
   Saving and Loading Selection *122*
   Refining the Edges of a Selection *122*
MASTERING THE MODIFY COMMANDS 124

CHAPTER TEN 125

WORKING WITH LAYERS 125

RECOGNIZING LAYERS 125
OVERVIEW OF THE LAYER PANEL 125
MASTERING THE LAYER MENU 126
MASTERING VARIOUS TYPES OF LAYERS 127
   The Image Layers *127*
   Using the Adjustment Layer *128*
   The Fill Layers *129*
   The Shape Layer *129*
   Text Layers *130*
MASTERING THE FUNDAMENTALS OF WORKING WITH LAYERS 130
   Creating a New Layer *130*
USING LAYER VIA COPY AND LAYER VIA CUT 131
   Duplicating Layers *131*
DRAGGING AND DROPPING LAYERS 132
   Transforming Layer *132*
MASTERING THE LAYER MASK 133
   Applying a Layer Mask to an Image *133*
   Additional Functions for Layer Masks *133*
   Flattening the Layers *134*
   Merging the Layers *134*

CHAPTER ELEVEN 135

SIMPLE IMAGE MAKEOVER 135

CROPPING IMAGES 135
    Mastering the Crop Tool *135*
    Using Selection Borders for Cropping *136*
RECOMPOSING IMAGES 137
    Adjust any settings in the Tool Options. *137*
PRESENTING ONE-STEP AUTO FIXES 137
    Auto Smart Fix *138*
    Auto Smart Tone *138*
    Auto Level *139*
    Auto Contrast *139*
    Auto Haze Removal *140*
    Auto Color Correction *140*
    Auto Shake Reduction *140*
    Auto Sharpen *141*
    Auto Red-Eye Fix *141*

CHAPTER TWELVE 142
CORRECTING CONTRAST, COLOR, AND CLARITY 142

CHANGING COLORS 142
    Removing Colors Cast Automatically *142*
ADJUSTING LIGHTING 142
    Resolving Lighting Issues through Shadows and Highlights *142*
WORKING WITH THE LEVELS 144
ADJUSTING COLOR 145
    Removing Colors Cast Automatically *145*
ADJUSTMENTS MADE USING HUE AND SATURATION 146
ELIMINATING COLOR WITH REMOVE COLOR COMMAND 148
CHANGING COLORS THROUGH THE USE OF REPLACE COLOR 148
USING COLOR CURVES TO MAKE CORRECTIONS 150
CHANGING PEOPLE'S SKIN TONE 151
DEFRINGING LAYERS 152
ELIMINATING HAZE 153
CHANGING THE COLOR TEMPERATURE WITH A PHOTO FILTER 153
HOW TO CREATE A COLOR MAP 154
ADJUSTING CLARITY 154
ELIMINATION NOISE, ARTIFACTS, DUST, AND SCRATCH 155
BLURRING YOU IMAGE 156
SHARPENING FOR BETTER FOCUS 157
UNSHARP MASK 158
OPEN CLOSED EYES 159
COLORIZING A PHOTO 160
SMOOTHING SKIN 162
ADJUSTING FACIAL FEATURES 163
REDUCING SHAKE 163
MOVING PHOTOS 164

    Moving Elements 164
    Moving Overlays 165
    Working Intelligently with the Smart Brush Tools 167
        Smart Brush Tool *167*
    The Detail Smart Brush Tool 168

CHAPTER THIRTEEN 169

TIPS AND TRICKS ON PHOTOSHOP ELEMENTS 169

    Viewing an Image in Two Windows 169
    Saving your Selections with your Photos 169
    Resetting a Dialog Box without Closing It 171
    Changing the Ruler Unit of Measurement 171
    Having Access to Additional Dialog Box Options 172
    Viewing Additional Files in the Recently Edited List 172
    Creating Fin Pieces 173
        How to Create an Organizer Slideshow *173*
    How to Create a Photo Calendar 174
    How to Create a Greeting Card 175
    Working Tips 176
    How to Create a Photo Collage 177
        How to make a collage of photos *177*
        Choose a theme in the middle of the Photo Collage Window *177*
        Specify whether you want Elements to add your photos to the collage automatically *178*
        Click OK after you've made your choices. *178*
        Select a layout. *178*
        Adjust the images *178*
        Customize the collage *179*
        Complete the collage *179*
    Adjusting Photos and Frames 179
    How to Create a Photo Book 180
        How to Create a Photo Reel *181*
    How to Create a Quote Prints 182
        Print each item separately using your local printer *183*
        Print a Picture Package or Contact Sheet using your local printer *183*
        Print a Picture Package *183*
    How to Create a Video Story 184
        Create a Video Story *184*
    Effects Collage 185

CHAPTER FOURTEEN 186

SHARE YOUR PHOTOS AND VIDEOS 186

    Share your Photos via email 186
        Add recipients *186*
    Share your Photos on Flickr 187

  Share your Video on Vimeo 187
  Choose the videos that you would want to share. 187
  Share your Video on YouTube 188
TROUBLESHOOTING ELEMENTS 2024 188
  Problems with saving files 189
  Adjusting dates to accommodate a variety of time zones 189
  Finding files that have been lost or disconnected 190
  Restoring your catalog 191
LIQUIFY FILTER 191
  Resolution Problems: Adding Pixels 192
FREQUENTLY ASKED QUESTIONS 193
  Frequently Asked Questions Regarding Adobe Photoshop Elements 193
  What are Adobe Photoshop Elements? 193
  Which of Adobe Photoshop Elements' major features are the most advantageous? ... 193
  What are the main differences between Adobe Photoshop and Adobe Photoshop Elements? 194
  To what extent are Adobe Photoshop Elements suitable for usage in professional settings? 194
  What are Guided Edits in Adobe Photoshop Elements? 195
  When it comes to removing backgrounds from photos, is it possible to use Adobe Photoshop Elements? 195
  Which steps should I take to install Adobe Photoshop Elements? 195
  Does Adobe Photoshop Elements include apps for both Windows and Mac operating systems? 195
  To edit raw pictures, is it possible to use Adobe Photoshop Elements? 196
  What are some ways that I may study Adobe Photoshop Elements? 196
  Can I use plugins from third-party developers with Adobe Photoshop Elements? 196
  In Adobe Photoshop Elements, what are the steps I need to take to resize images? .. 196
  What are the capabilities of Adobe Photoshop Elements for creating panoramas? ... 197
  To what extent is it possible to produce picture slideshows using Adobe Photoshop Elements? 197
  Is it possible to immediately share the modified photos that I have created using Adobe Photoshop Elements? 198
  CONCLUSION 198
INDEX 198

INTRODUCTION

Adobe Photoshop Elements is a versatile graphic editing software developed by the Adobe software community, appealing to photographers, videographers, image editors, and graphic designers. It provides a wide range of tools for editing and creating images and videos, allowing users to easily organize, modify, and share their creations on platforms like Email, Flickr, Twitter, Vimeo, and YouTube. Originally targeting casual photographers when it was launched in April 2001, the software has expanded to include a wider range of digital capabilities. Adobe Photoshop Elements is offered as a one-time purchase, providing users with continuous access to its features. Adobe Photoshop Elements 2024 is the newest version of this well-known software, with improved features designed to enhance user experience. Released on October 19, 2023, this version provides user-friendly assistance for crafting engaging image compositions, effects, designs, and prints.

CHAPTER ONE
NEW FEATURES IN ADOBE PHOTOSHOP ELEMENTS 2024

Discover the latest features in the 2024 version of Adobe Photoshop Elements, enhanced for improved performance compared to previous versions. Let's delve into the new features driven by Adobe Sensei.

The features include the following:

- **Match Color and Tone:** One of the latest additions to Adobe Photoshop Element is the Match Color and Tone feature. Use this feature to choose colors and tones from preloaded options or your image library.
- **Create Stylized Text:** Design professional-looking text with the Add Text Guided Edit. Align your text horizontally, vertically, or on a path, selection, or shape. Use gradients, textures, and patterns to enhance the appearance of your text. To use this feature, navigate to your photos, select Basic, choose Guided Mode, and then click on Add Text. Here is a guide to help you choose from the available options.
- **Free Access to Adobe Stock**: Gain access to thousands of free Adobe Stock photos with this feature. Consider using the complimentary Adobe Stock photo to swap out your background image. You can also access Adobe Stock from the Quote Graphics. Access the File menu, select Search on Adobe Stock, and locate the desired image in the library
- **Quick Actions:** This feature enables you to easily make one-click edits to your images. This feature allows you to easily select backgrounds for editing, enhance photo sharpness by removing JPEG fragments, and quickly add color to old photos. To use this feature, open any of your photos and select the Quick Action panel in the Quick Mode

- **Photo Reels**: Photo Reels are a powerful feature included with Element 2024. With this feature, you can remarkably showcase your top photos. To access this feature, open your images, click on **Create**, and then select Photo Reel. At last, you have the option to choose a layout from the available size options.
- **Web and Mobile Companion Apps:** Photoshop Element 2024 includes a web and mobile app. easily makes quick edits and adjustments from your devices and uploads them to the Cloud. This web app enables you to design a slideshow, contemporary collages, and unique text patterns.

How much does it cost to get Photoshop Elements?

You have the option of purchasing Photoshop Elements on its own for $99.99, or you can get it in a package with Premiere Elements, which is a video editing companion, for $149.99. If you are upgrading from an earlier version, the cost is $79.99. There is a trial version available for thirty days. However, in contrast to Adobe's Photoshop and Lightroom, which begin at $9.99 per month, Elements does not need a membership to continue using it. One of the closest competitors, Corel PaintShop Pro, has a one-time pricing of $79.99 and includes many of the same functions that are available in Photoshop. Another comparable alternative is ACDSee Photo Studio, which can be purchased for a one-time price of $149.99 or an annual subscription fee of $89 that includes four more applications for video editing and other features. The one-time pricing of CyberLink PhotoDirector is the same as that of Photoshop Elements, which is $99.99. However, it is also available as a subscription for $54.99 a year, which includes a large number of effects and stock content. CyberLink PhotoDirector offers features that are found in both Lightroom and Photoshop.

Photoshop Elements: What's New in the Version?

Not only does the 2024 update provide new creative tools, but it also adds new capabilities for the companion mobile app and web browser-based beta versions of the software. The application already has a plethora of picture tools and effects, but the 2024 upgrade adds even more. Any kind of generative artificial intelligence (AI), such as the recently introduced Firefly image-creation features in Photoshop, is conspicuously absent from the list.

This is a list of some highlights:

- **One-click photo selection**: Adobe Sensei AI now allows users to pick the backdrop or sky of a photograph with just one click.
- **Interface update with dark mode:** The appearance of Photoshop Elements has remained mostly unchanged for more than a decade. With this version, the user interface has been updated, and a Dark mode has been added, which is a very welcome addition.
- **Match color:** To generate a style that you can then fine-tune using hue, saturation, and brightness adjustments, you may either use a preset or one of your photos before beginning the process.

- **Photo Reels:** It is possible to generate films from your photos of an event or trip with this tool, which allows you to add text, effects, and graphics. These videos are ideal for use on Instagram Stories or YouTube Reels.
- **Quick Actions**: New one-click adjustments, which take a page from Photoshop, allow users to blur or erase a backdrop, smooth skin, dehaze, colorize, and do a variety of other editing tasks.
- **JPEG artifact removal:** Compression in this popular picture file format can result in distortions that are not realistic. This brand-new instrument eliminates them.
- **Guided Edits and Content:** Guided Edits are one of Elements' defining characteristics and a reason to pick it over full-fledged Photoshop. These edits walk you through the process of producing popular effects and edits in a step-by-step manner. You can now add compelling text to photographs for social media postings thanks to the new Guided Edits feature. In the Replace Background feature, new backgrounds are added, fresh skies are added to the Perfect Landscape feature, and new patterns are added to the Pattern Brush Guided Edit feature. The creative Effect tool also allows you to create new creative styles for your artistic expression.
- **Adobe Stock**: Within Elements, you can search for and make use of stock pictures from Adobe's stock service.
- **New features have been added to both the mobile and online versions**: In the beta version of Elements for the web, the production of picture collages and slideshows is joined by the addition of peek-through and pattern overlays. Among the fundamental editing features that have been added to the beta version of the Elements mobile app are the capabilities to crop, rotate, transform, and adjust the aspect ratio of a picture.

Moving Photos, which is driven by artificial intelligence and transforms still images into animated GIFs, and the Perfect Landscapes Guided Edit, were both included in Elements before those revisions. Users of Adobe Creative Cloud's online storage service now can share their work across Elements and other Creative Cloud applications, such as Adobe Lightroom and official Photoshop. Additional upgrades that have been released over the last several years have gradually included more sophisticated enhancements and capabilities, which are often inherited from Photoshop itself. Subject Select, Automatic Colorization, Object Removal, one-click skin smoothing, pattern objects, and the incredible Open Closed Eyes capabilities are some of the most notable features among them.

The Start Window and Organizer App

Two utilities are connected to the primary picture editing application. These utilities are the Home screen and the Organizer, and you often go through these before accessing the real editor.

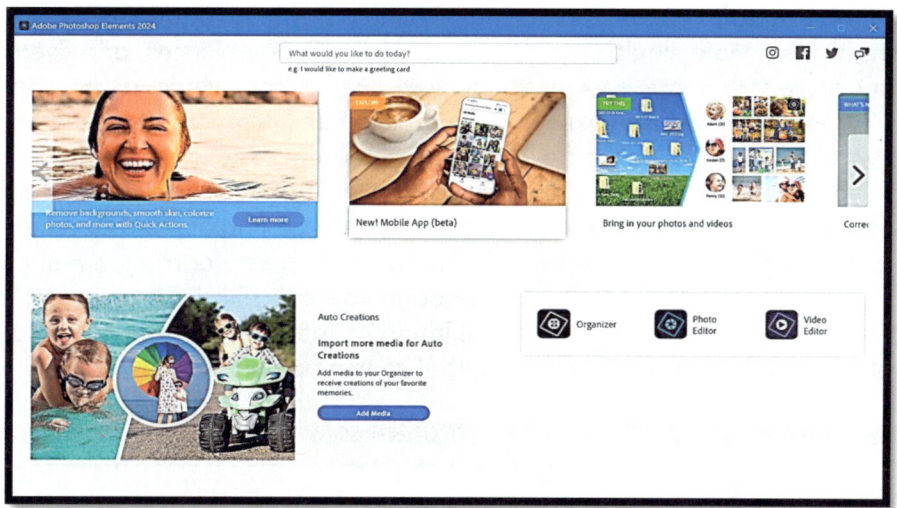

On top of serving as your entry point to both Photoshop Elements and Premiere Elements, the Start window also provides you with access to several tools that are incredibly helpful. This section provides you with hints on how to make use of new editing tools, links to the files you have worked on most recently, and Auto Creations, which are slide presentations and collages that the computer automatically creates based on the information you have uploaded.

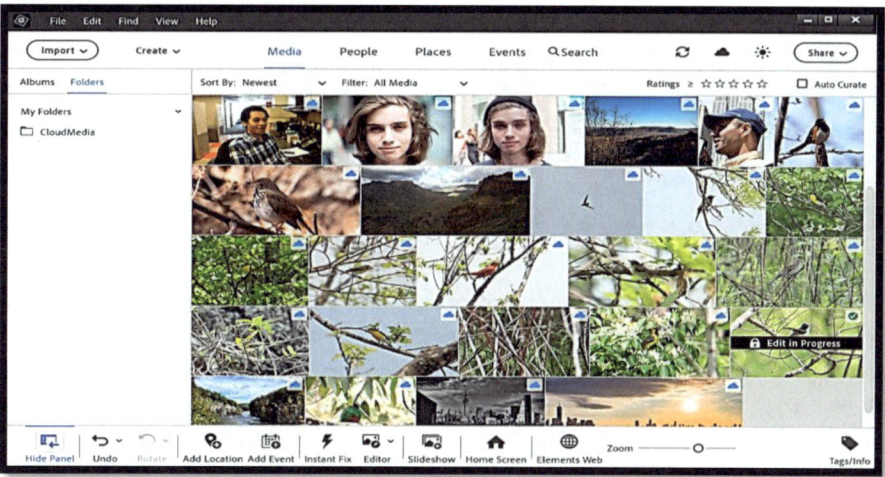

You can import, organize, tag, and export your images using the Organizer program, which is where the name of the application suggests it is. Although you are not required to use it, it has a great deal of features that would otherwise cause the primary editing program to become cluttered. The strong search, auto-curation, and sharing options that it offers may be helpful additions to the usual organizing tools that now exist. Corel PaintShop Pro and

ACDSee are two examples of competitors that eliminate the need for additional applications and perform all tasks via a single user interface. Media, People, Places, and Events are the four primary modes that are shown at the very top of the window that contains the Organizer. By the use of the Organizer search bar, you can filter material based on persons, places, keyword tags, types of media, dates, and folders. You also have the option of combining search criteria to reduce the results. Following in the footsteps of the AI and machine learning trend that we have seen in Flickr, Google Photos, and OneDrive, Smart Tags can automatically recognize what is included inside a photograph, whether it be an animal, a person, a scenery, or a flower. Although you can still do it yourself if you want more control, this cutting-edge technology eliminates the need for you to directly attach tags to photographs. However, you can still do it yourself otherwise.

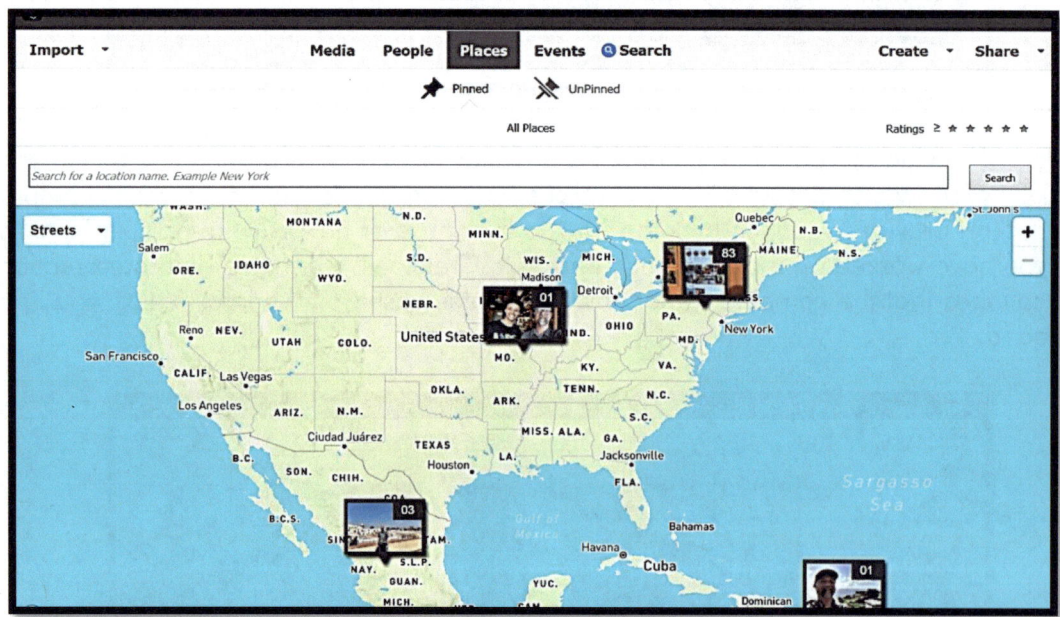

Organizer's Places mode displayed my position for images that were shot on a phone based on integrated GPS data; nevertheless, the Places part of the Search page informed me that there are no Places tags to search by; for anything to appear here, you will need to manually insert location tags. It may be quite frustrating when one section of a program has information that is not available in another section of the software. Our recommendation is for the built-in photo applications that come with Windows and macOS. These applications allow you to examine a little map in the Info panel while you are viewing a single shot. To do a search based on faces, you will first need to provide names in the People module. The software can recognize all faces and makes an attempt to match them to those that you have previously recognized; however, it is not completely accurate and may be deceived by side profiles or strange angles very often. Verifying the program's suggested pictures is a simple process that makes it simple to add photographs to a face tag.

The Auto Curate check box may be found just below the Share button. When there are fewer options available, the quality of the photographs that are shown is greater. Therefore, for instance, you can see what the computer considers to be your fifty greatest photographs or your one hundred finest photographs (ten is the minimum). The application searches for a variety of factors, including lighting, composition, focus, and even emotional effects, such as photographs of people hugging each other. It is not surprising that the majority of my findings involved human subjects, and the tool did bring to light several excellent photographs that we had overlooked. It is also possible to use Auto Curate for a search, which will allow you to locate, for instance, your most impressive photographs of cats or mountains. The Elements Organizer is equipped with no less than two cloud and syncing functions. For the mobile and web versions of Elements, which are both in beta, there is a cloud icon located in the upper right corner of the screen. This button allows you to synchronize your photographs and videos with Adobe's online storage service. To access the web address of Elements in your default browser, choose the button that is located on the rightmost side of the wide button row that is located at the bottom of the window. This button has the appearance of a globe.

Adjusting Photos

When moving from the Organizer to the full Editor software, Photoshop Elements truly comes into its own and becomes a powerful design tool. Although it does not have the same level of complexity as Photoshop, the tool has many of the high-end image modification features that Photoshop possesses. Adobe software is the only one that offers a significant number of tools, especially those that are content-aware and allow you to do tasks such as removing sections or objects without causing any disruption to the backdrop. In a significant way, the new Dark mode enhances the user interface. To facilitate the creation of slideshows, collages, reels, and other types of media, a new button labeled "**Create**" has been added next to the Open button. On the bottom-right toolbar, there is a new Quick Actions button that, when activated in Quick mode, allows you to access many of the most often required modifications, such as selecting the background, making color corrections, smoothing the skin, and removing the background.

At first glance, Elements Effects seems to be a squared version of Instagram, with capabilities that the mobile app just cannot compete with. Image analysis is used by the Smart Looks tool to choose an effect, and there are four different options available. Are three types of effects that you can choose from: Artistic, which are replicas of great painters driven by artificial intelligence; Classic, which includes Smart Looks, Tint, and Vintage; and the new Color Match, which is a feature that radically alters the colors of the picture, similar to LUTs? In the bottom panel, you will see four suggested crops when you choose the crop tool. These crops are based on the faces that were detected as well as other criteria. As a result of its amazing functionality, it frames group photographs and suggests innovative styles for landscapes. You can select conventional aspect ratios and even a target size in pixels using the crop tool, making it suited for a wide variety of professional use cases.

Filters, layers, actions (the ability to perform preset actions such as resizing and effects, rather than the capacity to create them), histograms, levels, and a large number of creative and visual effects are all included in the Expert mode, which provides you with capabilities that are comparable to those of Photoshop. As is the case with Photoshop, you will find a variety of tool buttons down the left side of the screen, and the files that you modify will be stored in the PSD format. For those who create websites, there is an option called "Save for Web," which optimizes (that is, minimizes the file size of) photographs for display on the internet. You have access to a wide variety of stuff, including backdrops, frames, and shapes that may be used to enhance the appearance of an image. Additionally, you can now get stock photographs from Adobe Stock, which can be accessed via the Search on Adobe Stock option accessed through the File menu. You can wrap text around a form using the Text tool, which ensures that it does not overrun any significant elements of a picture. On the other hand, the character-styling possibilities are somewhat less comprehensive than those found in Photoshop.

The Select Subject button is a simple button that shows at the bottom panel whenever you are using the selection brush. Additionally, it may be accessed using the Select function of the menu. All of the photographs, except for those with backgrounds that merged in with the subject by utilizing comparable colors, performed beautifully. When you pick Refine Edge, a second panel will show up. Within this panel, you will have the ability to alter the selection view (for instance, by using a red, white, or black backdrop), as well as use feathering and other sophisticated choices such as Decontaminate Colors, which eliminates color distortion from the selection. A separate Adobe Camera Raw (ACR) window is opened whenever a raw file is opened from a high-end mirrorless camera or a DSLR camera. This is because the software begins in a different window. Because it is a distinct plug-in, you will need to install it. Those individuals who will never make use of the space on their hard drive will benefit from this. Color, exposure, and detail adjustments are all accessible inside its window for your convenience. Not only does it include noise reduction, but it also includes Adobe's raw profiles, such as Color, Portrait, and Vivid. However, the Elements version of Adobe Creative Retouching does not have many of the features that are available in the Photoshop and Lightroom versions. These features include chromatic aberration correction, lens distortion correction, selection tools, and lens profile corrections. Red-eye removal and cropping are features that are included in the raw importer, which seems to be an unnecessary duplicate of what is available in the editing program.

Moving Pictures

Moving Elements, Moving Overlay, and Moving Photos are the three "Moving" tools that are now available in Photoshop Elements. These tools may be located at the bottom of the Enhance navigation menu. This is in addition to the newly added Photo Reel tool, which can be found in the Create menu. Without tools that are built expressly for animated GIFs, the process of creating them might be difficult. Moving Elements, which can be saved in either GIF or MP4 format, generates a highly special kind of animation in which the subject of the picture or the whole shot zooms, pans, rotates, or even flows. This animation may be saved in either format.

After selecting an area that may be animated based on logic, such as a sky or a river, you have the opportunity to further restrict your decision. Following that, you will need to click the arrow button and then drag the item that you have chosen in the direction that you want the motion to proceed. At long last, you can share your moving masterpiece with others by either downloading it as a GIF animation or an MP4 video clip by tapping the **Play arrow** that is located below the picture. To return to the Moving Pictures tool, there are eleven different movement options, each of which has a thumbnail that provides a glimpse of what it does for you. To apply them to your image, you need to double-click on one of them, which took around twenty seconds for some of the photos. The effect may be played by using a play arrow button, which is a conventional button.

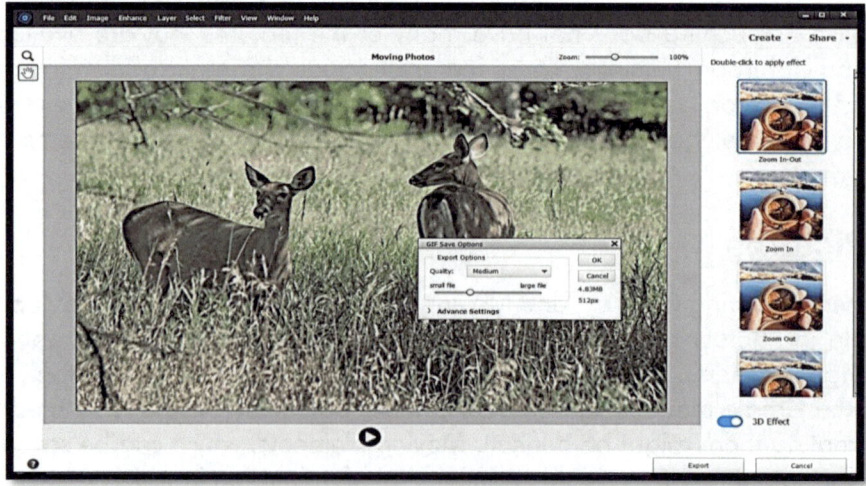

The 3D option is likely more stunning since it chooses the topic of the photograph and moves just that subject. It is not simply the subject of the photograph that moves when you turn off the 3D Effect slider; the whole photograph does so. It is still possible to get a nice 3D effect by selecting a photograph that does not have a distinct subject. This will give the impression that the camera is moving in a circle. Moving overlays, which include elements like snowflakes, hearts, and stars, add a touch of flair to your films that were originally photographed. Immediately above it, in the Enhance menu, there is a menu option that allows you to move photos. It is really easy to apply the effect, and you have a selection of 27 different sorts of overlay objects to choose from. You can superimpose frames and visuals, such as a flame or a balloon. A handy feature is the Protect Subject check box, which automatically recognizes a human or other picture subject and maintains it above the falling overlays. This option is available in the settings menu. A slider is used to adjust the degree of transparency of the overlay. These tools allow you to choose between a GIF or an MP4 as well as the dimensions of the exported file. Considering that one of the images we attempted to send was over 25 megabytes in size, which Facebook Messenger could not allow, this last choice is quite beneficial. With that being stated, it would be wonderful to have more choices when it comes to making the animation. Some examples of these possibilities include looping, refining the selection of what moves, and adjusting the distance of the motion.

Photo Reels

Online platforms such as Instagram, TikTok, YouTube, and Facebook have all contributed to the rise in popularity of short videos that resemble social memes and are vertical in orientation. This sort of material may now be easily created by non-professionals thanks to the new Photo Reels tools that are included in Photoshop Elements. Using the application, just open at least two photographs, go to the Create menu, and choose Photo Reel from the list of options. At the bottom of the page, you will find a timeline that contains all of your photos. After that, you choose a Layout, which includes options for Instagram, Facebook, TikTok, and other platforms. Additionally, you can modify the length of time that each picture is shown, as well as add text, effects (such as Vintage or Pastel), and visuals (such as birthday cakes and balloons). There is a restricted selection of visuals available; for instance, except for a basketball, there are no other types of sports balls available. You have the same two options for exporting as you did with the other motion pictures that were shown earlier: MP4 and GIF. Aside from the limited visuals, the tool is lacking in that it does not include any music or transitions. As a result, the reels that it generates do not compare to the greatest reels that you see on social video platforms. However, you are often able to choose background music when you are uploading your videos. Considering that most social applications allow you to do the majority of things with their built-in capabilities, Reels could be beneficial as a means to share a film with your friends that is compatible with smartphones.

AI Artistic Style Transfer Effects

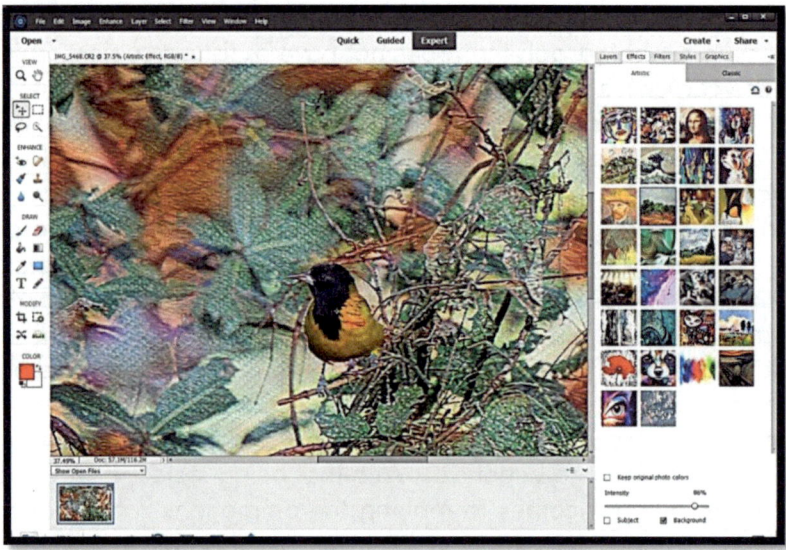

A tab on the Effects panel brings something to Photoshop Elements that has been available in other photo applications for a few years: artistic style transfers. These transfers make use of artificial intelligence to make your photo appear as though it was painted by Van Gogh or some other famous artist (instead of calling them things like Post-Impressionist). The software Elements presently contains thirty-five of these stylistic effects; but, unlike other applications, it does not identify the artists who created them. This is a decent assortment; in contrast, CyberLink PhotoDirector begins with eight options, but then it continues to add more options for subscribers or as additional purchases for those who do not have a subscription. The fact that this Elements feature allows you to change the intensity of the filter and tick a box if you want to maintain the colors of the original picture is something most people like, even though doing so takes away a lot of the allure of these filters. You can apply the effect solely to the subject (which is automatically chosen by Sensei AI) or only to the backdrop depending on the additional checkboxes that are located beneath the strength slider. In addition to these choices, PhotoDirector also can brush the effect on and off, as well as sliders for the brush option that control the feathering, size, and strength attributes.

Advanced Tools

A significant number of Photoshop effects require the exact selection of items, followed by the addition or removal of those objects from or inside a picture. Using the Auto Selection tool, you may choose an item by drawing a rectangle or shape over it, and the tool will then calculate the edges of the object using the shape or rectangle. The Quick Selection tool that was available before required you to write on the item that you wanted to choose.

My preference for Quick over Auto remains the same since it is more difficult to get the desired form size and location than it is to just scribble over the item. Both the Select Sky and Select Background buttons are brand-new additions to the selection tool for the year 2024. These buttons are shown whether you are using the Quick Selection tool in either the Quick or Advanced mode. You also have the option of accessing these using the Select menu system. There is a Refine Edge option available for each of the selection tools. This option makes use of a circle composed of inner and outer selection circumferences. Depending on whether you are within or outside of the initial selection, the tool will either add to or deduct from your selection. This is a brilliant feature that makes the tool so useful. If you move the tool such that it is hovering close over the edge, Photoshop Elements will automatically refine the selection for you. Adding those stray hairs to it is often included in this process.

The Photomerge Group Shot tool gives you the ability to choose the most flattering expression for each individual from a collection of group photographs. For instance, you can provide the eyes of one person's face to another person's face using another photo. Through the use of Scene Cleaner, you can eliminate people from a landscape or iconic location. By using two or more photographs, exposure, which is often referred to as high dynamic range (HDR), can improve the quality of photos by combining the most favorable version of, for example, the clouds in the sky from one photograph and the forest below from another one. You have a great deal of control over the Photomerge Panorama tool, which allows you to create a panorama that is complete rather than one that has twisted edges. In my testing, it even fills in empty regions left by the photographs and stitching, which resulted in an excellent appearance; nevertheless, it also takes a considerable amount of time to do its operation. That filling option is not available in any other program available to you. One such tool for improving photographs is called Smart Brushes, and it enables users to apply effects and modifications to certain regions of a photograph. These areas may include black and white, color, lighting, special effects, and creative treatments such as sketching. You can make the sky bluer or darken certain parts of a picture using these, which are a pretty neat and simple method to do it.

You can change a picture either manually or automatically to a selection of predefined forms, such as ovals, arcs, flags, and twists, with the help of warp tools, which have been a mainstay of Photoshop for quite some time. In conclusion, one of the tools that has been removed from Photoshop is the Shake Reduction button. It performs an automated sharpening process on photographs that you captured while gently shaking the camera. With this tool, you have the same level of flexibility as with the Photoshop tool, which allows you to choose the region that needs to be corrected.

System requirements for Adobe Photoshop Elements 2024 on Windows and Mac

Before downloading and installing Adobe Photoshop Element 2024, it's important to first check if your Windows or Mac system meets the requirements. It's important to note that the software now includes several new and advanced functions, so it's crucial to check if your Windows and Mac systems can support it. Knowing that the Adobe Photoshop Element Software application is not compatible with Windows 8 is crucial. **Below are the minimum system requirements for Photoshop Elements 2024 on Windows and Mac:**

Window

Basic Requirement

- Requires an Intel 6th Generation processor or newer, or an AMD equivalent with SSE4.1 support.
- Microsoft Windows 10 (version 22H2) or Windows 11 (version 22H2), 64-bit versions only; Windows 7, Windows 8.1 not supported
- 8 gigabytes of RAM
- Requires 8 GB of available hard-disk space for application installation, with extra space needed for downloading online content and temporary files during installation and use (not compatible with case-sensitive file systems or removable flash storage).
- Display resolution of 1280 x 800 (at 100% scale factor)
- Ensure your display driver is compatible with Microsoft DirectX 12.
- An Internet connection is necessary for product activation, downloading features, and accessing online content.

Mac

Basic Requirement

- 6th Generation Intel processor or newer; Apple silicon M1 processor or newer version
- macOS 12 and macOS 13 (version 13.4 or newer)
- 8 gigabytes of RAM

- Ensure you have at least 6 GB of hard-disc space available for installing the application. Additional space will be needed for downloading online content and temporary files during installation and usage. Note that the application cannot be installed on a volume using a case-sensitive file system or on removable flash storage devices.
- Display resolution of 1280 x 800 (at 100% scale factor)
- An Internet connection is necessary for product activation, downloading features, and accessing online content.

How to Download and Install Adobe Photoshop Element 2024

Once you have familiarized yourself with the minimal and recommended system requirements for downloading and installing Adobe Photoshop Elements, you can proceed with the download. **Before proceeding, carefully consider the following;**

1. Make sure you have the latest version of Internet Explorer, Firefox, Chrome, or Safari and administrative rights for your account.
2. You have disabled pop-up blockers in your web browser and temporarily deactivated firewalls, antivirus programs, and third-party security software. By following these steps, you can expedite the installation process.
3. You have administrative privileges for the account you are using.
4. Make sure you have a valid Adobe ID.
5. You possess a legitimate serial number for Photoshop Elements.
6. Connected to the internet to complete the installation.

Getting the Adobe Photoshop Elements 2023

Follow the steps provided to download Adobe Photoshop Elements

- Make sure to enter the URL link provided on your web browser page to download Adobe Photoshop Elements from the official website.
- Click on the **Download button** for Windows or Mac

For Windows	For macOS
Download 64-bit	**Download**
Languages: Czech, Dutch, English, French, German, Italian, Japanese, Polish, Spanish, and Swedish	Languages: English, French, German, and Japanese

15

Setting up Adobe Photoshop Element 2024

Once you have downloaded Photoshop Element on your computer, the next step is to proceed with the installation.

Here are the steps:

1. Begin by opening the Adobe Photoshop Element installer on your computer.
2. Sign in with your Adobe ID.
3. Proceed by clicking on **Continue** when the next screen appears.
4. When you get to the Installation Options screen, choose the **language and installation location**, then proceed by selecting **Continue**.

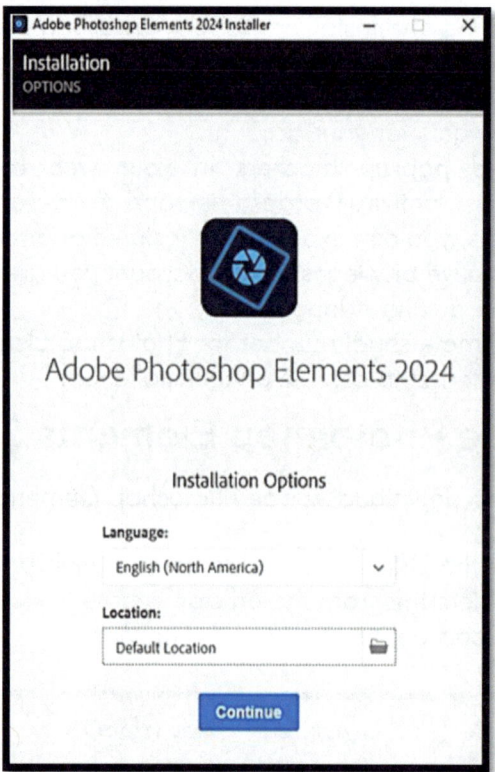

5. Choose your previous version of Photoshop Element in the following screen and click on **Confirm**.
6. Make sure to open the Photo Editor on the next screen to access the Adobe Photoshop Editor Workspace.
7. Make sure to sign in again with your Adobe ID and password.
8. Proceed to the next page and select **Activate Now** on the Welcome screen.

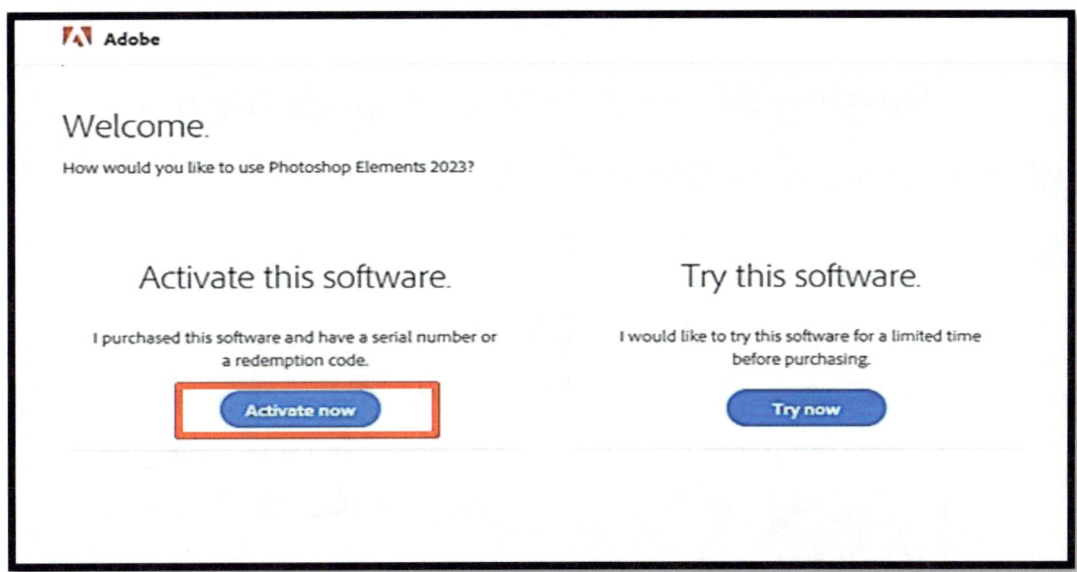

9. Make sure to input the serial number in the following screen and then proceed by clicking on **Next**.

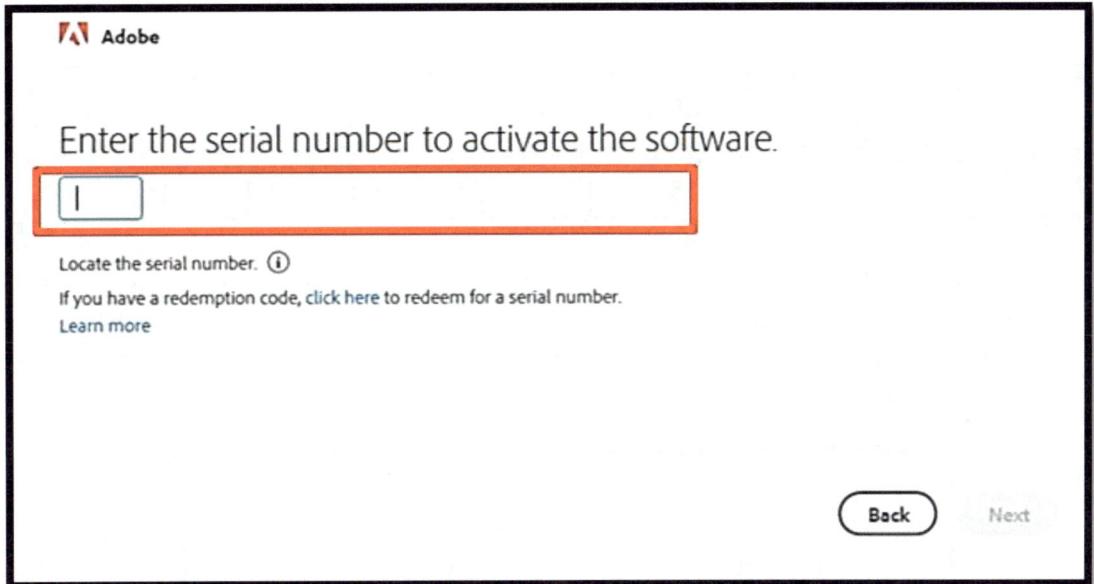

10. From there, your Photo Editor will open.

CHAPTER TWO
Getting Started with Image Editing

Exploring the Home Screen

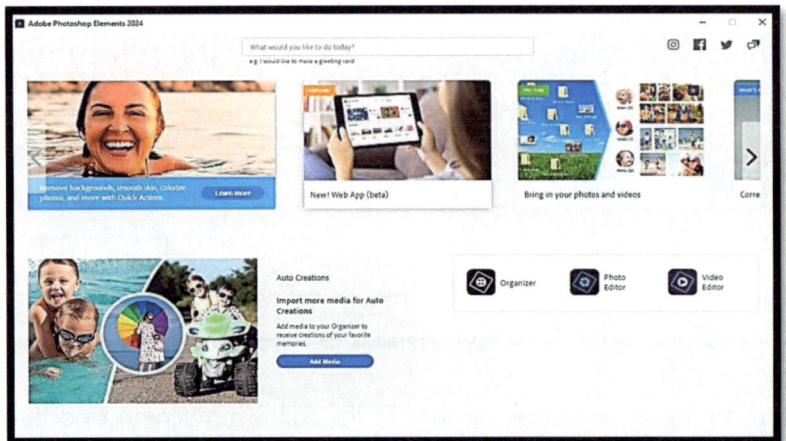

After downloading and installing Photoshop Element 2024 on your PC, the first thing you'll see is the Home Screen. The Home Screen features automatically generated photos, videos, and slideshows tailored by the software to work with the imported media. Discover engaging editing projects, collect creative ideas, change workspaces, view recently opened files, and seek help from the Adobe community on the home screen.

Here are the main icons on the Home Screen:

- **The Search Bar**: Use the search bar at the top of the Home Screen to quickly find Help documents and tutorials for different features. Simply type the keyword into the search bar and press Enter on your keyboard. The Home Screen will display the pertinent results as thumbnails and hyperlinks in this location.

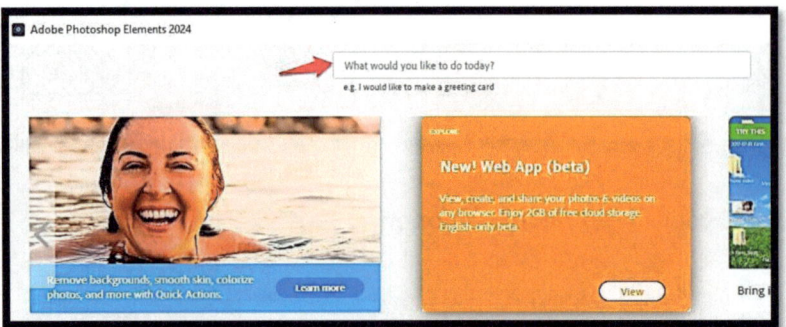

- **The Carousel of Cards:** The upper part of the Home Screen features a carousel of cards that offer access to information about new features, tasks, and inspirational ideas. You can navigate through the carousel by clicking the arrows on the right and left sides.

Here are some common elements often found in the carousel:

- **Explore:** This tag allows you to tour around certain features in the Photoshop Element application. To use this feature, simply click on the **View button**.
- **What's New:** Information about new features in the Photoshop Element application is provided by the blue tag. Be sure to click on the Open Link button to access these resources.
- **Try This:** This tag is colored green and provides access to a range of fascinating features. Your use of actions and features in Photoshop Elements determines which features are displayed and updated regularly. Click on the Try button to test out any of these features.

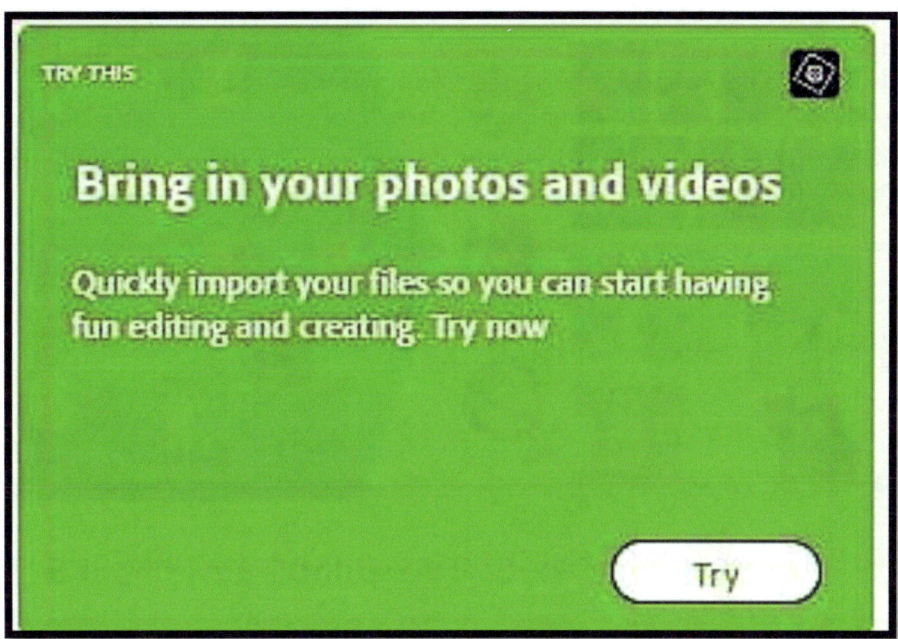

- **Auto Creations:** Auto Creations are located at the bottom of the Home Screen and are regularly generated by the software using the imported media in the Elements. Adding media to Auto Creations is easily done by selecting Add media from the Auto Creation menu. When you choose **View all** or the number icon below the Auto Creations thumbnail, you can see all the auto-created projects, such as picture collages, slideshows, and video collages.

- **Organizer:** Located at the right-hand side of the Home Screen is The Organizer. Here is where you can import, browse, and organize photographs to keep your image collection effective and well-organized. Organize your photos efficiently with tools for tagging, rating, sorting, and finding in the Organizer.
- **The Photo Editor:** Photo editing tools are provided for creating and modifying images. These tools cover brightness adjustments, color enhancements, effects, image corrections, and more.

- **Video Editor:** Access Photoshop Elements video editing tools with The Video Editor.

- **Recent Files:** Access project files that have recently been worked on from the Home Screen under Recent Files. You can seamlessly pick up where you left off on the

20

project by using this symbol. Every image you open in this window will be displayed in the Photo Editor.

Opening the Photo Editor

The Photo Editor plays a vital role in Photoshop Element. As previously stated, the Photo Editor offers features for applying effects, adjusting brightness and color, fixing photographs, and more.

Opening the Photo Editor in Photoshop Elements 2024

Here are the steps:

1. Click on Photo Editor from the right-hand side of the Home Screen Interface.
2. On the next page, you will find the main interface of the Photo Editor, showcasing a range of tools for creating and editing photos.

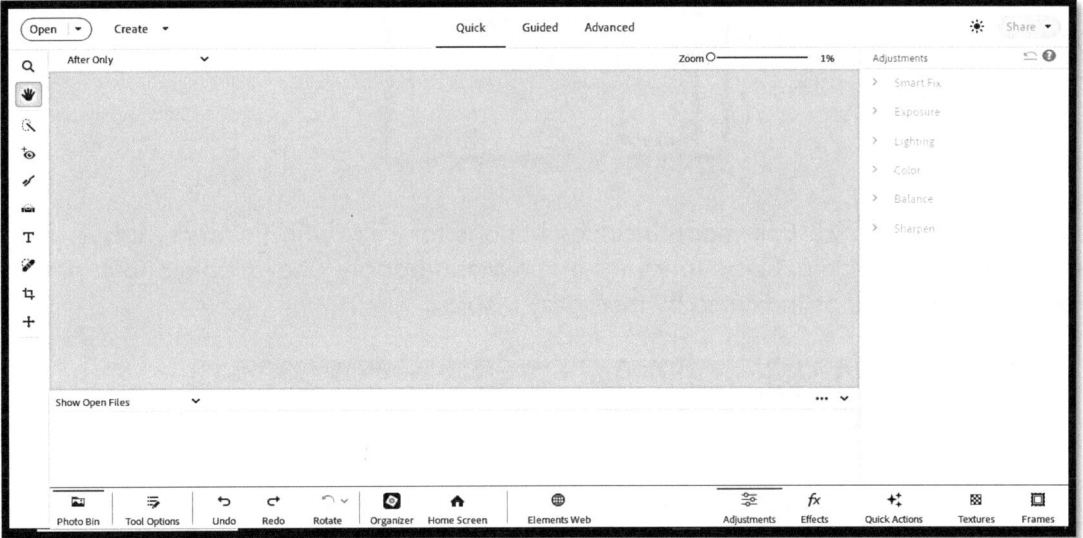

3. The Photo Editor is set to Quick mode when the Quick tab is selected by default at the top of the workspace, along with the other modes (Guided and Advanced, previously known as Expert). Unfortunately, Quick mode lacks sufficient controls for adjusting brightness, color, contrast, and sharpness.
4. **The workspace is structured into three editing modes:** Quick, Guided, and Advanced. The Adjustments panel is located in the panel Bin on the right side of the workspace. The Tools panel can be found on the left side of the workspace. When combined with items in the Panel Bin and the tools available, the Tools panel provides a wide range of options for enhancing, editing, and customizing photos.

Carrying our Basic Edits in Elements' Quick Mode

Quick Edit is a mode in Photo Editor that provides fewer options compared to Expert Edit. Only the essential tools are available in the Toolbox's Quick Edit mode, including the Zoom Tool, Hand Tool, Selection Tools, Healing Brush Tools, Red Eye Removal Tool, Whiten Teeth, Straighten Tool, Text Tools, Healing Brush Tools, Crop Tool, and Move Tool. All these tools operate similarly in the Edit modes (**Quick or Advanced**).

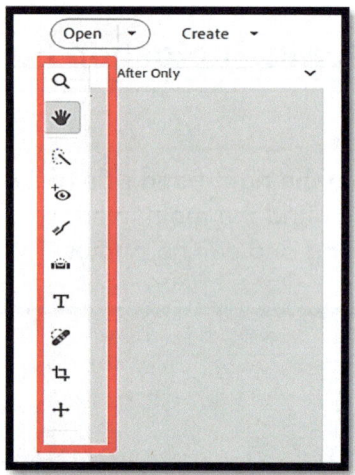

The Menu bar in Quick Edit mode includes buttons for File, Edit, Enhance, Layer, Filter, View Windows, and Help. Some functions in the Menu bar are unavailable and cannot be selected or accessed, as indicated by their gray display.

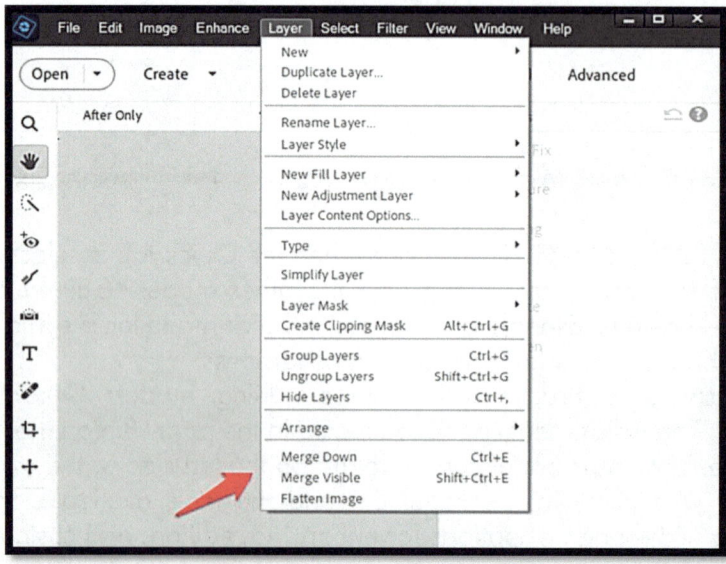

22

Another feature in the Quick Edit mode is the **Panel Bin**. This feature includes various tools like Photo Bin, Tool Options, Undo, and Redo, Rotate, Organizer, Element Web, Adjustment, Effects, Quick Actions, Textures, and Frames

Editing and making changes in Quick Edit Mode

- Make sure to open the Photo Editor and select the Quick tab at the top of the screen.
- Click on a file in Windows Explorer or the Mac Finder to open it in Elements.
- Find the file you want on your hard drive, select it, and then click **Open** in the Open dialog box that appears.
- Choose **Before & After-Horizontal** from the View drop-down menu.
- Adjust your photo by cropping it or using Smart Fix.
- Make sure to navigate to **File > Save As**, provide a new name for the picture in the Save As dialog box, and then save it by clicking **Save**.

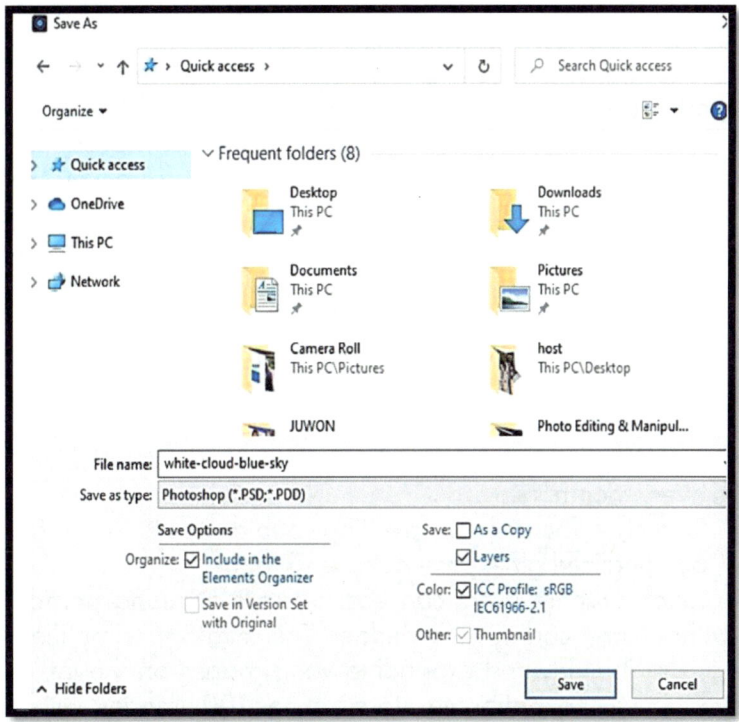

Sharing a Photo

The Adobe Photoshop Element 2024 is a versatile tool for sharing media files (photos, videos, and projects) online through various platforms such as Flickr, Facebook, Twitter, and more.

In addition to sharing individual photo files online, you can also share the following.

- **Albums**: Creating albums allows you to compile multiple images for easy sharing or uploading to other platforms.
- **Slideshow**: Create a slideshow and export it as a movie file (.wmv) or a PDF. Before posting or distributing slideshows on the internet, you have the option to add audio files as well.
- **Video Files**: Video files can be uploaded using Adobe Element for online viewing on various websites.

Photo Sharing Providers on Photoshop Elements

You have the option to upload or share your images on a wide variety of photo-sharing platforms. Photoshop Element is linked to certain photo-sharing websites.

Here is a list of the web pages for Photoshop Element.

- **Behance**: Behance is a platform for displaying your creative work and exploring beautiful designs and photography from other creators.
- **DotPhoto**: DotPhoto is an extra platform for sharing images that require a club membership fee.
- **FaceBook**: Facebook is a popular social media platform designed for sharing an endless number of photos and videos. Here on this platform, you create an account.
- **Flickr**: A platform for sharing photos and connecting with others through uploaded images. This online photo management and sharing application is among the top choices worldwide, offering 1TB of photo upload capacity with no restrictions.
- **Google +:** Google + is an online platform for sharing photos with unlimited storage. In addition, you have the option to browse through images uploaded by other users
- **Photobucket**: Photobucket is a user-friendly and robust platform for sharing and hosting images. You have the option to share a maximum of 2GB worth of photos and videos every month
- **Shutterfly**: Shutterfly focuses on creating photo books, wall art, photo cards, invitations, personalized gifts, calendars, and more.
- **SlicPic:** A platform where users can easily create stunning portfolio websites and galleries without any coding knowledge. This platform simplifies the process of showcasing, distributing, and expanding your images on the internet. For the free account, you have the option to store up to 200 images with size limitations. However, with the paid account, you can enjoy 50 GB of storage space without any size restrictions.
- **SmugMug**: SmugMug is a photo-sharing website where users can store, share, and sell their photos online. The monthly fee for an account on this platform is $3.84 at minimum.
- **Twitter**: Twitter is a platform where you can share up to 100 images, with each image being a maximum of 3MB. On this website, newly uploaded pictures are showcased for everyone to view

- **Vimeo**: Vimeo is a video-sharing platform where users can effortlessly create and share high-quality videos with their audience.
- **YouTube**: YouTube is a popular video-sharing platform that allows users to watch, create, and share videos online.

Sharing Photos on Photoshop Elements

Two applications on the Home Screen are Organizer and Photo Editor for sharing photos.

Sharing photo files with the organizer

Follow the detailed guide below to understand how to share photos using the Organizer.

1. Launch Organizer from the Home Screen.

2. Click on **Media** and choose the picture you want to share once the Organizer opens.
3. Click on **Share** and choose an option from the Share drop-down menu.

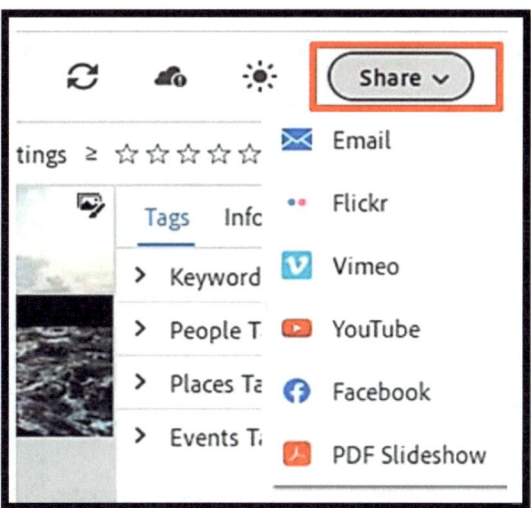

Sharing Photos with the Photo Editor

Follow the detailed guide below to master sharing photos with the Photo Editor

1. Open the **Photo Editor application** on the Home Screen.

2. When the Photo Editor is launched, choose the image you want to share
3. Select the **Share button** and choose an option from the Share drop-down menu

Revisiting Your Actions

There may be times when errors occur during photo editing or when you're not satisfied with the changes you've made. **You can efficiently retrace your steps using the Undo and Redo commands.**

- Head to Edit in the **Menu bar** and choose **Undo (Ctrl + Z) or Redo (Ctrl + Y)** to make use of the command.

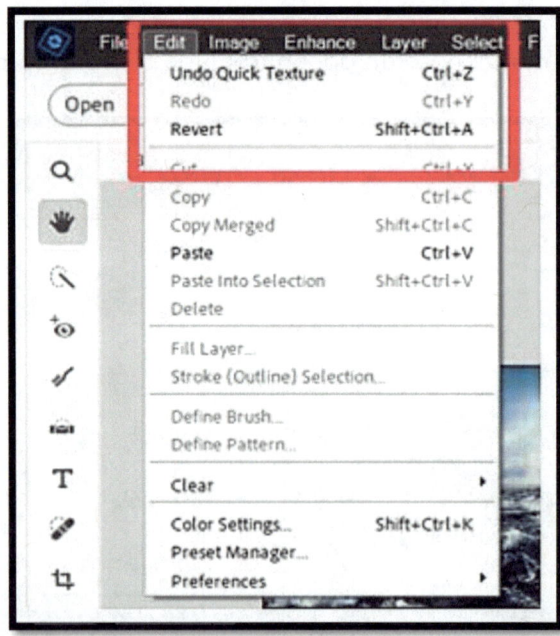

Exploring the History panel

Understanding the editing history of an image or project is simplified with the assistance of the History panel. You can easily move through the History panel to adjust your work during the current session, and it offers a detailed record of all the edits made to the image.

To open the History panel, follow these steps:

1. Head to **Windows** and choose **History** to open the History panel. Next, you will find the list of edits that have been made.

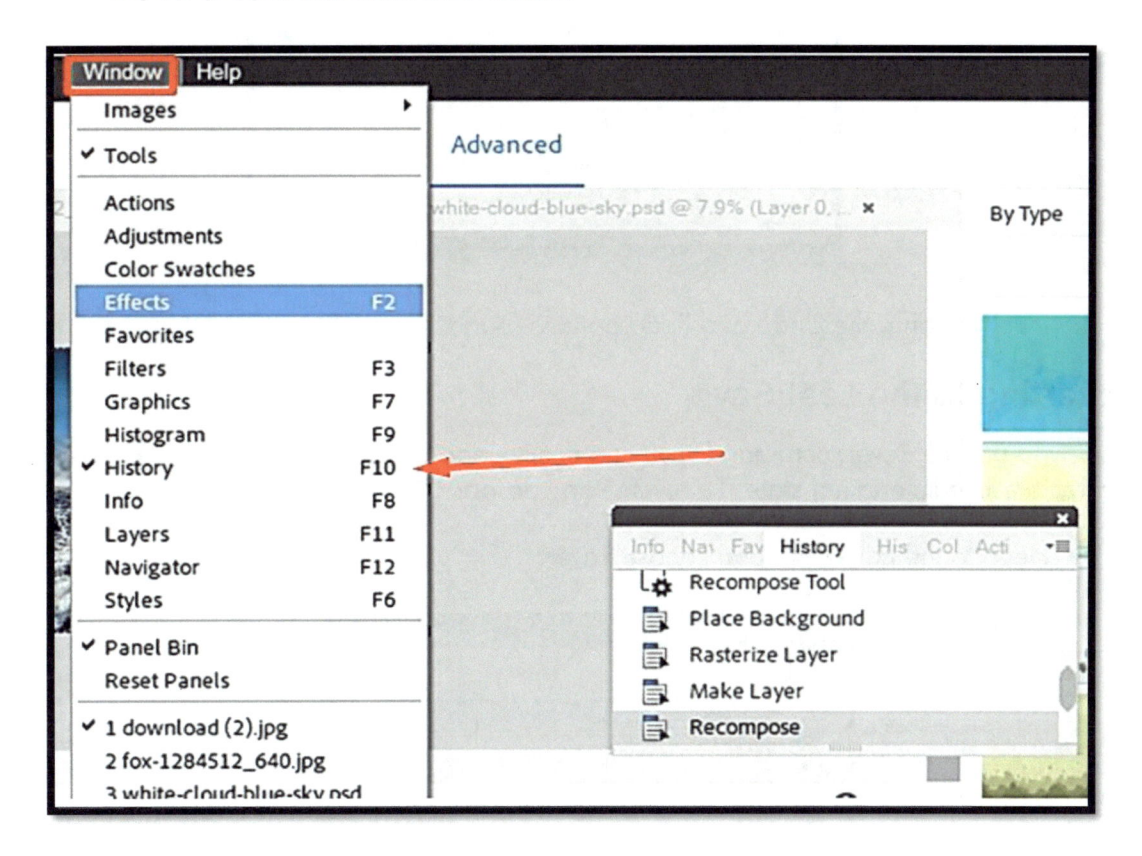

Reverting To a Previous State of an Image

If you need to revert an image to its previous state, there are three straightforward methods available in both Quick and Expert modes, as outlined below.

1. Select the state from the History Panel.
2. Access the **Undo or Redo button** in the Taskbar.

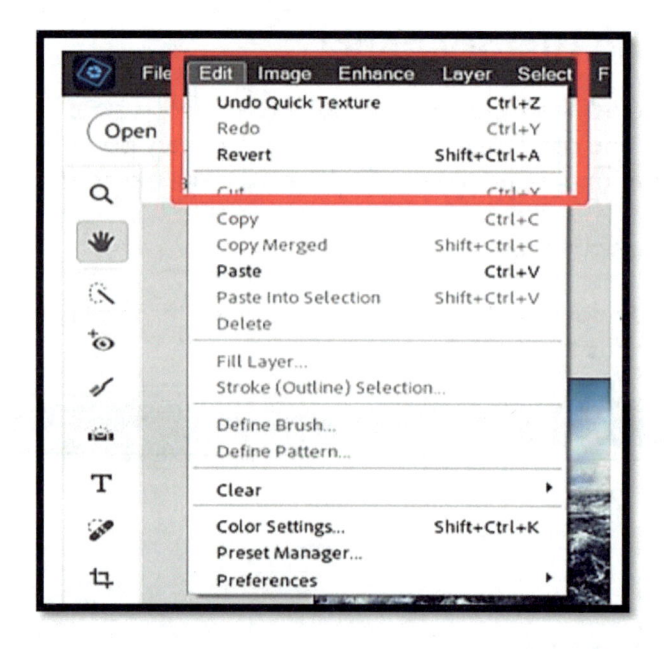

3. Involves using the Undo and Redo options found in the Edit Menu.

Reverting to the Last Save

When you use the Revert command, you can easily undo any changes made to the image and restore it to its original state. To reverse any action:

- Head to the **Edit Menu** and choose **Revert**.

Erasing and Deleting States from The History panel

If you wish to remove any alterations from the list that are no longer needed in your image, follow these steps

- Right-click on the action and choose the **Delete option**.
- Make sure to choose **Yes** from the menu bar that appears to confirm the deletion.

Follow these steps to eliminate the list of states from the History panel without affecting the visual appearance:

- Make sure to right-click on the action and choose **Clear History**.
- Click "**Ok**" to confirm the deletion.

Follow these guidelines carefully when using the History panel:

- The History panel in Photoshop Element only displays the most recent 50 states by default. Any states beyond that limit are automatically removed to free up space. You can set the number of states to a maximum of 1000, but feel free to adjust it to your preference.

Here are the steps to complete this task:

- Choose **Preference** from the **Edit menu** and then select **Performance**.

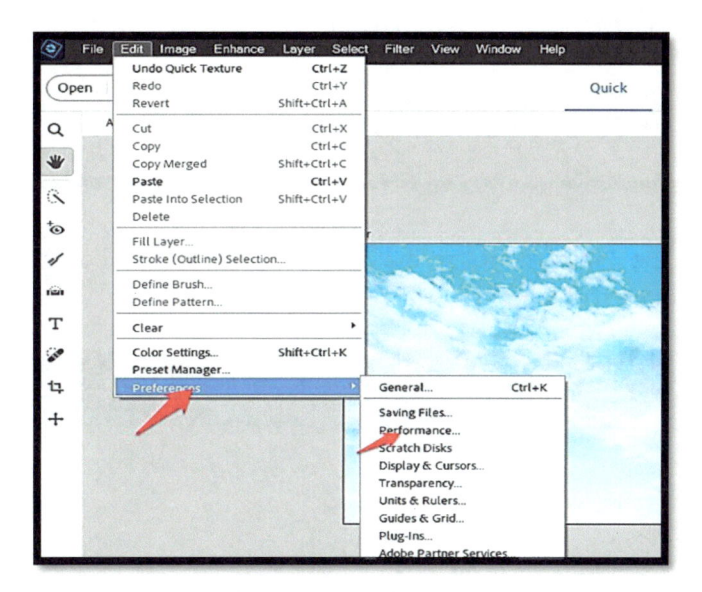

- Adjust the statistics number in the Performance tab's History & Cache section to your preference and then select "Ok."

- Keeping more states in your History panel will result in the element using more memory.
- The initial state of the photo is always displayed at the top of the History panel. Clicking on the top state will easily revert the image to its initial state.
- The name of the tool or command used to change the image is listed next to each state in the History panel.
- The state listed at the top of the History panel is the oldest, with the most recent state at the bottom.
- After closing a document, all the states in the History panel are cleared.
- All subsequent states change when you modify the selected state in the image. Furthermore, deleting state results in the deletion of all subsequent states.
- When selecting a state, the previous states are dimmed to help you focus on the chosen state.

Getting a Helping Hand

If you encounter any issues while using Photoshop Elements, you may need some assistance.

Below are additional tools created by Adobe for use in comparable scenarios.

The Help Menu

For professional assistance with Photoshop, the **Help menu** is the initial resource to consult.

You can locate the Help menu at the top of the Photo Editor or Organizer interface, alongside the other menus.

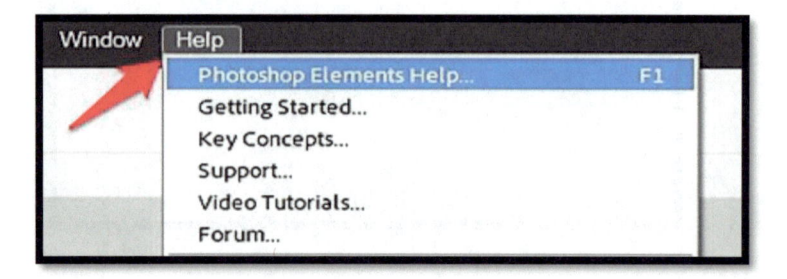

Upon selecting the Help menu, the commands will be displayed, allowing you to access the necessary information.

Let's now explore some of the commands in the Help menu.

- **Photoshop Element Help:** For Photoshop Element assistance, use the search box to find relevant topics and search results. To access the Element Help file, simply press the F1 shortcut key.
- **Getting Started**: This command provides advice and information on how to start in Elements.
- **Key Concepts**: Understanding key concepts is essential when encountering unfamiliar words or phrases. By selecting this option, a web page will open and your default web browser will be launched, displaying various web pages that explain the key concepts.
- **Support**: For assistance, use this command to open your web browser and access the Adobe website. Discover current information about Elements, reported issues from users, and useful tips for using Adobe Element on the Adobe website. There are plenty of resources available on the Adobe website to help enhance the use of Adobe Elements and provide solutions for any potential issues.
- **Video Tutorials**: Check out the video tutorials to open a web page on Adobe's website with helpful videos on using Adobe Element.
- **Forum**: Access the forum to find user comments, queries, and solutions to common issues encountered while using the Element.

Tooltips

Hover your mouse over any object in Photoshop Element to reveal additional help resources displayed as text below your cursor. The displayed texts offer detailed descriptions of the object in focus.

The Dialog Box Links

The dialog box is a useful tool. Some words in the dialog box are highlighted in bright blue and can be clicked to access the Elements Help page.

Saving Files with Purpose

We are now going to explore how to use Adobe Photoshop Element to save any file. Let's explore two methods for saving data in this section.

- Save command
- Save as command

The Save Command

To save the changes made to the file being worked on, simply use the Save command. Simply follow these steps:

- Choose the **File option** and then click on **Save**, or you can use the shortcut (Ctrl+S)

The Save As Command

When saving photos, you can use the Save As command to set preferences like the file name, file type, layers, and more.

When saving files, use the Save As Command

- Begin by opening Photoshop Element and choosing the image you want to save as a file.
- Open the File menu and select **Save As**.
- Choose the directory where you want to save the file and type in the desired name in the Save As text box.
- Choose the **File Format option** and pick the desired file format for saving (JPEG, GIF, PNG, etc.)
- Next, proceed to **Save**.

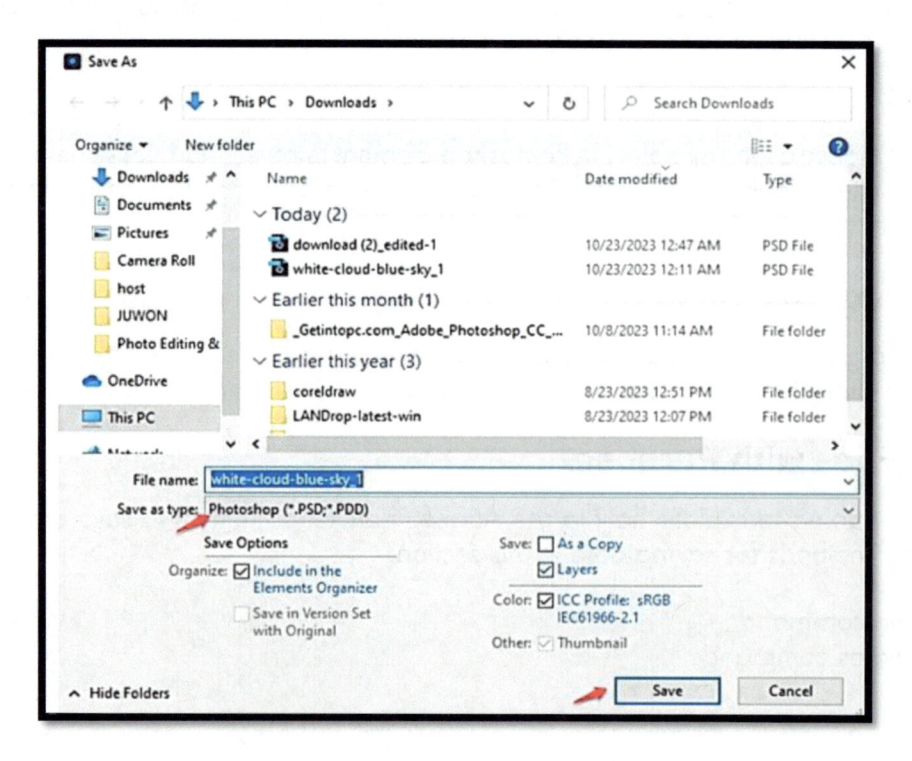

Here are some extra features that certain file-saving options might provide when using the Save As command.

- **Include in the Element Organizer**: Make sure to include the file in the Element Organizer to have it readily available for viewing in the Photo Browser. Nevertheless, various file formats, such as the EPS file format, are not compatible with the Element organizer.
- **Save In Version Set with Original**: Save the file and add it to a version set in the Photo Browser to keep the various image versions organized. To access this option, you must select "**Include in the Organizer.**"
- **Layer**: Enhance the preservation of layers in the image with this option. If the Layer option is turned off or not accessible, it means there are no layers present in the image. When the layer in the image needs to be flattened or merged for the chosen format, a warning icon will appear in the Layer checkbox. If you wish to retain the layers in an image, consider selecting an alternative format.
- **As a Copy**: When choosing the selected option, a duplicate of the open file will be saved. The folder where the file is saved will also receive a copy of the open file.
- **ICC Profile**: By adding a color profile to the image, you can enhance the quality for certain formats.
- **Thumbnail**: This feature saves the thumbnail data of the file. When the Ask when saving option for Image Preview is activated in the Preferences dialog box, this choice becomes available.
- **Use Lowercase Extension**: Make sure to select the "**Lower Case Extension**" setting to choose between lowercase or uppercase for the file extension.

File Format Options for Saving Files

When saving files in Adobe Photoshop Element, you have a variety of file types to choose from.

Let's examine the file types supported by Adobe Element for saving files:

- **JPEG (Joint Photographic Expert Group):** Photos are stored in the JPEG (Joint Photographic Expert Group) file format. This file format efficiently reduces data to decrease file size without compromising the image's color information. Reducing compression leads to improved image quality but larger file sizes, while increasing compression leads to reduced image quality but smaller file sizes. JPEG is the ideal format for showcasing images on websites.
- **TIFF (Tagged Image File Format):** This is a versatile bitmap image format supported by various programs for transferring files between different platforms. Many desktop scanners are capable of generating TIFF files.
- **PNG (Portable Network Graphics):** On the internet, PNG (Portable Network Graphics) is the most widely used uncompressed raster image format. Moreover, it is commonly utilized for storing digital photos, website designs, and images with

transparent backgrounds. The PNG file format replaced the Graphics Interchange Format (GIF). The PNG image can display a transparent background, similar to the GIF picture. Both grayscale and 24-bit RGB color palettes are commonly found in PNG files.
- **Photoshop (PSD):** The default file format for Photoshop Elements. This file format allows you to make changes to an image while preserving its layers, data, and size.
- **BMP (Bitmap):** Developed by Microsoft Corporation, the BMP (Bitmap) standard image format is used to save bitmap digital images for MS Windows and OS/2. Uncompressed files, like BMP files, are easier to interpret. Moreover, the BMP picture file format is no longer compatible.
- **CompuServe GIF (Graphics Interchange Format):** Small animations and pictures are commonly displayed on web pages using the GIF format. This file format was developed to efficiently reduce file sizes and save time. Only images in 8-bit color are compatible. Utilize the Save As Web feature to save an image in GIF format.
- **Photo Creation Format (PSE):** The standard file format for creating multiple pages is also this one. Save your work in this file format to preserve all image data and layer information in a multi-page file.
- **PDF:** Photoshop PDFs display and preserve fonts, page layouts, vector, and bitmap graphics across different platforms and applications.
- **Pixar**: Computers with Pixar image files can share files in this format. The Pixar workstations were designed and manufactured for sophisticated graphics applications, like those used for 3D animation and three-dimensional imagery. Moreover, this layout accommodates grayscale and RGB.

How to Save a File in JPEG Format

Here are the steps to save your file in JPEG format:

1. Head to the File menu and select **Save As**.

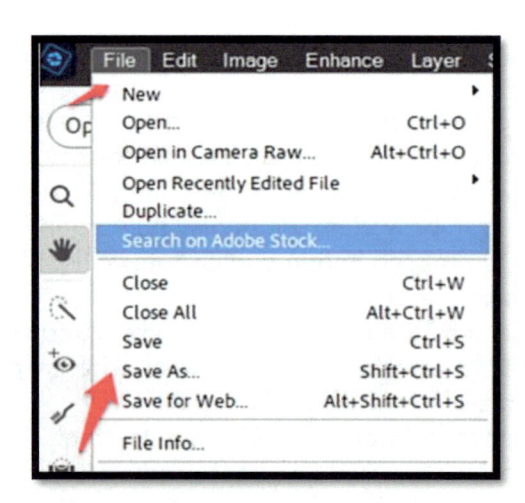

2. Choose the folder where you want to save the file and type in the name in the Save As text box.
3. Choose **JPEG** in the file format.
4. Next, simply click on **Save**.

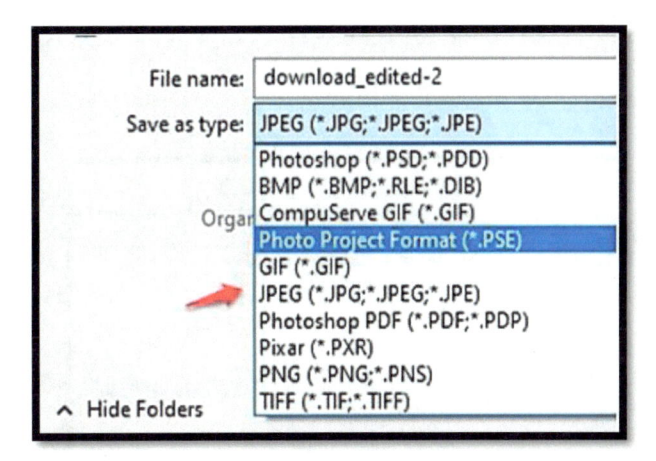

5. When the JPEG dialog box appears on this page, choose a matte color to enhance the background opacity when the image file has transparency.
6. Identify the image compression and resolution by choosing from the Quality menu. Choose the image quality level by inputting a value from 1 to 12 or by adjusting the Quality Slider.
7. Choose Baseline ("standard"), Baseline Optimized, or Progressive from the Quality Menu.

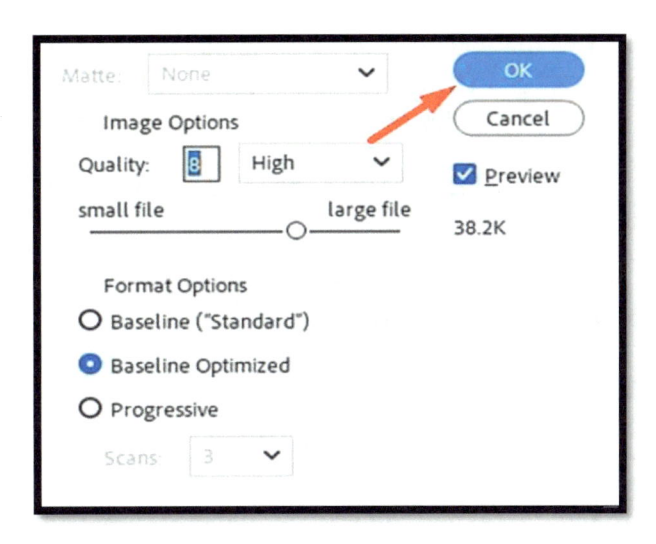

8. Next, simply click on Ok.

35

How to Save a File in Photoshop as a PDF

Follow the detailed instructions to save your file in Photoshop PDF format.

1. Head to the **File menu** and select **Save As**.
2. Choose the folder where you want to save the file and type in the desired name in the Save As text box.
3. Choose **Photoshop PDF** in the File format.

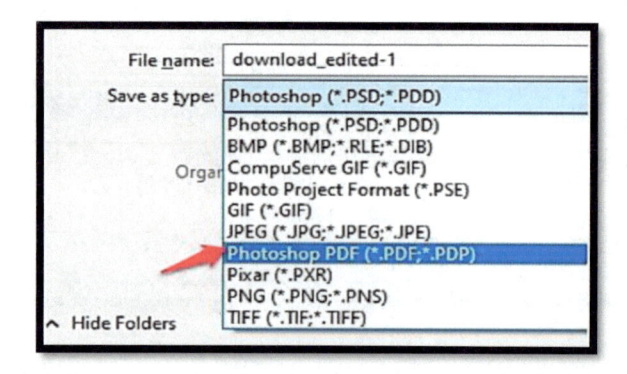

4. Next, simply click on Save

How to Save a File in PNG Format

Follow the detailed instructions to save your file as a PNG:

1. Click on **Save As** from the File menu.
2. Choose the folder where you want to save the file and type in the desired name in the Save As text box.
3. Choose Photoshop PDF in the File format.
4. Next, proceed to Save.
5. On this page, the PNG dialog box will open, and when it does, choose the Interlace option to select either None or Interlaced.

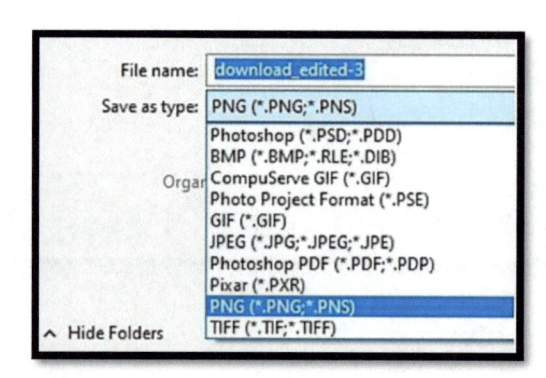

- **None**: Displays the image in a browser once the download is complete.
- **Interlaced**: The Interlay option shows the image in low resolution for faster download times but results in a larger file size.

6. Next, proceed by clicking on Ok

Saving File in GIF format

Follow the detailed instructions to save your file in GIF format:

1. Head to the **File Menu** and select **Save As**.
2. Choose the folder location where you want to save the file and type the name in the Save As text box.
3. Choose **GIF format** in the File format section.
4. Next, proceed to **Save**.
5. Make selections in the GIF option dialog box and then confirm by clicking Ok.

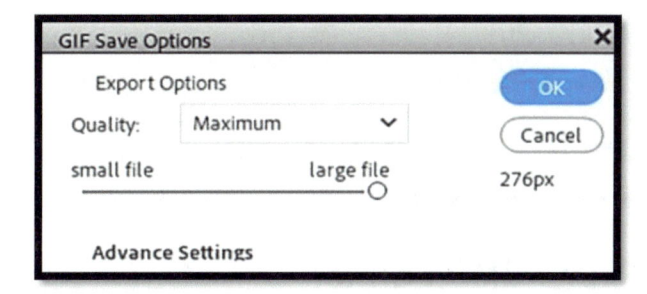

How to Save a File in TIFF Format

Follow the detailed instructions to save your file in TIFF format:

1. Head to the File menu and select **Save As**.
2. Choose the folder where you want to save the file and type in the desired name in the Save As text box.
3. Choose **TIFF format** in the File format section.
4. Next, proceed to Save

When the TIFF Options dialog box appears, you can choose from the listed options below:

- **Image Compression**: This option is utilized to indicate or choose the method for compressing the image data
- **Pixel Order**: Choose the Pixel Order option to add the photo to the Element organizer.
- **Byte Order**: Choose the Byte Order option to specify the platform for reading the file, particularly if you are unsure about the program that will be used to open the file.

- **Save Image Pyramid**: Preserve multiresolution information by selecting the Save Image Pyramid option in Adobe Element. This feature enables the image to open in the highest resolution available in the file.
- **Save Transparency:** This option maintains transparency in a file when opened in another application.
- **Layer Compression**: This option specifies the method for compressing data for pixels in layers. When files contain layers, they tend to be larger. Compressing the layers can help reduce the overall file size.

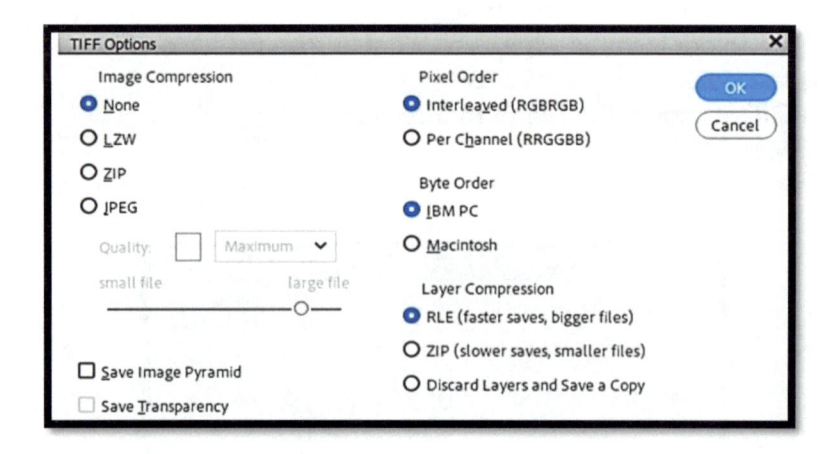

How to Save a File in BMP Format

Follow the detailed instructions to save your file in BIMP Format:

1. Head to the File menu and select **Save As**.
2. Choose the location where you want to save the file and type in the desired name in the Save As text box.
3. Choose the **BMP format** under File Format.

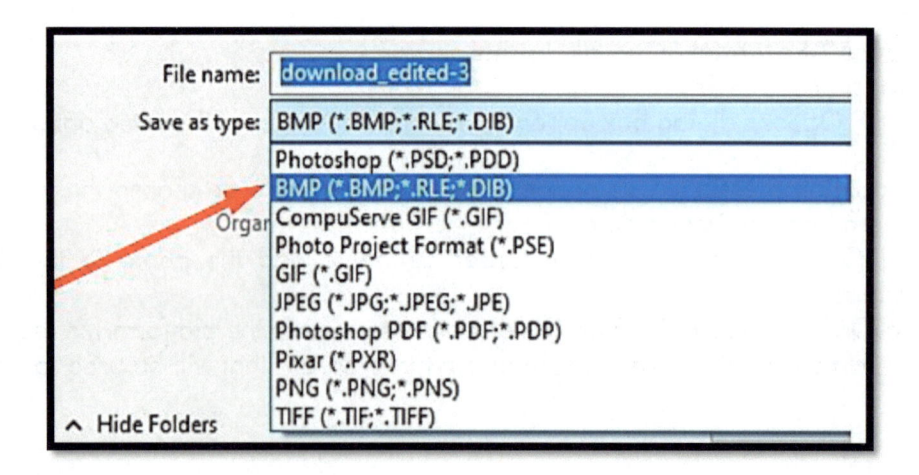

4. Next, proceed to **Save**.
5. Make sure to choose the file format, specify the bit depth, and opt for the Flip Row Order in the BMP Options dialog box. For additional options, simply select **Advanced Modes**.
6. Click the OK button.

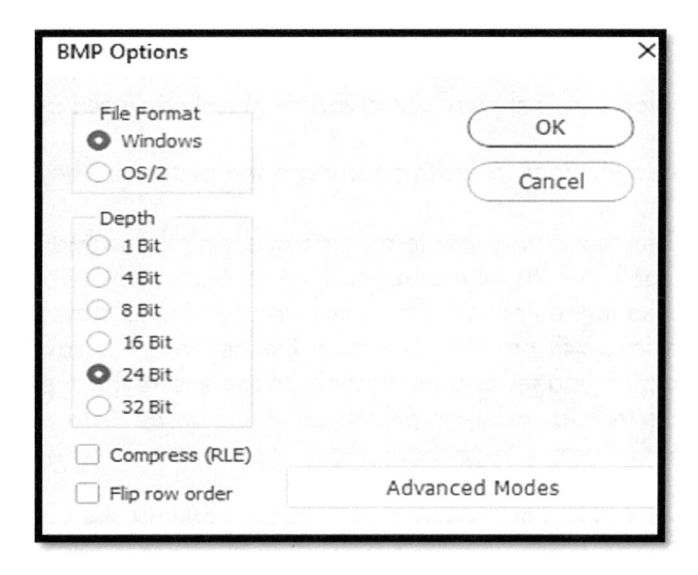

File Format Compression

Various image file formats are used for compressing picture data when saving files in different formats. There are two main types of file compression: lossy and lossless. Lossless compression retains all picture data by eliminating specific features, whereas lossy compression

Here are the commonly utilized compression techniques or formats:

- **RLE (Run Length Encoding):** The lossless compression technique used for transparent regions of layers in an image with multiple layers is RLE (Run Length Encoding).
- **LZW (Lemple-Zif-Welch):** A lossless compression algorithm commonly used for compressing images with large areas of uniform color.
- **JPEG**: JPEG is a compression method that effectively reduces the file size of photos.
- **CCIT**: CCIT is another lossless compression technique for black-and-white photos.
- **ZIP**: ZIP is a lossless compression method used for images with a large area of uniform color.

Web File Saving

The Save for Web tool is used for compressing photos and adjusting display parameters to fine-tune images for web-based media like blogs and webpages. Before posting an image online, it's important to take into account the file size. It should be kept small enough for easy downloading while still maintaining image quality. When it comes to the web, three main file formats are commonly used: GIF, JPEG, and PNG.

For optimal web file saving, adhere to the following steps:

1. Head to the **File menu** and select **Save for Web**.

The Save for Web dialog box is shown with a variety of options listed below:

- **Hand Tool**: Use this tool to navigate around the picture in the Preview area when zoomed in.
- **Zoom Tool:** This tool allows you to enlarge or shrink the preview image.
- **Eyedropper Tool:** Use the Eyedropper Tool to accurately select a color from an image displayed in the Preview area. Here is a preview of how the image will look.
- **Previews**: Previews will be available once the document is saved. The first image displays the actual image, and the second image shows the preview.
- **Preset**: Choose from a variety of presets available in the drop-down menu with the Preset option. Creating pre-configured settings for the dialog box's choices is done using the preset.
- **Image Format:** Select a file format (GIF, JPEG, or PNG) from the drop-down menu.
- **Quality Settings:** Select the image quality before saving it. When saving a file as a JPEG, the Quality option will be available; for GIF and PNG, you can specify the color number.
- **Image Attributes:** The field labeled Original Size displays the original dimensions. Within the New Size Area, adjust the image's dimensions in pixels or percentages.
- **Animation**: This feature is exclusively accessible for animated GIFs.
- **Preview Menu:** Here is where you can view a preview of the output.

CHAPTER THREE
BASIC IMAGE EDITING CONCEPTS

Mastering the Art of Pixels

It is essential to grasp the concept of pixels before you can proficiently edit photos in Photoshop Element. Pixels are the fundamental components of all digital images. These tiny elements are essential for all digital images. "**Picture element**" is simply a shorter term for "**pixel**." When looking at a photo at a standard zoom level (100 percent or less), the pixels are usually too small to notice, but upon closer inspection, we can see a lot of tiny squares. To calculate the total number of pixels in a photograph, simply multiply the width by the height. For example, multiplying 300 by 239 equals 71,700. Keep in mind that the pixels within an image determine its resolution and dimensions.

Understanding Resolution

The image resolution dictates the size at which an image will be reproduced. The resolution of an image is determined by the number of pixels per inch in the image file (PPI). With 200 pixels in a 1-inch horizontal line, the picture resolution will be 200 PPI. **Image resolution plays a crucial role in the following tasks:**

- **Printing Images:** For printing images, it is advised to use a print resolution of 300 PPI. If the image resolution is too high, the printer will take longer to process the data, while if the resolution is too low, the printed picture quality will be poor.
- **Displaying Image Screen**: The image resolution depends on the monitor in use.

Understanding Image Dimension

Picture dimension is related to the width and height of the image. Picture dimensions can be displayed in various units including Pixels, Inches, Percentages, Centimeters, Millimeters, Points, and Picas.

Display the Image Resolution and Dimensions

The Image Size dialog box is the optimal location to view the image resolution and dimensions. You can adjust the image size in the Image Size dialog box.

You can adjust four aspects of the picture in the Image Size dialog box:

- **Pixel Dimension**: Refers to the width and height of the image.
- **Image Size**: Displayed at the top of the dialog box is the value indicating the image's size.
- **Document Size:** Refers to the physical dimensions of the image when printed.
- **Image Resolution When Printed**: Refers to the pixel density on the printed image.

Follow these steps to open the Image Size dialog box:

- Head to the Image Menu and select **Resize**.
- Next, select **Image Size**.
- On this page, the Image Size dialog box is displayed with options to adjust the settings.

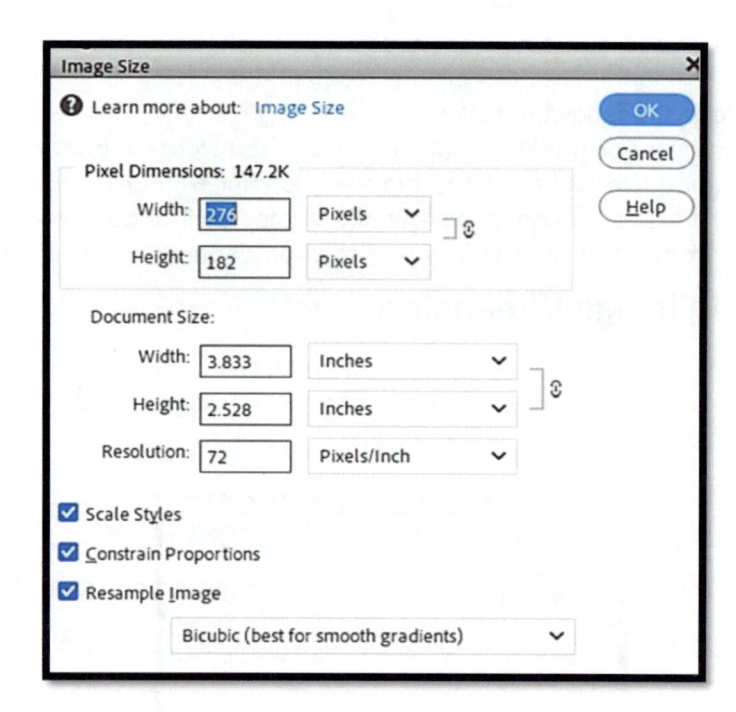

Photoshop Elements determines an image's size, resolution, and pixel measurements.

- Physical size is determined by multiplying resolution by pixel dimensions.
- Resolution is determined by the physical size and pixel dimensions.
- Pixel dimensions are calculated by dividing the physical size by the resolution.

42

Resampling Techniques

Resampling involves adjusting the size of a file by adding or removing pixels. When downsampling, the number of pixels decreases, and when upsampling, the number of pixels increases. The photographs' quality decreases with each resample. Scan or create an image at a high resolution to avoid resampling.

How to Resample an Image

For optimal image resampling, adhere to the following steps:

- Head to the **Image Menu** and select **Image Size**.

Make sure to click on the Resample Image checkbox in the Image Size dialog box, and then choose one of the resampling methods:

- **Nearest Neighbor**: Nearest Neighbor is a resampling approach used when dealing with numerous files of the same color that need to be combined into a smaller file. This process is the fastest of them all.
- **Billnear**: Bilinear interpolation generates a medium-quality image and is ideal for grayscale and line art.
- **Bicubic**: Bicubic is the default resampling method, providing satisfactory results.
- **Bicubic Smoother**: This method is an enhanced version of the Bicubic technique, with a slight softening of the edges. When you need to increase the resolution of an image, this is the technique to use.
- **Bicubic Sharper**: This is ideal for producing high-quality images and is most effective when reducing the size of an image.

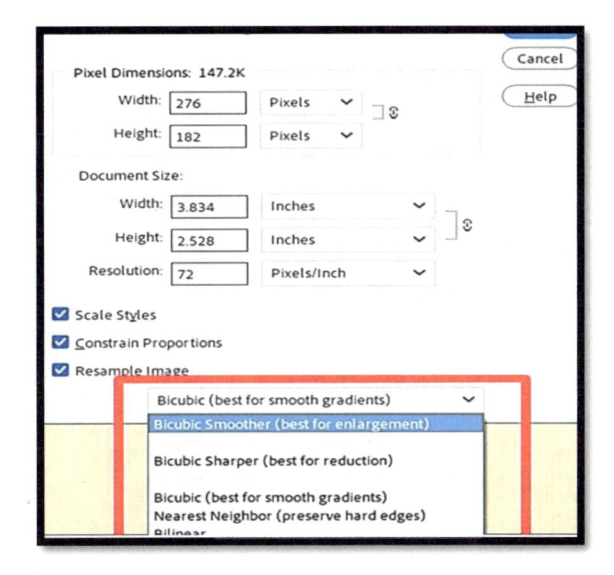

43

- Make sure to check the Scale Styles box in the Image Size dialog box to apply different style effects to the image.
- Make sure to check the Constraint Proportions box to keep the current aspect ratio.
- Select the **Ok button**.

Choosing between Print and On Screen Resolutions

Choosing the correct resolution for your image is essential before printing or displaying it. Ensuring high image quality. Display resolution is typically measured in pixels per inch, while printer resolution is measured in ink dots per inch (dpi). Here are the recommended print and on screen resolutions for different output devices

Output Devices	Optimum Resolution	Acceptable Resolution
Desktop color inkjet and laser printers	300 PPI	180 PPI
Large-format inkjet printer	150 PPI	120 PPI
Professional photo lab printer	300 PPI	200 PPI
Desktop laser printer (Black and white)	170 PPI	100 PPI
Magazine quality (offset press)	300 PPI	225 PPI
Screen image (web, slide show, video)	72 PPI	72 PPI
Tablet devices and smartphones	150 + PPI	150 PPI

Getting Familiar and Proficient with the Use of Color

Understanding RGB (Red, Green, and Blue) is essential for mastering color in Adobe Photoshop Elements. RGB colors, also called additive primaries, are the main colors used in Element. Lighting, video, and displays all use these colors. The RGB colors form the color channels. The color data for a specific channel is stored in the color channels. When evaluating the color channels on a scale of 0 to 255, the red channel, green channel, and blue channel each hold specific color information. When examining the red channel, the brighter area appears to have a stronger red hue, while the darker section appears less red.

Follow these steps to view the color channels:

- Head to the Enhance Menu and choose **Adjust Lighting**.
- Access the Levels dialog box by clicking on **Levels**.

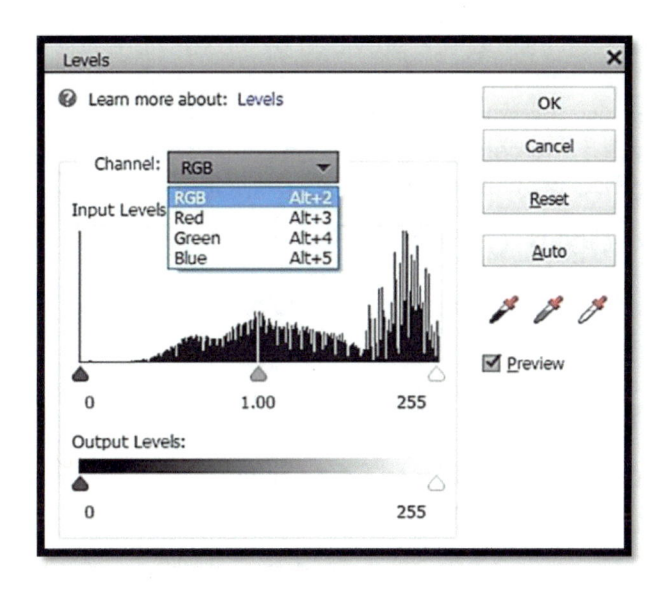

Calibrating Your Monitor

Imagine spending hours perfecting an image, only to print it out or see it displayed on another device and notice that the colors are not accurate. This is how we proceed with calibrating your monitor. Calibrating your monitor involves measuring and adjusting the colors on your computer screen to align with a standard reference. Not calibrating your monitor can lead to inaccurate color display on your screen, affecting how images look on other devices or when printed. If your monitor requires calibration, one way to tell is by noticing an overall color cast in your images, making them appear washed out or flat on different devices. Calibrating your monitor involves using a device called a Spectrophotometer, which operates in conjunction with computer software to ensure accurate image color.

Here's how to calibrate a monitor:

One of the most effective and accurate methods for calibrating the monitor is by using a spectrometer. This device is attached to the screen and works with computer software to analyze colors, brightness, contrast, and gamma for creating and saving an ICC (International Color Consortium) profile.

Here are the steps to calibrate your monitor:

1. Make sure to allow the monitor to warm up for at least 20-30 minutes before use, and avoid any direct light (daylight or ambient light) on it.
2. Make sure to connect the spectrometer to the computer using a USB connection and place it on top of the screen.

3. Follow the on-screen instructions provided by the software and wait for it to complete the process.
4. It's important to use the spectrometer to calibrate the monitor, which will capture all types of grayscales and colors displayed on the screen. This information is then used to generate an ICC profile stored on the computer.

Choosing the Right Color Scheme for Your Workspace

Once the display is calibrated, ensure to set the color workspace to either sRGB or Adobe RGB.

Here are the steps to access the color workplace settings:

- Head to the Edit menu and choose **Color Settings** from the drop-down menu.
- Choose one of the options in the Color Settings dialog box, as shown in the image below.

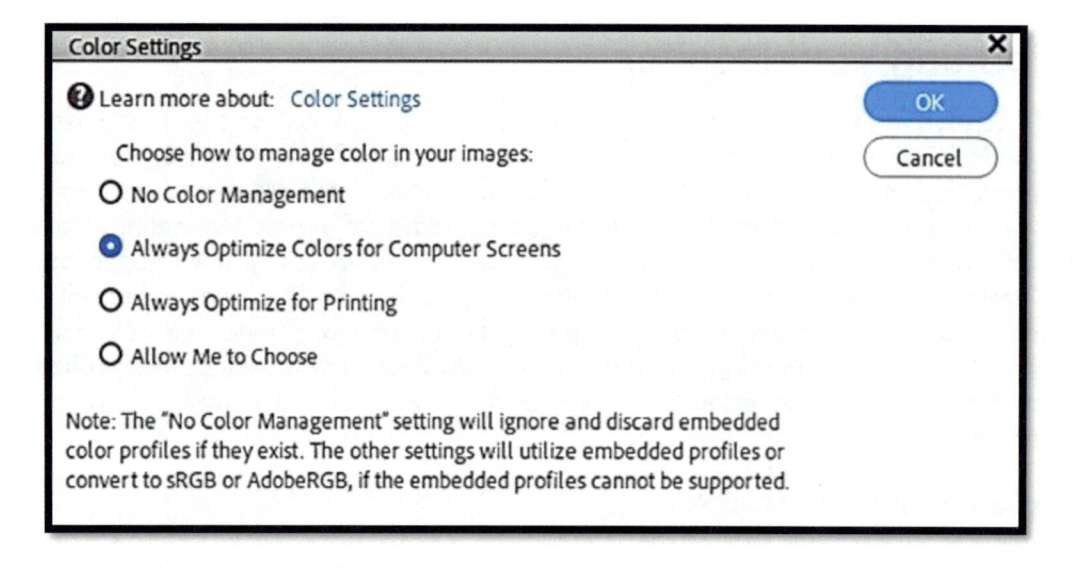

Here is a description of each option in the Color Settings dialog box.

- **No Color Management**: When you choose this option, color management is turned off, and the display profile is used as the working space. When viewing photos, this feature removes any embedded profiles and does not add tags when saving.
- **Always Optimize Colors for Computer Screen**: Make sure to optimize colors for the computer screen by selecting the sRGB option using the ratio button. The sRGB color space is perfect for viewing images on a monitor and for printing purposes.
- **Always Optimize for Printing**: Make sure to always optimize for printing by setting your workspace to Adobe RGB (1998) to retain embedded profiles and assign

Adobe RGB to untagged files when you open them. Monitors and inkjet printers excel in this setting due to the vibrant colors. It is set to this option by default
- **Allow Me to Choose:** Choose between sRGB or Adobe RGB when opening untagged files with this option.

Understanding the functions of a profile

To ensure precise and uniform color management, each color device in your system should possess a precise ICC-compliant profile. For instance, the image shown on the monitor might look different without a specific monitor profile. To avoid any confusion and save time and effort, a thorough profile is necessary.

It offers a variety of profiles, including:

- **Monitor Profiles:** Creating the monitor profile first is crucial for accurate color representation on the display. This explanation clarifies how the monitor is displaying a color.
- **Input Device Profile:** The profile specifies the color range that the input device is capable of capturing or scanning. For optimal results when selecting a profile on your digital camera, Adobe recommends using Adobe RGB or sRGB (the default option).
- **Output Device Profile:** This section specifies the color space used by output devices such as desktop printers and printing presses. The color management system utilizes the output device to match the colors in a document with the colors in the output device's color space. Consider specific printing factors like paper type and ink when creating the output profile.
- **Document Profiles:** This outlines the specific RGB or CMYK color space for the page. When a document is assigned or tagged with a profile, the program will display an accurate description of the document's true color appearance. Adobe programs utilize the Working Space choices set in the Color Settings dialog box to determine which profile to apply to a new document when Color Management is enabled. Untagged documents only display a raw color number without any assigned profile. Adobe program efficiently uses the current working space profile to display and modify colors in untagged documents.

CHAPTER FOUR
EXPLORING THE PHOTO EDITOR

Delving further into Photo Editor with the Advanced Edit Mode

When you first enter Advanced Edit mode, the screen displays the image. If you have experience working in a Windows environment, you will find some of the tools familiar. It is essential to gain familiarity with the various tools, panels, and objects in the environment by understanding their names and locations. Begin using the various tools, panels, and resources available to you.

After opening the Photo Editor, you can access the following features in Expert Mode.

- **System Menu Button**: Located on the left side of the menu bar, you can access the System Menu Button. Just click the button to use this feature and choose an option from the list that pops up.
- **The Menu Bar**: Task-execution commands are available in the Menu Bar section. The menu bar contains various commands such as File, Edit, Image, Enhance, Layer, Select, Filter, View, and Help. The shortcut keys can be found in the menu bar next to the different subcommands.

- **The Open Bar:** Located beneath the menu bar on the left-hand side of the status bar is The Open Bar. You can use the Open option on the far left of the shortcuts bar to access previously opened photos or create new files.
- **The Edit Buttons:** These buttons are at the heart of the shortcut bar in the Photo Editor. You have the option to select between Quick, Guided, and Advanced modes

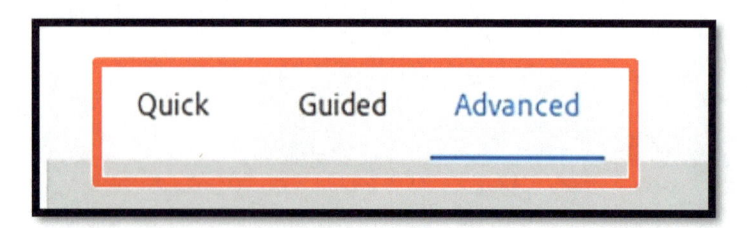

- **The Share:** Located on the far-right side of the Home screen is The Share. Feel free to use this button for creating and sharing calendars, collages, and other items.
- **The Create Button:** Located next to the Open bar is the Create Button. This tool is used to generate various types of content like slideshows, photo collages, photo reels, quote graphics, and more.

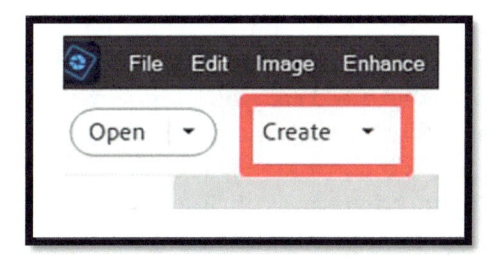

- **Status Bar:** It is the bar that provides information about the picture you are currently working on.

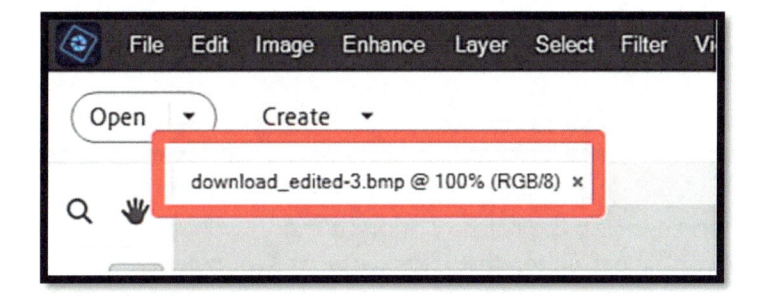

- **The Tool Box/Panel:** This section provides the tools necessary for editing photos in the Photo Editor. There are various tools available such as the Zoom Tool, Hand Tool, Move Tool, Lasso Tool, Quick Selection, Spot Healing, Clone Stamp, Eraser, Gradients, Red Eye, Smart Brush, Blur, Paint Bucket, Color Picker, Horizontal Type, and more. You can find this option on the left side of the Home screen.

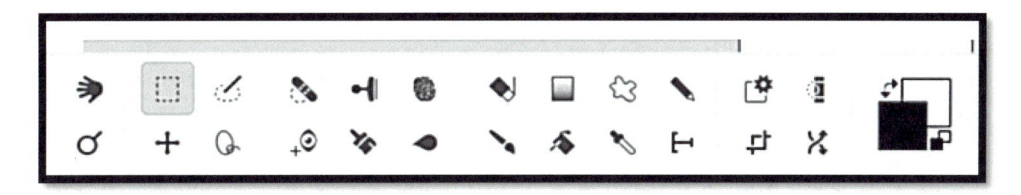

- **The Tool Options and Photo Bin:** Located below the Status bar are the Tool Options and Photo Bin. Customize the options for the various tools in the Toolbox using the Tool Options menu. You can view or access photos in the Photo Bin by clicking on

the Photo Bin Button. To access the Photo Bin, click on the button located at the bottom left of the window. The Tool Options can also be found similarly.
- **Image Window**: The Image Window serves as the main workspace in the Photoshop Element program. Countless photos are opened and displayed in the image window at the top.
- **Photo Tabs**: In contrast to the status bar, which only shows details about the current tab, the Photo Tab showcases all the photos opened in the Photo Editor. These images are conveniently arranged in multiple tabs at the window's top.
- **Panel Bin**: The Layer panels are displayed here. Simply select the symbol located at the bottom of the Panel Bin to switch the panel. All the panels such as Layers, Effect, Graphics, and Favorites are conveniently located in the Panel Bin.
- **Undo/Redo**: Undo/Redo commands in the Photo Editor are crucial and can be found next to the Photo Bin/Tool Options.

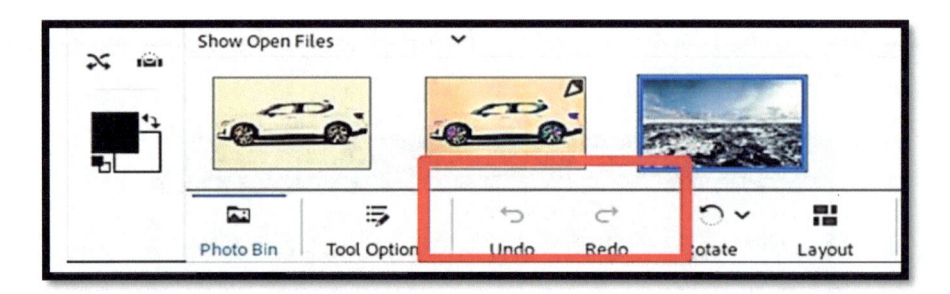

- **Rotate**: When choosing the rotate option, a menu will appear in the Image Window where you can select either the Clockwise or Counterclockwise tool to rotate the picture.
- **Layout**: Arranging the layout of your image files in the Photo Editor allows you to choose how they will appear - in rows, columns, or as a grid in the image window.
- **Organizer**: Located on the right side of the Home Screen is the Organizer. For a polished and efficient image collection, use this tool for importing, viewing, and organizing pictures. Organize your photographs with features for categorizing, ranking, sorting, and locating in the Organizer.
- **Home Screen**: The Home Screen feature allows users to access the Photoshop Element's home screen.
- **Elements Web:** Access the official Adobe Elements website through the Elements Web option.
- **Photo Bin Options Menu:** When you select the Photo Bin Options Menu button, a menu of choices will pop up. These options include printing selected images and making a creation from photos chosen in the Photo Bin.

How to Open the Image Window

The image window serves as the main workspace for the Photoshop Element program. The many images that are created are shown in the top section of the Image Window. Opening a picture in the Image Windows provides access to a wide range of advanced tools and capabilities.

Follow these steps to open an image in an Image Window:

1. Head to the File menu and select **Open**.
2. When the Open dialog box appears, you can easily navigate through the folder and select the photos you want.
3. Choose the picture you want and click on the Open button.

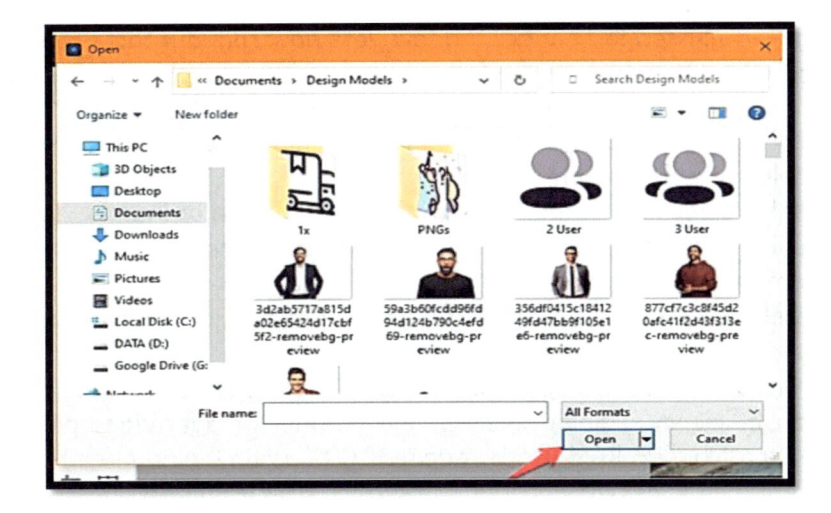

Here are the key items that will be showcased in the Image Window:

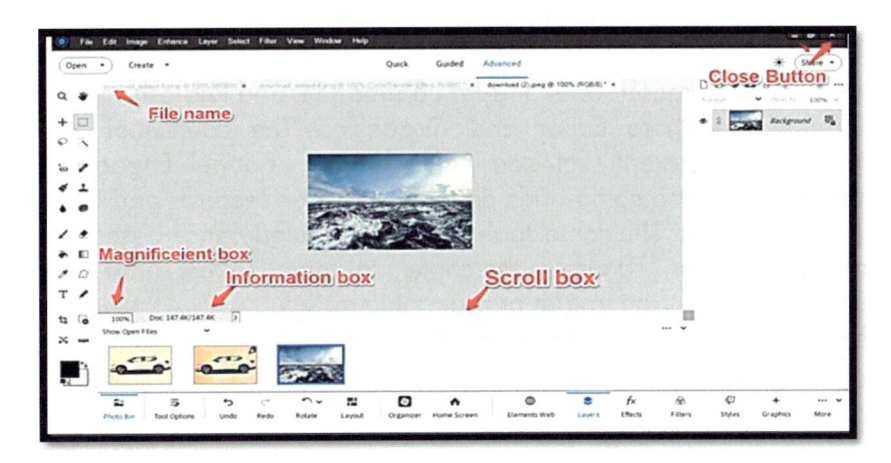

- **File Name**: Each file opened in the image window displays its filename. Above the image window in the Photo Editor, you will find the filename displayed.
- **Close Button**: The X symbol located to the left of the filename indicates the option to close the file.
- **Scroll Bars:** When zooming in on an image, the scroll bar becomes active. Feel free to use the scroll arrows, scroll bar, or the Hand tool in the Tools pane to navigate the picture within the window
- **Magnificent Box:** Check out the Magnificent Box feature to easily see how a picture is zoomed in or out.
- **Information Box**: This feature enables you to select the information you want to display by choosing from the available options in the pop-up menu.
- **Sizing the Window**: When resizing the window, simply drag any corner in or out while the image is undocked and not viewed as a tab.

Having thoroughly discussed the Image Window, let's now shift our focus to the pop-menu of the Information Box. They include the following;

- **Document Sizes**: Displaying information about the size and resolution of stored files is available in the Document Sizes option.
- **Document Profile:** This feature displays the color profile of the file.
- **Document Dimension**: It shows the physical size of the document in your chosen measurement unit, like inches.
- **Present Selected Layer:** Choose the Current Selected Layer as a display by clicking on a layer in the Layer panel and selecting it.
- **Scratch Sizes**: This feature displays the Memory usage of each open document.
- **Efficiency**: Efficiency is determined by the number of operations performed when using the scratch disk. RAM usage reaches 100% when the number increases. When the percentage drops below 100%, the scratch disk is utilized.
- **Timing**: Reflects the duration of the preceding operation.
- **Current Tool:** Displaying the selected tool name from the Touch panel.

Identifying Contextual Menus

Many apps use contextual menus for standard commands, and Photoshop Element follows suit, particularly in the Photo Editor and Organizer. The contextual menu displays commands related to the currently selected tool, selection, or panel. Engage the contextual menu to access varying menu commands depending on the features and tools being used and the location of the click. The contextual menu provides guidance based on the objects, tools, and areas you click on. **To access the contextual menu, follow these steps:**

- Hover the cursor over an image or a panel item.
- Make a selection by right-clicking and choosing a command from the menu.

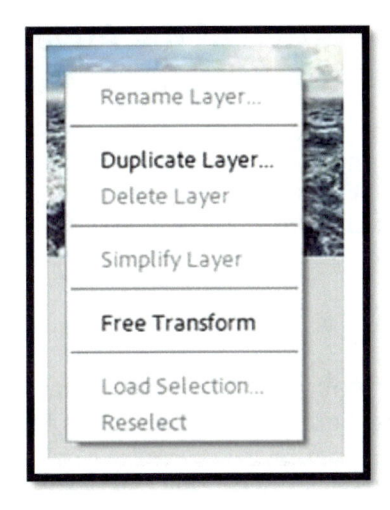

- Remember to access the contextual menu from the Menu bar.
- Several panel objects are currently missing the context menu.

Choosing the right tools

First, let's explore the different tools available in the Tools Panel; particularly in the Advanced Edit Mode, before moving on to selecting the appropriate ones.

Using the Toolbox in the Quick Mode

The Quick mode toolbox contains several sets of tools that can be used efficiently. There are various tools available such as Zoom, Hand, Quick Selection, Eye, Whiten Teeth, Straighten, Type, Spot Healing Brush, Crop, and Move.

The Toolbox in the Advanced Mode

The toolbox in the Advanced mode is more powerful and sophisticated compared to the toolbox in the Quick mode. The toolbox in Expert mode is categorized as follows.

- View
- Draw
- Select
- Enhance
- Modify

Tool located in the View group of the Advanced Mode toolbox

- **Zoom Tool:** Use the Zoom tool to adjust the size of an image.

- **The Hand Tool:** This tool in the Photoshop Element workspace is used for repositioning images. You can use this tool to easily move your image around.

Tools in the Select Group of the Advanced Mode

- **Move Tool (V):** This tool is used for adjusting layers and selections within Photoshop Element.

- **Rectangular Marquee Tool (M):** Used for outlining a rectangular area within an image. Remember to hold down the Shift key to create a square selection.

- **Elliptical Marquee Tool (M):** This tool is used for generating an elliptical selection. Remember to hold down the Shift key to create a circular selection.

- **Lasso Tool (L):** This feature enables you to create a free-form selection within a specific area of the image.

- **Magnetic Lasso Tool (L):** When selecting a shape in an image, this tool assists in creating a bold outline with high contrast.

- **Polygonal Lasso Tool (L):** Used for creating selection border segments with straight edges.

- **Quick Selection Tool:** This tool generates a color and texture selection for any part of the picture that is selected or dragged.

- **Selection Brush Tool (A):** You can select the specific area you wish to paint by using the brush tool with this feature.

- **Magic Wand Tool (A):** Used for quickly selecting pixels with similar hues.

- **Refine Selection Brush Tool (Y):** This function allows for the automatic detection of edges to add or remove areas from a selection.

- **Auto Selection Tool (A):** This tool is designed to automatically detect the margins of an area and adjust the selection accordingly.

Tools within the Enhanced Group of the Advanced Mode Toolbox

They include the following;

- **Eye Tool:** This feature helps to remove the red-eye effect and pet-eye appearance, and corrects closed eyelids in your photos.

- **Spot Healing Brush (J):** This tool is used to remove imperfections from an image by selecting a specific area of the picture.

- **Smart Brush Tool (F):** This tool allows you to fine-tune the tone and color balance of specific areas in a picture.

- **Detail Smart Brush Tool (F):** This tool, similar to the painting tool, enables you to paint specific sections of a photo with adjustments.

- **Clone Stamp Tool (S):** This tool uses an image sample to paint over elements in your image, allowing you to replicate objects, remove image imperfections, or paint over objects.

- **Pattern Stamp Tool (S):** This tool is used for generating a design over an image.

- **Blur Tool (R):** This tool is used to smooth out rough edges or areas by eliminating some of the edges.

- **Sharpen Tool (R):** Enhance images by focusing on soft edges to boost clarity and sharpness.

- **Smudge Tool (R):** This tool helps stimulate a wet paint-smearing brush. This tool transfers the color from the starting point of the stroke to wherever you move it.

- **Sponge Tool (O):** This tool is used to adjust the color saturation of a particular area within an image.

- **Dodge Tool (O):** This tool is used to brighten specific areas of an image. This tool can also be used to enhance features in shadows.

- **Burn Tool (O):** This tool is used to shade parts of an image. This tool is great for enhancing details in the highlight.

Tools located in the Draw group of the Advanced Mode

They include the following:

- **Brush Tool (B):** This tool is used to create color strokes with varying levels of intensity. It can also be used to enhance retouching abilities.

- **Impressionist Brush Tool (B):** This tool is used for fine-tuning the color and enhancing the details of the image.

- **Color Replacement Tool (B):** This tool helps decrease the amount of specific colors in your photo.

- **Eraser Tool (E):** While exploring the images in the photo, this tool helps remove pixels.

- **Background Eraser Tool (E):** This tool is used for converting the color of a pixel to transparent pixels, making it simple to remove an item from its background.

- **Magic Eraser Tool (E):** This tool is perfect for adjusting similar pixels when moved around within an image.

- **Paint Bucket Tool (K):** This tool is used to fill an area with a color value that matches the pixels you select.

- **Pattern Tool (K):** Instead of using one of the brush tools, you can use this tool to apply a fill or pattern to your picture.

- **Gradient Tool (G):** This tool generates a gradient within a designated area of an image.

- **Color Picker Tool (I):** This tool duplicates the color of a section in an image and applies it to create a new background or foreground.

- **Custom Shape Tool (U):** This tool enables you to create a wide range of shapes. You can locate these forms in the Tool Options bar once you select the Custom Shape tool. The Tool Options bar provides a variety of shape tools such as rectangle, rounded rectangle, ellipse, polygon, star, line, and selection.

- **Type Tool (T):** This program enables you to create and modify captions on a picture. Additional type-related options in the Tool Options bar include Vertical Type, Horizontal Mask Type, Vertical Type Mask, Text on Shape, and Text on Custom Path.

- **Pencil Tool (N):** This tool is perfect for creating precise, clean lines without any restrictions.

Tools found in the Modify group of the Advanced Mode Toolbox

They include the following:

- **Crop Tool (C):** With this tool, you can easily crop a specific section of an image.

- **Cookie Cutter Tool (C):** This tool allows you to easily crop images into any shape you want.

- **Perspective Crop Tool (C):** When cropping a picture, this tool is used to adjust the perspective of the image.

- **Recompose Tool (W):** This tool is designed to resize images while preserving all their original features.

- **Content-Aware Move Tool (Q):** This function is typically used to choose an item before relocating it.

- **Straighten Tool (P):** This function is used to adjust the position of a picture either vertically or horizontally.

Simply follow any of the steps provided to select one of the tools mentioned.

- Choose a tool from the toolbox.
- When selecting tools, simply use the keyboard shortcut of your choice. As an illustration, pressing P will activate the Straighten tool.

One can configure a Shift key to select a tool. The preferences settings control this. Follow these instructions to change the default settings and avoid pressing the **Shift key** in the future.

- From the Edit menu, navigate to **Preferences**.
- Choose **General** and uncheck the box for the Use **Shift key** for the Tool Switch.

Choosing from the Tool Options

The Tool Options bar is displayed at the bottom of the Element window. Various options in the Tool Options section can be used with a selected tool. When you select the Lasso Tool, the Tool Options menu will display options such as the Polygonal Lasso Tool and Magnetic Lasso Tool.

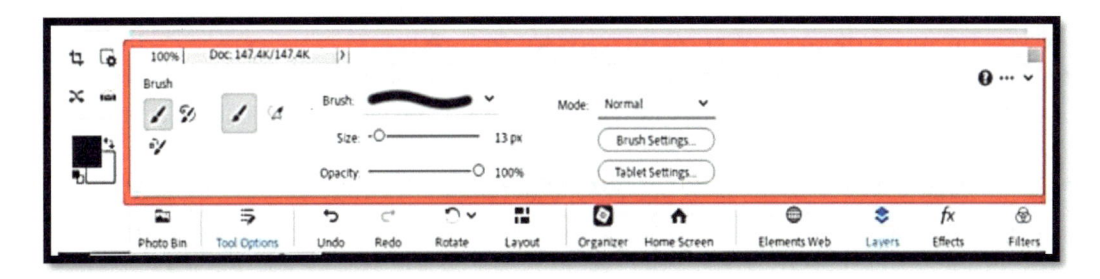

Using the Panels

The panels can be found on the right-hand side of the main screen, in both Quick and Advanced Edit modes. The Quick Edit mode includes an Adjustment panel, Effects, Textures, and Frames. When using the Advanced edit mode, you'll have access to a wider variety of panels such as Layers, Effects, Filters, Styles, Graphics, and More.

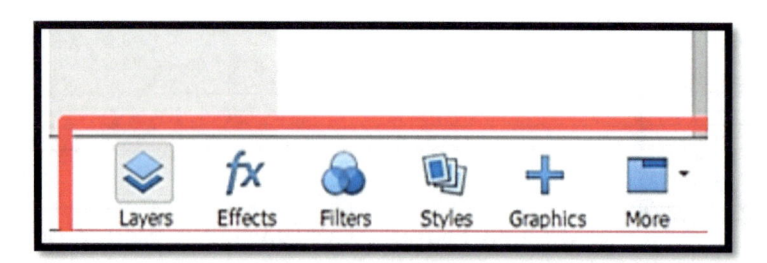

Let's efficiently go over the panels in both Quick Edit and Expert Edit modes.

- **Layers**: Layers are crucial and stand out as the most significant panel among all the others. You can enhance your document by adding text, multiple photographs, and other elements to various layers using the layer panel while working on a creative project. With the layer's panel, you can make edits to your project at any stage of the production process. In the top-left corner of the layer panel, you will find access to various tools, while the top-right corner features an icon with horizontal lines.
- **Effects**: Effects are available in this section through menus and tabs for selecting various effects to apply to images. This panel provides users with intricate recipes that can be easily applied to any image with just one click, offering automatic color adjustments, special effects, and other advanced features.
- **Graphics**: Graphics options include clip art, text effects, scalable vector shapes, and various picture frame designs that can be easily applied to images with just one click. Objects in the panel can be sorted and filtered by Type, Activity, Mood, Event, Object, Season, and various other criteria. You can find some features for download on Adobe's official websites.
- **Filter**: Here is a small thumbnail demonstrating the functionality of each FX filter. Just click on the thumbnail to activate the effect. With 98 unique filters available, you have a vast array of combinations to explore.
- **Styles**: Styles are used to modify the image by applying a filter to the entire layer. You can find drop shadows, glow, bevels, patterns, and glass button effects in the Styles tab. There are a total of 176 unique styles available in the Styles section.
- **Textures**: This collection offers a range of creative elements such as sun beams and light leaks that can be used for backgrounds, web pages, and beyond. By simply clicking once, you can easily apply a textured overlay to your image. Feel free to utilize your Adobe account to access new textures or overlays.

Additional Information

The More panels can be found to the right of the Graphics panel in the bottom right corner of the main window. Clicking the More panels reveals a pop-up menu with access to additional panels not displayed in the Panel bin. **Here is a brief overview of the extra panels.**

- **Actions**: Element inherited this function from Adobe Photoshop. This function allows you to automatically make various adjustments to your photo. Replaying specific actions or interactions captured in the images is a key feature of this functionality. There are additional actions available online for download and integration with the Elements, such as cropping, resizing, copying, and adding a border to photos.
- **Adjustments**: Adjustments can be made using sliders for exposure, lighting, color, balance, and sharpness in the adjustment panels.
- **Color Swatches:** Choose the color type by using the Color Swatches panels. You can use either a paintbrush or a pencil to create this backdrop color. Create a custom color swatch using these panels to finish a specific project.
- **Histogram**: Upon opening the Histogram panel, a range of tones are presented for adding or applying to foreground images. Midtone, highlights, whites, blacks, underexposed, and overexposed are some of these elements.
- **Info**: This panel provides the readout for various color values and the physical dimensions of your photographs.
- **Navigator**: The Navigator feature allows you to zoom in and move around an image within the image window.
- **Custom Workspace:** Customize your workspace by docking and undocking panels here. Moreover, this panel allows you to customize your workspace based on your preferences.
- **Create/Share Panel:** The Create panel is used for various creations like calendars, greeting cards, photo books, and more. The share panel is equipped with numerous tools for easily sharing photos

Working with the Photo Bin

You can locate the Photo Bin below the Element window and above the taskbar. It serves various functions such as opening and closing photos, hiding photos, rotating photos, and viewing file metadata. Images opened in the Image window are shown as thumbnails in the Photo Bin. You can easily transfer multiple open photographs between different locations using the Photo Bin.

Showing Different Views of the Same Image

Follow these steps to ensure the image is displayed consistently:

1. Choose the image's thumbnail in the Photo Bin and navigate to the View menu
2. Choose "**New Window**" for the image name.

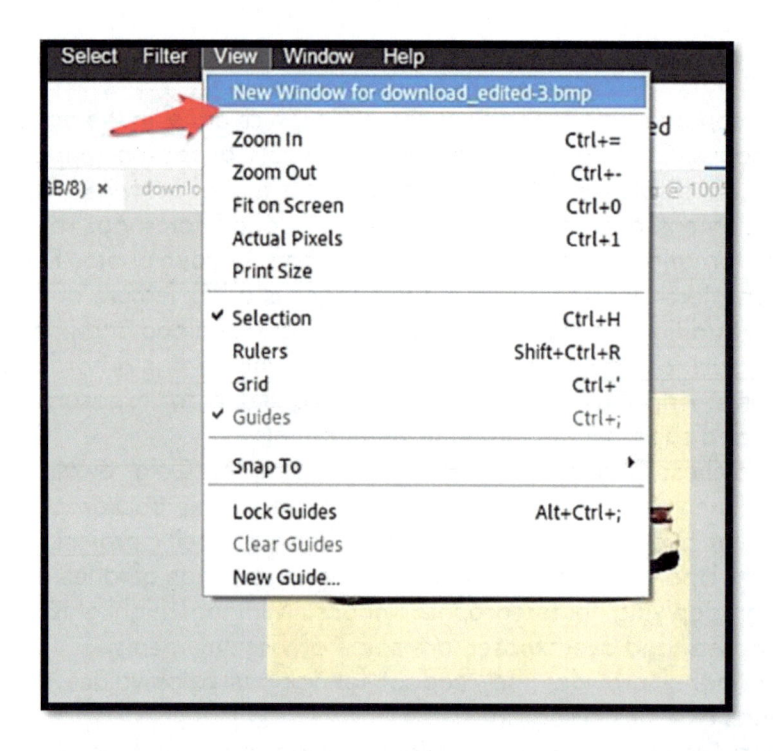

3. There is a new image shown on the Image window with an additional thumbnail in the Photo Bin
4. For a different view of the same image, simply double-click on the Thumbnails in the Photo bin.
5. Click on the **Zoom tool** in the Tool panels to zoom in on the image.

Getting Very Familiar with the Photo Bin Actions

There are additional options available for managing the images in the Photo Bin through the Photo Bin Actions menu. To access these options, refer to the image below and click on the small square with four lines located in the top right corner of the bin.

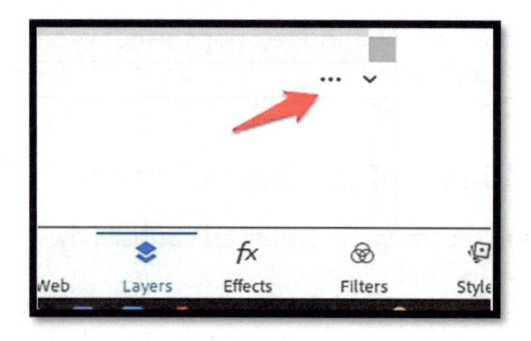

The Photo Bin Actions perform the following tasks:

64

- **Printing Bin Files**: This option is helpful when you need to print a file from the Photo Bin. Start by selecting the file you wish to print, and then choose Print Bin Files from the drop-down menu. Once you reach the Print dialog box, you can easily print the photo prints of the selected file.
- **Save Bin As An Album**: Use this tool to add additional images to an existing album or create a new one.
- **Show Grid**: Used for generating a grid around photos in the Photo bin.

Exploring the Guided Mode

With Photoshop Elements advanced Guided Edit mode, you can easily make decisions about your photos and let the computer handle the rest. The purpose of the Guided Edit mode is to assist you in various editing activities by providing step-by-step guidance. Head to the Shortcut bar and choose **Guided** to access the Guided Edit mode.

There are six categories in the Guide Edit mode, listed below:

- **Basics Edit:** Enhance your images by adjusting features like brightness, contrast, skin tone correction, cropping, levels, and more.
- **Color Edit:** Enhance your images by adjusting the color using features like enhanced color, lomo camera effect, removing a cast color, saturated film effect, and more.
- **The Black Edit and White Edit:** This edition enables you to effortlessly transform your photo into black and white by using features like B&W color pop, B&W selection, and more.
- **The Fun Edit:** Enhance your images with unique features like meme maker, double exposure, and multi-photo text using the Fun Edit.
- **The Special Edits:** Enhance your photos with creative and artistic effects like depth of field, frame creator, Orton effect, and perfect landscape using the Special Edits feature.
- **The Photomerge Edit**: Combine or connect multiple images or photos to produce a new image using the Photomerge Edit feature. The Photomerge edit includes Photomerge compose, Photomerge exposure, Photomerge faces, and Photomerge group.

Mastering the Editing Environment

Using preference options allows you to customize a program to match your unique working style and tailor your job experience. Adobe Photoshop Element has two Preference dialog boxes: one in the Organizer and one in the Photo Editor.

Launching and navigating preferences in the photo editor

The Preference dialog box in the Photo Editor organizes the options into panes for efficiently completing tasks in Photoshop Element. Upon opening the Preference dialog box, the General pane is the initial one to appear.

Opening the Preference dialog box:

- Head to the **Edit menu**, choose **Preference**, and then **General**.
- The Preference dialog box will now appear on the screen.

Let's quickly examine the features in the Preference dialog box and how they operate:

- **Panelists**: Located on the left-hand side of the Preference dialog box are the panelists, which display various panels like General, Saving files, Scratch disks, etc. When you click on any of these pages, you will be presented with more options to explore.
- **Ok**: This is used to verify any modification in any of the panes and close the Preference dialog box
- **Cancel**: Clicking on "**Cancel**" will revert to the original settings when you first open the pane and then close the dialog box.
- **Reset**: Resetting this option will restore the Preference dialog box to its original settings. After resetting, the dialog box remains open for you to configure the new settings.
- **Previous**: Used for navigating to the previous pane
- **Next**: This function allows you to navigate to the following pane.

Just a reminder: Panes are sections within the Preference dialog box.

Exploring all the Preference Panes thoroughly

There are multiple panes with a range of functions in the preference panes. Let's thoroughly analyze each pane and its specific functions.

- **General Preference**: Adjust the general settings for the editing environment here.
- **Saving Files References**: When it comes to saving files, this section covers the available file-saving choices. Extensions can be added to filenames and files can be saved with picture previews, layers, and compatibility options in this section.

- **Performance Preference**: This window displays historical statistics and memory settings for allocating memory in Photoshop Element.
- **Scratch Disks:** This panel uses the hard drive as an extension of the RAM.
- **Display and Cursor Preferences:** Customize the display and cursor preferences to adjust how different tool cursors and Crop tools are shown while cropping photos.
- **Transparency Preferences:** Choose your transparency preferences in these panes to control how transparency is displayed in the Element.
- **Units and Ruler Preferences**: Specify your column guide, and ruler units, and document default resolutions for precise control.
- **Guides & Grid Preferences:** This feature allows you to customize gridline color, divisions, and subdivisions.
- **Plugins Preference**: Responsible for choosing a different Plug-Ins folder. This Plug-Ins are third-party programs that help you carry out tasks not included in Element. You can easily locate the Photoshop Element Plug-Ins online.
- **Adobe Partner Services**: Adobe Partner Services allows Elements to search for new services, remove any stored data online, and reset all account information.
- **Application Updates**: You can choose to automatically update the Element application or get notified when a new version is available.
- **Type Preferences**: Adjust text attributes in the Type Preferences section. Preview font sizes and use different font types, including Asian characters displaying the font name in English.
- **Country/Region**: Choose a country or region from the drop-down menu.

CHAPTER FIVE
MOVING ALONG WITH THE ORGANIZER

The Organizer, which can be found on the right side of the Home Screen and was previously covered in this book, is the place where you may import, browse, and arrange images to maintain an efficient and well-organized image collection. In addition to identifying your photographs, the Organizer provides you with options for classifying, rating, and sorting them.

Sorting Images and Media on the Hard Drive

The bulk of the space on the hard drive is taken up by the photographs and media. For reference, it would be necessary to classify the photographs if there are a great number of them. Making a folder a designated location is the most prudent line of action. There is no restriction on the name that can be used for the folder; it can include dates, places, events, and several other things. As soon as you have completed everything, you can begin organizing the photographs into folders. One other thing that may be done with the Organizer is to import files.

Adding pictures to the organizer

Before you can import any picture into your organizer, you must first save it to the hard disk of your computer. **When you want to upload photographs from a camera or another device to the actual components of your computer, you can use the following ways:**

- Simply go to the File menu inside the Organizer, click on the **Get Photo and Videos option,** and then select **From Files and Folder** from the right-hand side of the menu.

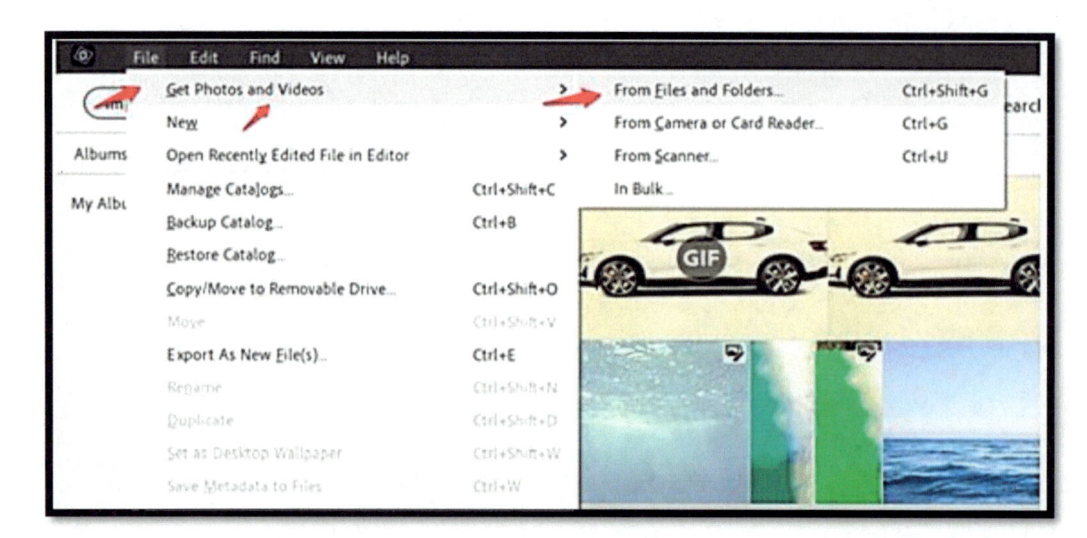

- Go through your hard drive and choose the picture you want to add to the Get Photo and Videos dialog box. Once you have made your selection, proceed to click on the **Get Media** button.

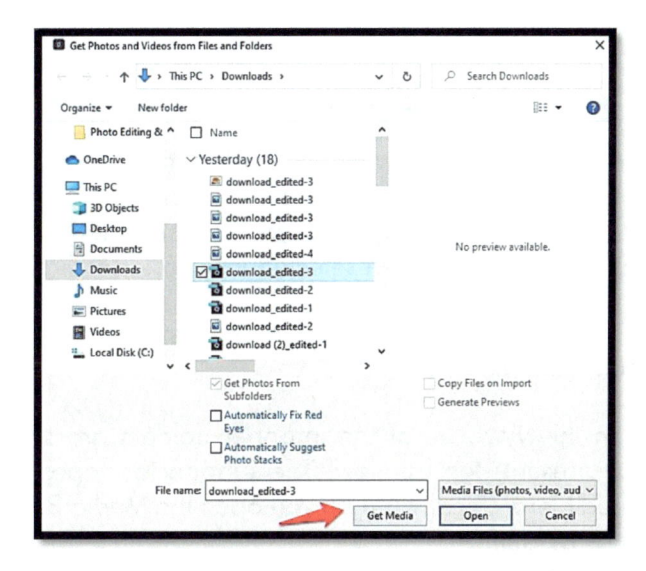

Using the Element Downloader to Download Images from a Camera

Following the steps outlined below will allow you to transfer photos from your camera to your organizer.

1. Step one is to either insert the media card from the camera or connect the camera to your computer using a USB connection.
2. Proceed to open the Organizer Window.
3. Open the File menu, select **Get Photo and Videos**, and then click on **From Camera or Card Reader**.

4. To download photos from a media card, go to the Get Photos from drop-down list inside the Adobe Photo Downloader dialog box and choose the media card.
5. Choose the **Browse button** to locate the folder from which you desire to copy the picture. After that, proceed to click on the **Get Media button** to import the photographs.

Working with the Media Browser

Through the use of the Media Browser, which is located inside the Organizer itself, every picture or photo that is imported into the Organizer is shown as thumbnails in the middle of the Media Browser. Inside the Import panel, you will be able to see photos that have been imported from a folder that has been selected inside the Media browser.

An Import panel that contains a list of folders can be found on the left side of the Media browser, as can be seen in the below:

- **The List View:** In this view, all of the imported folders are shown in alphabetical order. This view presents the list view. The subdirectory does not include any files that are structured hierarchically. When you open the Media Browser, this is the view that is selected by default.
- **The Tree View:** This mode allows the photographs in the Media Browser to be presented in a hierarchical arrangement. The Tree View mode is where you can find it. This view may be accessed by selecting View as Tree from the drop-down menu located in the Menu section.

Using the Scanner in the Organizer

You may acquire scans of your slides, negatives, and photographs by utilizing the organizer that is included with Photoshop Element. Through the use of the same USB or FireWire connections, the scanner may be linked to both the card readers and the camera together.

Image Requirements for Scanning in Photoshop Elements

Before starting the scanning process, you can modify the resolution and color settings on the scanner device itself. You can also choose the resolution that you want to use before scanning a file.

Be sure to take into consideration the following components to assist you with scanning.

- **Grayscale Images:** Grayscale images or grayscale graphics are visuals that do not include any color, but instead depend on gradients, such as varying shades of black, to form an image. Because of this, the grayscale picture has to be scanned at a resolution of 600 dots per inch or higher and then saved as a PNG file.
- **Line Art:** An example of line art is a sort of visual representation that consists simply of lines and curves, without any colors or shadings. There are many different types

of line art, including glyphs, cartoons, comics, and ideographs. The suggested resolution for scanning line art is 900 dots per inch (dpi) for print and 300 dpi for the web.
- **Halftone**: Halftones are types of images that are composed of very little dots. It is recommended that tone mapping photographs be scanned at a resolution of 1200 dots per inch or higher to guarantee that the scanner will accurately capture the halftone.
- **Color**: Colored photographs are the ones that are scanned the most often for scanning purposes. Ensure that the scan resolution is set to 600 dpi for photographs and 300 dpi for the web. For colorful images, save them in PNG format.

Importing Images Through the Use of the Scanner

If you want to import images from your scanner into the Organizer, you will need to follow the procedures that are described below. Before you use your scanner to acquire **any photographs, you should first ensure that the Scanner program has been properly installed on your computer by following the instructions that are given here:**

1. To begin, it is important to verify that your scanner is both activated and connected to your computer.
2. From the File menu, choose the option to **Get Photo and Videos**, and then proceed to click on **With Scanner**.
3. In the dialog box titled "**Get Photos from Scanner**," select the name of the scanner that you intend to use from the drop-down menu labeled "**Scanner**." Next, click on the Browse button to alter the location where the photos will be saved.
4. Click on the **Save button** to alter the file format of the photos. Finally, drag the Quality slider to either increase or decrease the quality of the scan. Finally, click on the Ok button.

5. You can make further modifications to the scanned picture inside the dialog box that appears, and after you have finished, you can proceed to click on the **Scan** button.

Exporting Images with your Mobile Devices

It is possible to transfer media files from a wide range of mobile devices, including iPhones, iPods, and other mobile devices among others.

By following the instructions below, you will be able to import photos from your phone into your Organizer file.

1. Navigate to the **File menu**, choose the option to **Get Photos and Videos**, and then proceed to click on the **From Files and Folder option**.
2. To transfer the files to the organizer, you must first go through the folder in which you copied them. After that, you must connect the device to the organizer using a USB connection.
3. Once the Photo Downloader has been opened, you should click on the **Browse button** and then open the box that opens the **Select Directory to Store Files**.
4. To see the location where the photographs are stored, you must first choose a target folder and then click on the **Select Folder button**. After that, you must click on the Get Media button to get the photos onto your computer.

There is also the possibility of using iTunes, which is offered by Apple, to transfer images from Element to the iPhone, iPod touch, or iPad. To do this, you will need to follow these instructions.

- Open the **iTunes application** and choose the option to **Add Files to the Library** from the menu. The iPhone or iPad should be connected.
- The photos will be accessed by clicking on them from the folder on the hard drive where they are stored.
- The first step is to choose Photos and Videos from the menu located at the top of iTunes. Next, verify the items you want to upload by checking the boxes next to them, and finally, click the Sync button.

Setting the Organizer Preferences

To adjust the settings of the organizer, all you need to do is follow the steps that are listed below.

- Go to the **Edit menu** and choose the **Preference option**. The dialog box provides you with the opportunity to make the required adjustments to the Organizer Preference. When you are finished, choose the OK button.

CHAPTER SIX
ORGANIZING YOUR PICTURES WITH ORGANIZER

First, let's have a look at the Organizer workspace before we go on to learning how to successfully arrange images using it.

When you open an organizer, the following features are displayed: the ability to use custom tags, among other features and functions:

- **Menu Bar:** The instructions that are necessary to carry out activities or operations inside the Organizer are located in the Menu bar as well. A file. The commands that are located in the menu bar are as follows: File, Edit, Find, View, and Help Menu for the Help Menu.

- **Search Bar:** It is possible to find images and other media assets by using the Search Bar facility. To locate photos or media, enter a search word into the drop-down box labeled "**Search**."

- **Sort By:** With the Sort By option, you can organize your media in a manner that prioritizes the most current, oldest, names, and batches of photographs that have been loaded or imported into the Organizer.

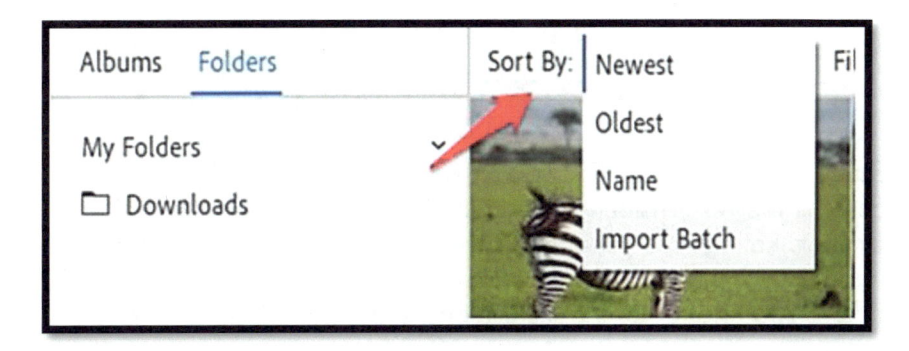

- **Features Buttons:** The buttons that include the Maximize, Minimize, and Close buttons are referred to as the Features Buttons. In Windows, these buttons are located in the upper-right-hand corner of the Organizer window. These buttons are located on the left-hand side of the Mac OS X operating system.
- **Import:** You can import media files from a variety of sources, including computers, folders, cameras, card readers, and scanners.
- **The Share**: This feature may be found on the far-right side of the Home screen. You can create and share calendars, collages, and other types of content by using this button.
- **The Create Button**: In addition to the Open bar, there is a button that is referred to as the Create button. The creation of things such as Slide shows, Photo Collages, Photo Reels, Quote Graphics, and so on may be accomplished with this.

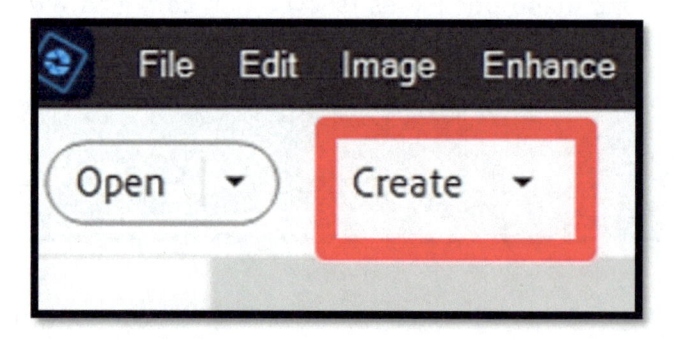

- **Albums and Folders Tabs:** Every picture album that you have made in your Organizer may be located in the Album/Folder Tab

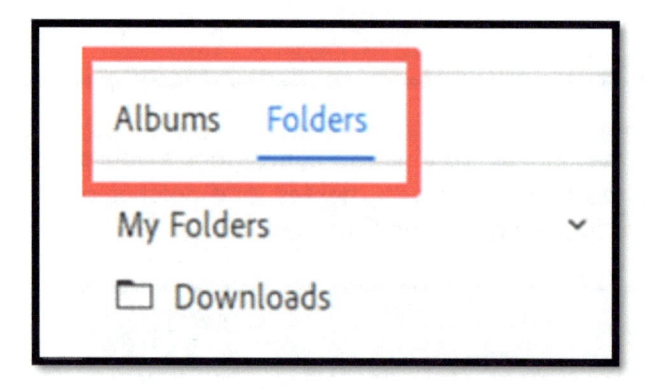

- **Ratings/Auto Curator:** The task of assigning a star rating to your picture or media asset is the responsibility of the rating function, which is also known as the auto curator. Ratings are yet another tool that may be used to organize and categorize images and media assets. You have the option of using the Auto Curator to do an automated analysis of the picture and search for visual patterns.

- **Folder View:** To gain access to the photographs included inside each folder, just choose the folder name to see them.
- **Media Browsers:** The Media browser is responsible for displaying thumbnails of the photos that have been loaded into the organizer.
- **Keynote/Information**: This feature allows users to access the Panel bin via which they may choose Options from the Tags or information.
- **Hide Panel:** In the Media Browser, you can hide the left panel by selecting the Hide Panel option. This option is helpful in situations when you want to see all of the thumbnails of the photos.
- **Undo/Rotate**: With the Undo/Rotate option, you can rotate a picture in both the clockwise and counterclockwise directions. You can also undo or redo an action by clicking on a very small arrow in this section as well.
- **Add Location**: Within the Organizer, you can establish a new place by selecting the "Add Location" option. When you choose this option, a window will emerge at the very top of the Organizer. This window will show the new location, and it will then be added to the Places panel.
- **Add Event:** You may arrange photographs by using the Organizer's Add Event tool, which is another feature that enables you to organize images.
- **Instant Fix:** Instant Fix is a tool that can assist in the process of applying Quick Edit edits to your photos. Through the use of Instant Fix, you can crop, correct red-eye, alter lighting, and more.
- **Editor**: The symbol that represents the Editor allows you to return to the Photo Editor.
- **Slideshow**: It is necessary to click on the Slideshow button to build a project that is referred to as Memory. Inside the Slideshow, the photographs are presented in the form of movies.
- **Home Screen:** When you click on this button, you will be sent back to the Home page. Thank you for your attention.
- **Zoom**: One of the features that may be used to decrease or magnify the size of thumbnails is the Zoom component.

The Views Tabs in the Organizer

When using Photoshop Element, the organizer has four different view tabs to choose from. With the help of these perspective tabs, you will be able to arrange and display your media following the individuals who are shown in the photographs, the locations where the photographs were taken, and the events that took place while the photographs were being shot. **The following is a list of the different views tabs that the Organizer offers.**

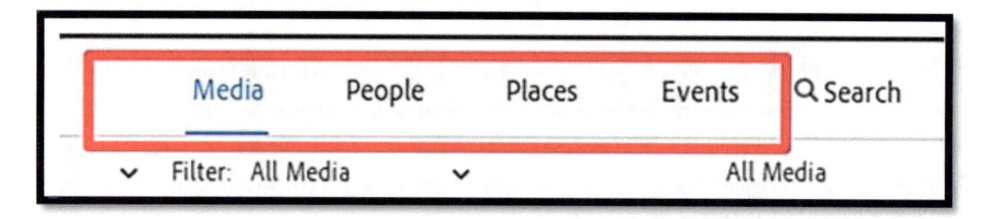

- **Media**: One of the locations where all of the media files are shown or exhibited is located in the media section. In this view, you can also make adjustments to the photographs you have.
- **People**: There is a tab called "People" that gives you the ability to examine photographs depending on the individuals who are present in them. Additionally, you can categorize the pictures of the persons who feature in them.
- **Places**: This view tab gives you the ability to examine photographs depending on the location or locations where they were shot. You also have the option of organizing the photographs following the area or location where they were shot.
- **Events**: Within this view, you can build a stack of events, each of which includes a picture of the event. To provide an example, you might create an event for a birthday celebration and then tag the photographs that are associated with the event inside that event.

Using Tags to Sort Images into Groups

When photographs are arranged in categories, it is often simpler to handle them inside the organizer. Tags are an excellent method for maintaining the organization of your photographs. The time at which a picture was taken can be used for a variety of purposes, including analysis and classification of the image. Keywords, People Tags, Places Tags, and Events Tags are the four categories that are separated into these four groups by the Tags panel.

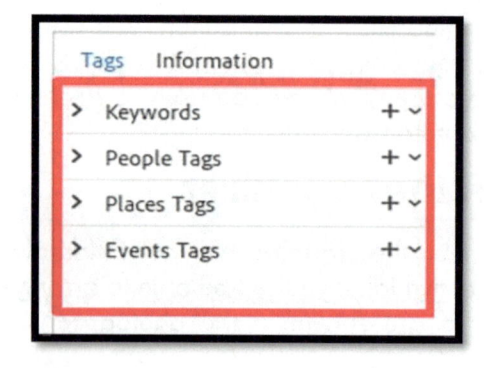

76

Creating and Viewing Tag

To create a new tag, follow the procedures that are listed below.

1. The first step is to open your media browser and choose the photographs that you want to tag.
2. To create a new tag, you can do so by clicking on the drop-down arrow that is located next to the New button, which is represented by a plus symbol.
3. To create a new category, choose it from the drop-down menu.

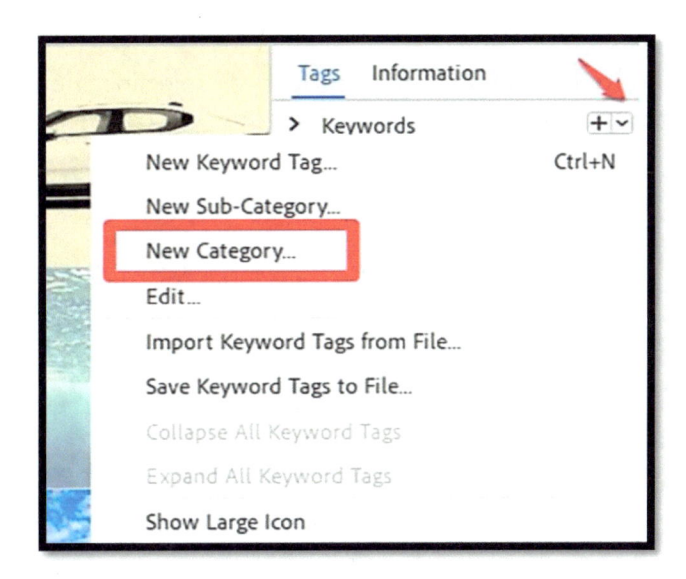

4. You may choose the category that you want to be included in the category that is listed by clicking on the drop-down menu labeled "**Category**."
5. After entering the name of the tag in the Name text box, proceed to describe it in the Note text box. Finally, proceed to click on the Ok button.

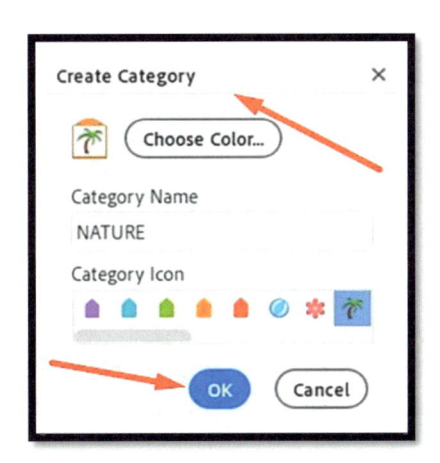

Adding Icons to Tags

To properly add an icon to a tag, follow the procedures that are listed below:

1. Go to the Tags area and click on the **New button**, which is a button that looks like a green plus sign.
2. Choose the New Keyword Tag option from the drop-down menu, and then choose the **Edit Icon option** from the Create Keyword Tag dialog box.
3. Click on the Import button located inside the Edit Keyword Tag Icon dialog box. This will allow you to search through the folder and locate the picture that you want to use as the icon.
4. You may return to the Edit Keyword Tag Icon by selecting the picture you want to edit and then clicking the **Open button**. After that, choose the OK button.

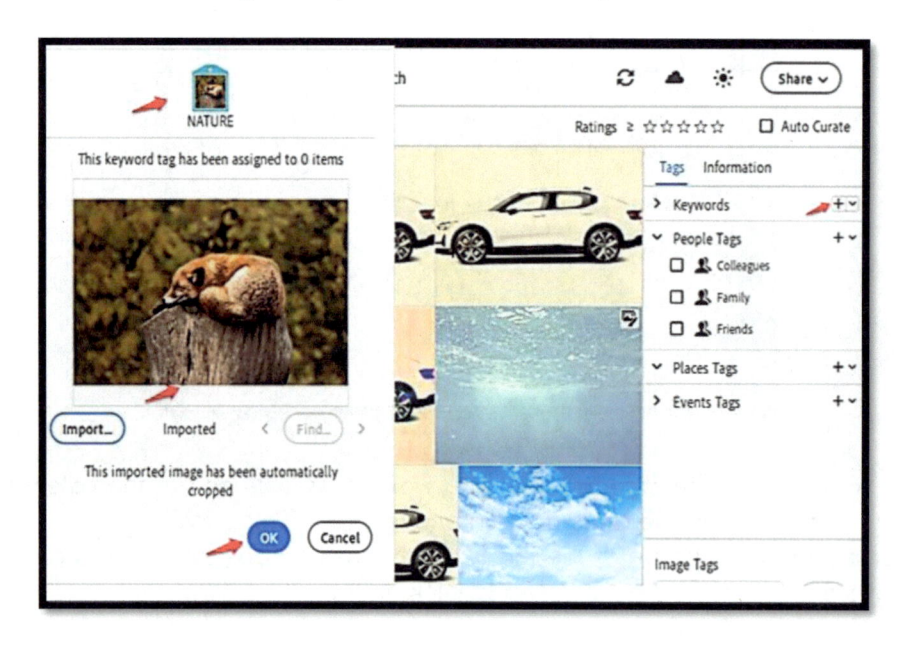

Custom Tags and their Uses

The Tags panel is where you can create your unique tags. In this part, we will go over a few commands that can be found in the drop-down menu of the Tag panel.

These commands are helpful when it comes to producing custom tags.

- **New Keyword Tag**: Following what was previously said, the New Keyword Tag is used to generate a new tag.
- **New Sub Category**: One of the tags that are included inside another tag is referred to as a "**new sub category**." Follow the procedures to create a subcategory. Choose

78

the New Sub-Category option from the menu labeled "**New**." In the dialogue box, enter the name of the new subcategory that you want to create.
- **New Category:** You have the option to create a new category by selecting the "**New Category**" option at this point. After opening the dialog box by selecting the New Category button, you will need to put in the name of the new category to create a new category.
- **Edit**: You may access the Edit Keyword dialog box by selecting this option, which is referred to as Edit. This Edit option allows you to add icons to a tag, and it is located here.
- **Import Keyword Tags from File:** When you have committed time and work into classifying files, establishing a new catalog, importing images, and also importing tags for the photographs, it is helpful to have the option to import keyword tags from the file. An XML file is associated with every tag that is exported or imported. This is true for all tags.
- **Save Keyword Tags to a File:** When you choose this option, you will have the ability to save keyword tags to a file, allowing you to access them at a later time. When you open a separate catalog file, you can import the identical collection names that were generated in one catalog file into another catalog file.
- **Collapse All Keyword Tags:** The option known as "**Collapse All keyword Tags**" gives you the ability to collapse the list in which the Tags are presented.
- **Expand All Keyword Tags**: To enlarge the collapsed list that includes the tag, there is a feature called enlarges All Keyword Tags.
- **Show Large Icon:** When you click on this option, the tags icon that is shown in the Tags panel will be transformed into a larger icon inside the panel.

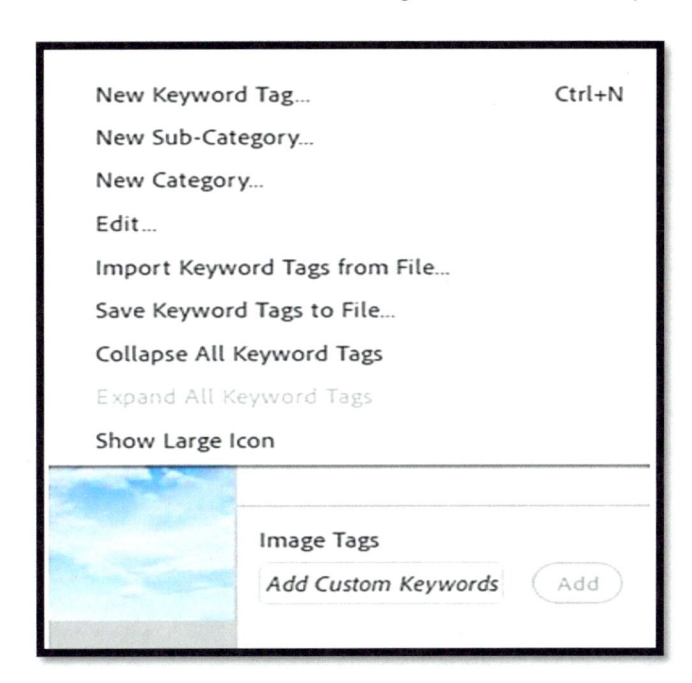

Auto Curating Images

When comparing photos, the Auto Curator searches for visual commonalities between them. As soon as the evaluations are finished, the Media Browser will show the photographs that were deemed to be the best. Within the Organizer pane, the check box for Auto Curator may be found in the upper-right corner of the window.

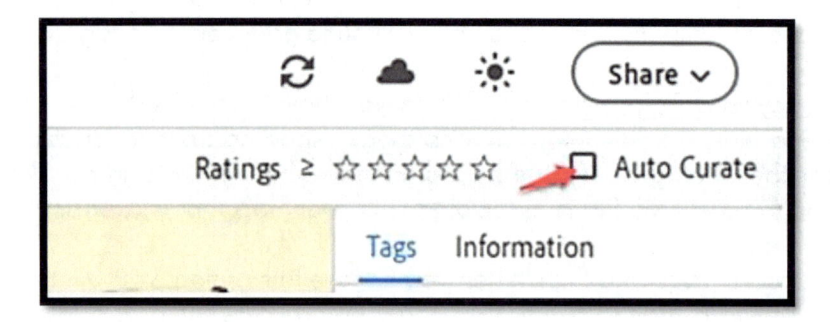

Auto Creation at Work

To get a comprehensive grasp of the possibilities of Auto Creation, it is recommended that you become acquainted with the program Auto Creation, which facilitates the creation of a variety of events inside your photographs.

- From the Edit menu, go to the Organizer Preferences section, and then choose **Media Analysis**.
- To activate Auto Creation, choose the Enable Auto Creation button and then select the Generate Auto Creations option.

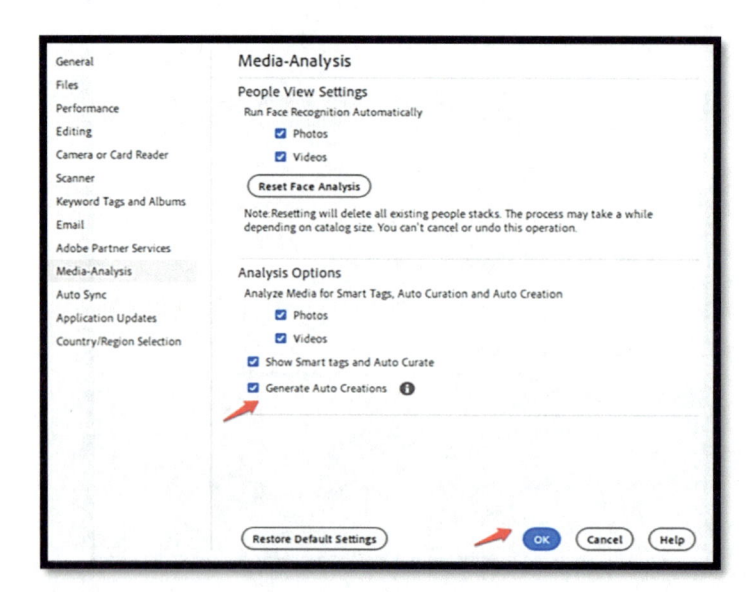

Adding New Events

There is the ability to add a brand-new event inside your Media Browser. To do this, all you need to do is click the Add New Event button that is located in the bottom left corner of the organizer. Following the completion of the entry of the name, the beginning date, the ending date, and the description in the dialogue box click the OK button.

Using Stars to Rate Images

Through the usage of the Organizer, users can assign photographs a rating ranging from one to five stars. The lowest possible rating is one star, while the highest possible rating is five stars. On top of that, you can organize your pictures according to the ratings they receive. **To assign a star rating to an image:**
1. Once you have selected the picture from the Media Browser, go to the Rating option located on the right-hand side of the screen.
2. From there, you can choose to click either one or two stars, depending on the rating you are giving.

Using Photo Albums

The albums that are accessible via the Element Organizer are, to a large extent, analogous to the traditional albums that are often used for storing and organizing your photographs. Albums allow you to organize your photographs in a variety of ways, such as by tagging them and assigning them star ratings. Not only is it possible to add many photographs to the album, but it is also possible to remove them.

Creating an Album

Using the Organizer, you can create an album of your choosing by following the procedures that are listed below.

1. To add photos to the album, you must first pick the images you want to include. Next, click on Album, which is located on the left-hand side of the Organizer. Finally, click on the plus symbol, and then select **New Album**.

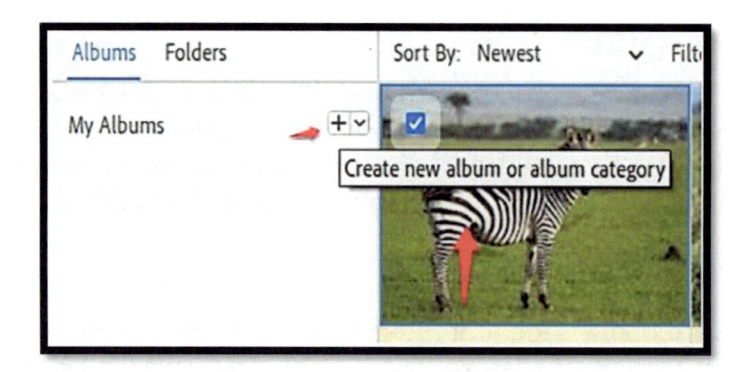

2. Enter the name of the album into the text box labeled "**Name**" located on the right-hand side of the panel. Additionally, choose the category that the album falls under from the drop-down menu labeled "**Category**."

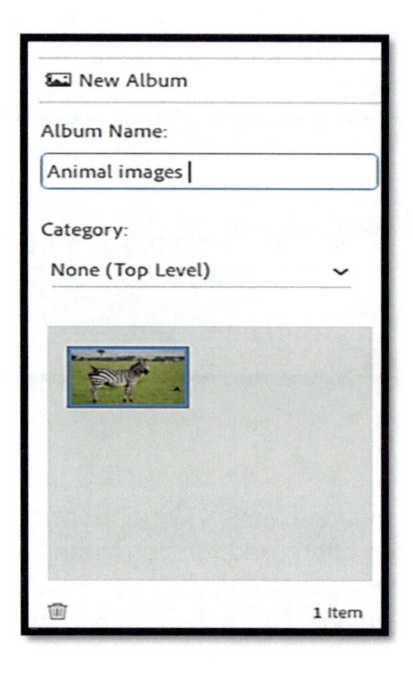

3. Once you have completed the process, you will need to click the OK button. The images will then be shown on the left side of the Media browser.

Creating an Album Category

Here are the actions you need to do to create an album category:

1. Click on the **Album option** located on the left-hand side of the Organizer. Next, click on the plus symbol, and then select the option for New Album Category.

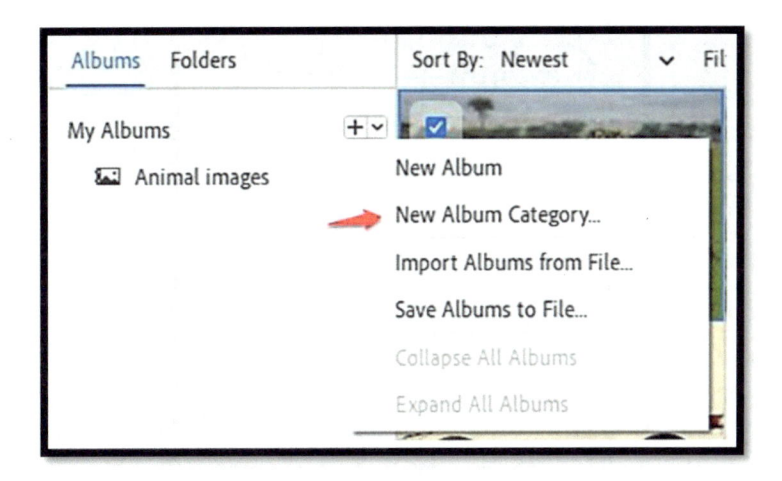

2. On the right-hand side of the panel, in the text box labeled "**Name**" and the drop-down menu labeled "**Category**," respectively, enter the name of the album and the category it falls under. Click OK after that.

It is important to note that you can add images to an album by performing any of the following:

- You have the option to choose the stack and then drag it to the album.
- You can drag the photos from the Media view into the album in the Album panel.
- You can also drag the album from the Album panel to the photo in the Media view.

Browsing Through an Album of Photos

Double-clicking on an album will allow you to see the accompanying images.

Deleting an Album

To remove an album from the Album panel, you will need to follow the instructions that are listed below:

- Right-click on the album, and then select the **Delete option**.

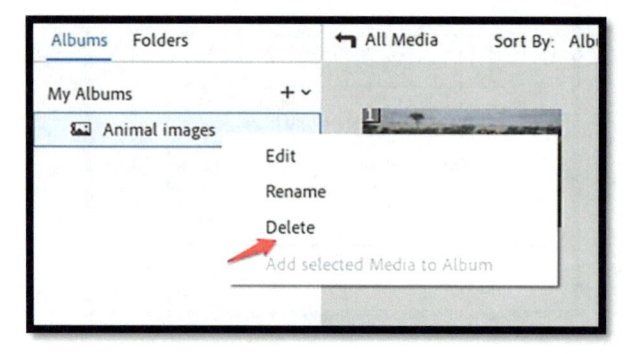

- To remove the album, you must first click the OK button in the dialog box labeled "**Confirm Album Deletion**."

Removing an Image from an Album

To delete a photo from an album, you will need to follow the procedures that are listed below:

1. Right-click on the picture that you want to remove from the album.
2. Select **Remove from Album** from the menu that appears.
3. Click on the **Remove button**.

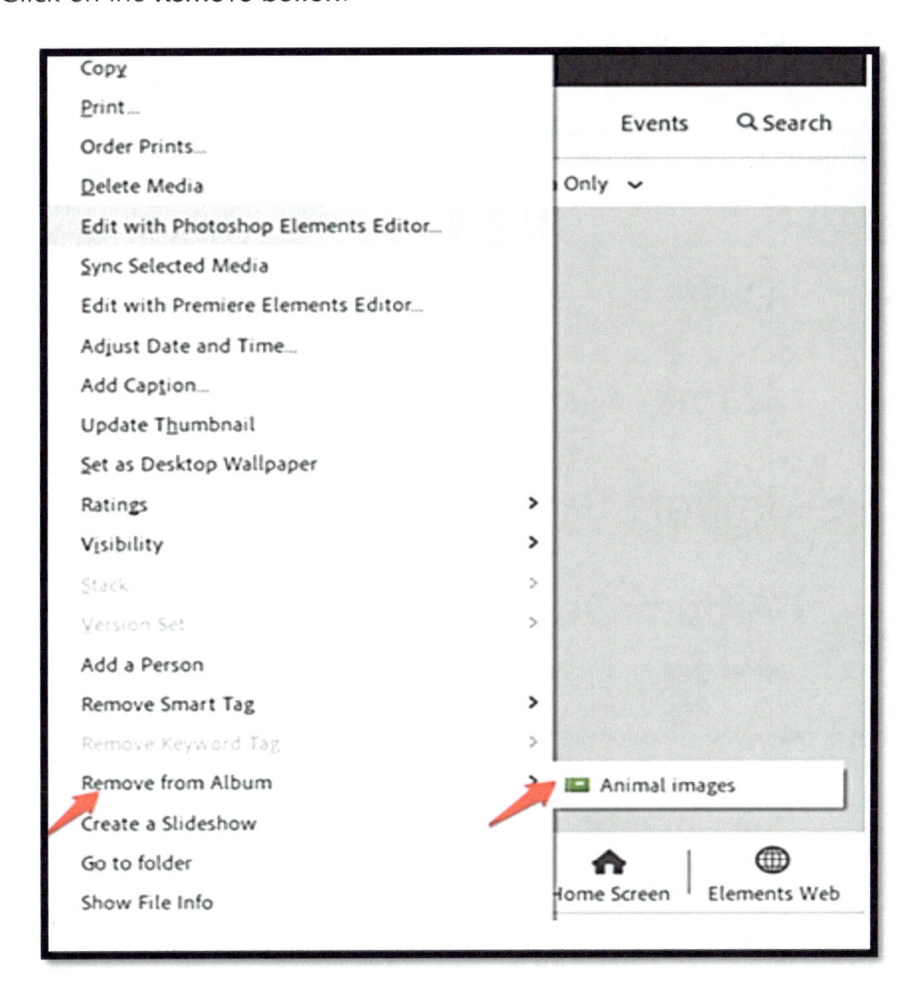

Sorting Photos in an Album

When organizing the photographs in your album, you have the option of using either the reverse chronological, chronological, or album sorting techniques. The following steps may be used to organize the photographs included in an album. Make a selection from the Album and Folders tab to choose an album. Choose one of the following options from the drop-down menu labeled "**Sort By**" in the Media view.

85

- **Newest**: In the "**Newest**" option, the images are organized in chronological order, beginning with the most current and working their way backward.
- **Oldest**: The photos in this collection are sorted chronologically, beginning with the earliest and working their way up to the most recent.
- **Name**: If you choose this option, the media will be alphabetized from A to Z based on their names.
- **Import Batch**: On the other hand, the Import Batch option organizes the photographs in batches according to the date that they were imported.
- **Album Order:** Album Order is a feature that allows the user to order the photographs in a manner that best suits their tastes.

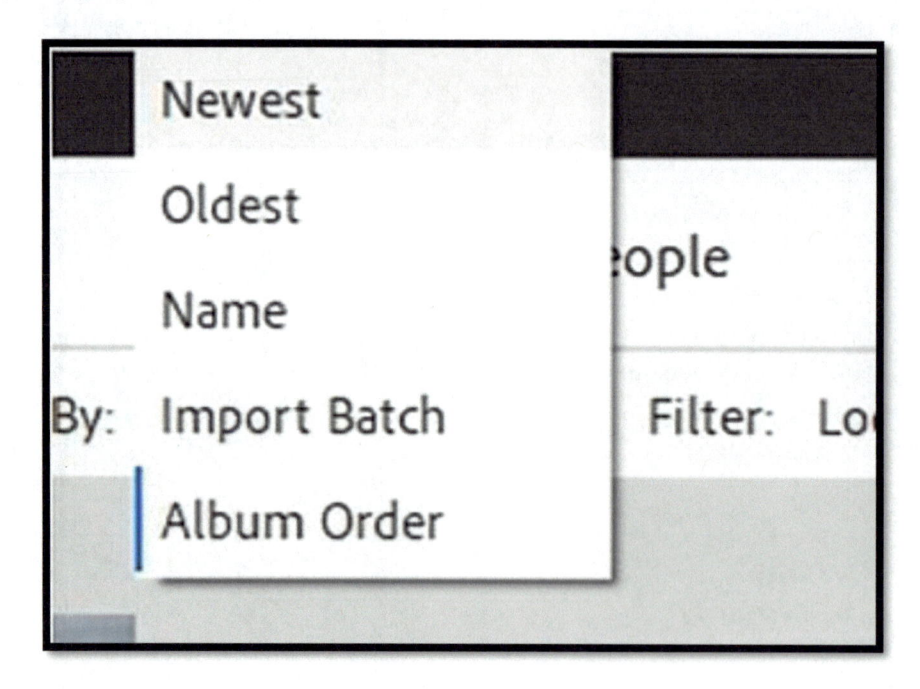

CHAPTER SEVEN
VIEWING AND LOCATING YOUR IMAGES

You can view and locate your images in the fastest way possible by using Adobe Photoshop Elements 2024.

Cataloging a File

An Element file contains a catalog that keeps track of all imported content, with the default name set as My Catalog. When media is loaded, the catalog is automatically updated with basic information about the imported material, including its location and filename.

The catalog file includes the following information:

- Provide the name and location of any related audio files.
- Ensure to provide the exact location of the original and full-resolution file, along with its filename and volume name.
- Provide the original file's location and name.
- Ensure the camera or scanner title is connected to the group of imported media files.
- Adding captions to the media file.
- The modifications to the media file's notes.
- The media file contains images, videos, audio files, and projects.
- When the media file was created, both the date and time.
- Tagging the media file with keywords.
- The album contains the media file.
- Exploring the background of a media file.
- The changes to the media file. Editing techniques such as cropping, red-eye removal, and rotation are commonly employed.
- Providing the dimensions in pixels for each image and video file.
- Project parameters.
- Metadata such as pixel sizes, EXIF, copyright, IPTC data, and file format data are included.

Creating a Catalog

Get familiar with the Catalog Manager before you start creating a new catalog. Catalogs are generated, deleted, and overseen by the catalog manager. **Simply follow the clear instructions provided below to create a catalog.**

1. Head to the **File menu** and select **Manage Catalogs**.

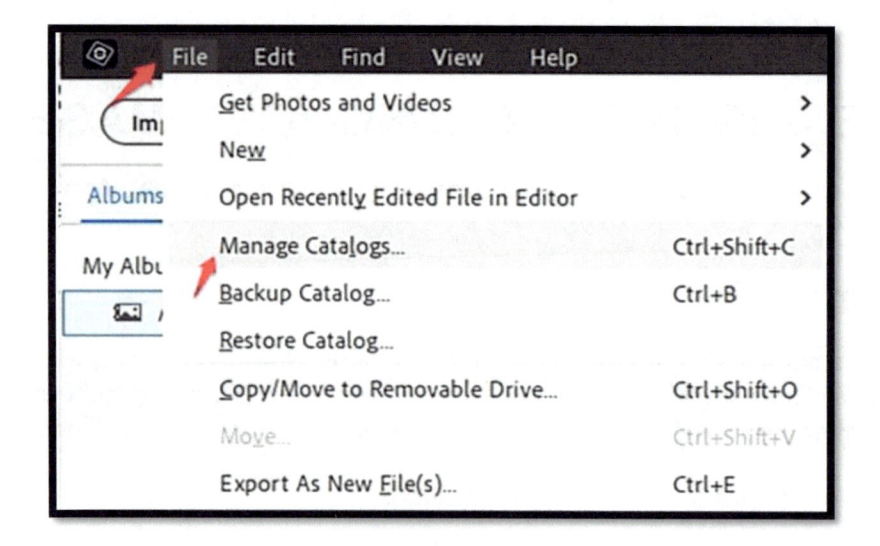

2. Click on "**New**" in the Catalog Manager dialog box.

3. Fill in the File Name text box with the name of the new catalog and proceed by clicking on Ok. Now you can include images in the catalogs you create. Follow these steps to include images in the catalog you've created.
4. Explore your hard drive to choose the image you want to add in the Get Photo and Videos dialog box by selecting it from the right-hand side of the Get Photo and Videos menu located under the File menu.
5. Next, click on the **Get Media button**.

Opening a Catalog

Follow the steps provided to open/launch a catalog.

1. Head to the **File menu** and select **Manage Catalogs**.
2. Click on **My Catalog** within the Catalog Manager dialog box.

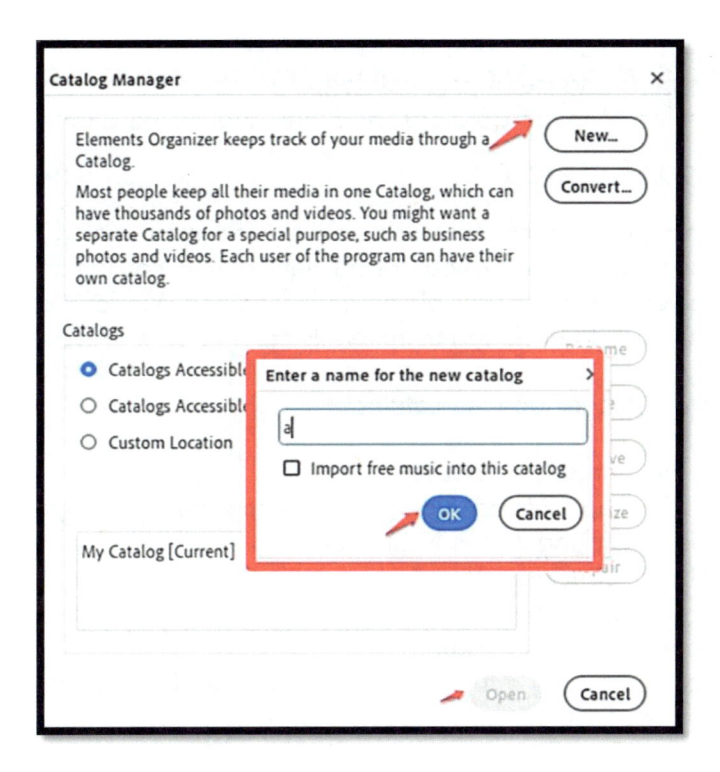

3. Then, click on **Open**.

Using the Catalog

Remember these key points as you continue to work with the catalog you've created.

- Make sure to properly categorize your photos after creating a catalog. You must manually divide catalogs into smaller or larger categories by copying and pasting photos from an older catalog into the new one because Element does not by default have a method for doing so.
- It is essential to consider how to transition from one topic to another smoothly. Access File, select **Manage Catalogs**, choose the desired catalog, and then click **Open** to switch between them.
- Once you have created your initial catalog, think about how to fix a catalog that has been damaged. If you're having trouble opening your photos in editing mode or viewing the thumbnail preview, the catalog may be corrupted. We will repair the damaged catalog by using the Repairs button. For this task, navigate to File, select Manage Catalogs, and then click on the names of the catalogs you wish to access, edit, and open. Once you've made your selection, simply click on the **Repair button** located next to the catalog.

- Enhancing your catalog's performance can optimize its speed and efficiency. To enhance the performance of your catalog, it is important to consistently optimize it. Go to **File**, select **Manage Catalogs**, and then choose the **Optimize option**.

Backing up Your Catalog

Backing up a catalog takes precedence over creating and maintaining it. Backing up your catalog can help eliminate worries about losing data due to corruption or errors on your devices. Backing up your library is possible on both Mac and Windows computers, but only a CD or DVD can be used to back up the Elements catalog on a Windows computer.

Follow the steps below to back up your catalog:

1. Navigate to **File** and select **Backup Catalog**.
2. When in the Backup Catalog dialog box, select one of the options provided and then proceed by clicking on the **Next button**.
- **Backup Catalog Structure**: This feature enables you to efficiently back up your catalog's structure, encompassing tags, people, places, and events. Photos and videos are not part of the backup.
- **Full Back up**: Performing a full backup is recommended when initiating your initial backup or saving files to a new storage device. This option thoroughly backs up all items in your catalog, including photos and images.
- **Incremental Backup:** Once you have performed a backup and need to update the previously backed-up files, choose this option.

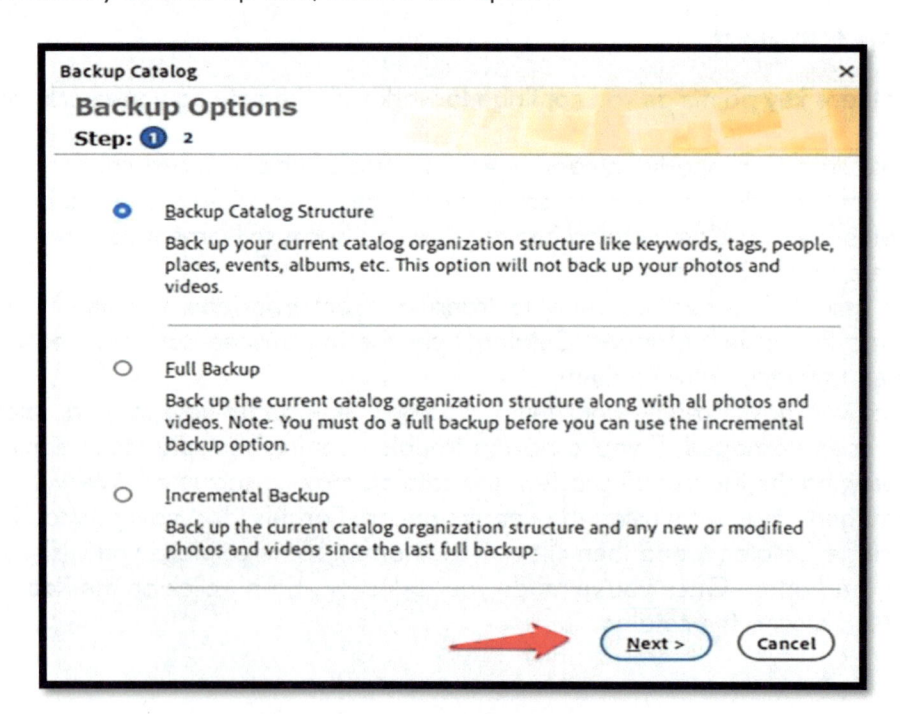

3. Choose the Destination Drive in the following screen by clicking on the preferred drive letter.
4. Click on **Browse** under Options to select where to save the backup catalog, then click Ok.
5. Once you're done, simply click on the Save Backup button to complete the backup process.

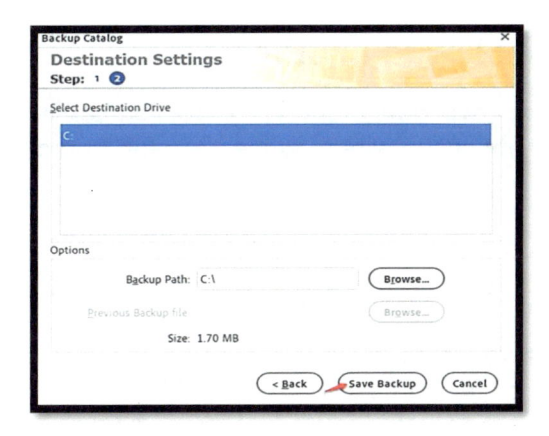

Restoring a Catalog

It's crucial to understand that only backed-up catalogs can be recovered or restored. Follow the steps outlined below to restore a catalog.

1. Go to the **File menu** and select **Restore Catalog**.
2. Click on CD/DVD, Hard Drive, or Other Volume from the Restore Catalog dialog box. Click on browse to locate the backup file if you selected Hard Drive.
3. Once you've chosen the backup file, simply click on **Browse** in the Restore Files and Catalog window to specify where you want to restore the file.
4. Click on **Restore Original Folder Structure** to preserve the files within the catalog
5. Next, select the Restore button.

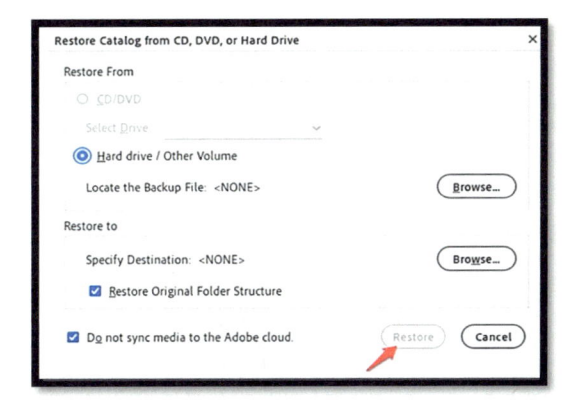

Backing up your photos and files

Follow the steps below to back up your photos and files:

1. Go to the File menu and select **Copy/Move** to removable.
2. Click on **Copy Files** in the dialog box that appears, and then choose **Next**.
3. Choose a hard drive, enter the name of the backup folder, and click OK.

Switching from one view to another

With various viewing options available in the View tab, you can easily organize your work. **To access various viewing options, navigate to the View tab and choose from the available options.**

- **Media Types:** This feature enables you to easily switch between different types of media files in the Media Browser. Access View, Media Browser, and choose the submenu.
- **Hidden Files:** Hide your files in the View tab to keep them out of sight. To see all files, navigate to the View tab and choose All Files.
- **Details**: File information like file creation dates and star ratings is hidden by default. To view the details of a file, navigate to View and choose Details.
- **File Name:** View the filename of your photos in the Media browser by selecting View and choosing Files Names. Photo filenames are not displayed by default.
- **Timeline**: The horizontal bar at the top of the Organizer displays the timeline. You can adjust the slider to select the time the picture was taken. To access this feature, navigate to View and select **Timeline**.

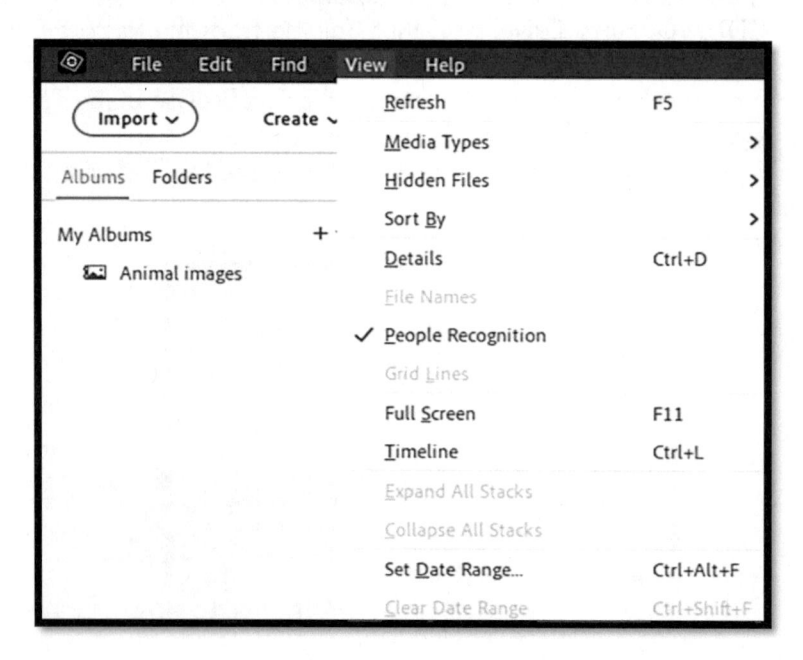

Using a Slide Show (Memories) to browse through PAt

A slide show is what a still-image-based video is called. The slideshow allows for smooth transitions between images, ensuring they are presented in a coherent sequence. Presenting your photos through a slide show is a visually impactful way to showcase them. Consider adding activities or sounds to enhance the experience.

You can locate the slide show in three different places.

- Located at the bottom left of the Media Browser is the Editor.
- Within the Create Panel in the Media Browser.
- When viewing selected photos in the View tab.

Here are the steps to showcase images in a slideshow:

- Choose the images you want to include in the slideshow, click on the **Create button**, and then select **Slideshow** from the Create drop-down menu.

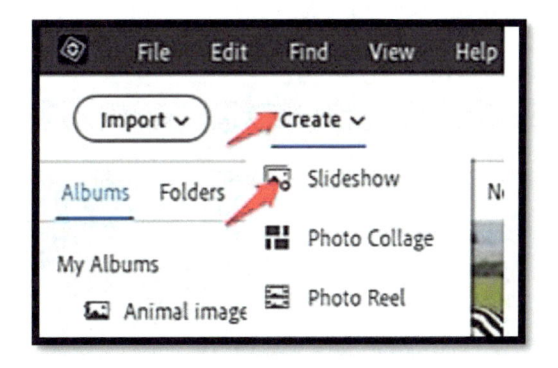

- Access the slideshow preview by using the images currently displayed in the slideshow window.

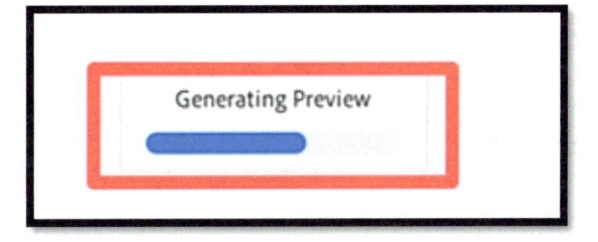

- Make your slideshow stand out by incorporating audio, themes, and media. Simply click on Audio, Themes, or Media in the Toolbar on the left side of the slideshow.

- Remember to save the slide show by clicking on **Save**.
- In the Element Organizer dialog box, input the name of the slide show and then select the **Save button**.

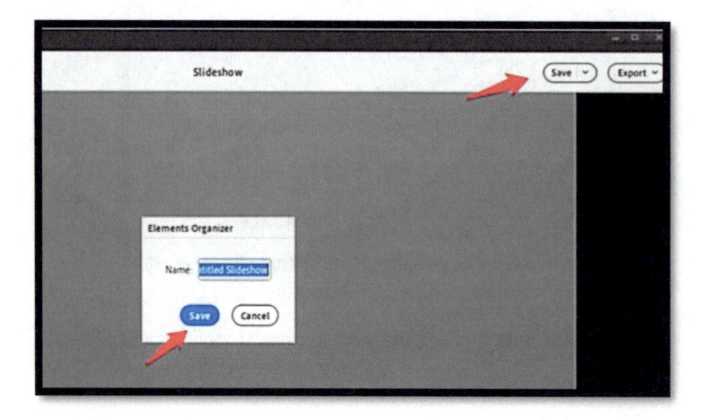

Searching for Photos

When searching for your photos in the same location where you stored them, you may need to use the Element search function.

Using the Search Icon

One of the initial aspects to keep in mind when browsing through photos is the Search Icon. In the upper right corner is the Media Browser's search bar. The Search icon features a text area and a magnifying glass. Enter the image name in the Search icon to find it.

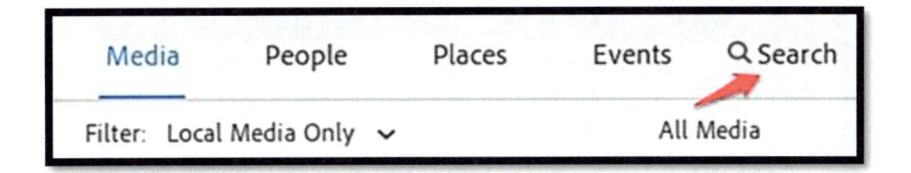

After clicking the Search icon, a window will appear on the left-hand side, presenting a list of parameters for conducting your search.

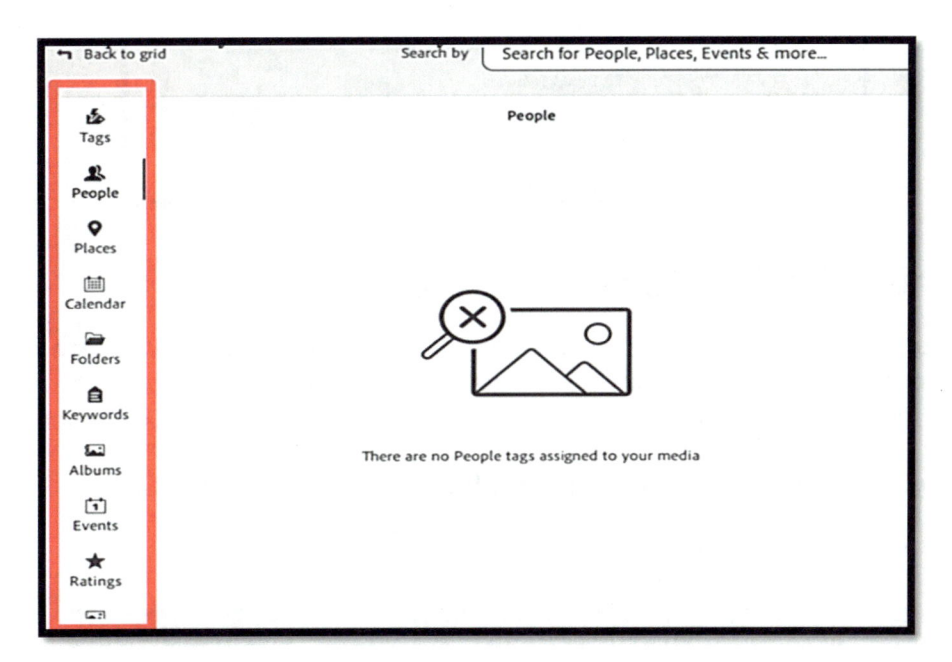

Showing Recent Searches

The section for Recent Searches shows a list of your most recent search queries. Simply click on the search text bar to view your past search history.

Looking for Untagged Items

Another method to find your photos in Element is by utilizing the Untagged Command. Head to the **Find menu** and select **Untagged Items** to make use of the Untagged Items command for locating photos.

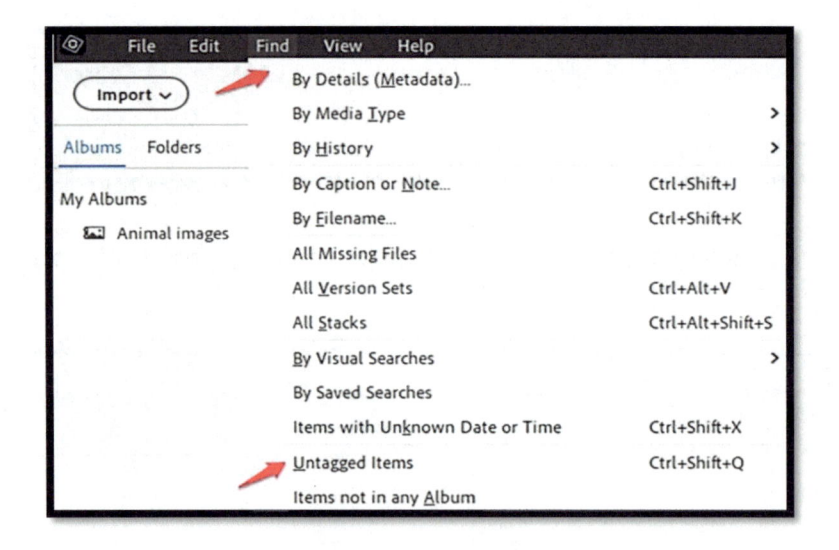

Searching for Captions and Notes

By using captions and annotations, you can search for photos. More details can be found in the Information panel through the captions and notes. When a caption or note is included, you have the option to search for the image using the title of the caption or note.

Here is a guide to searching for photographs based on captions and notes.

1. Head to the **File menu** and select **Captions and Notes**.

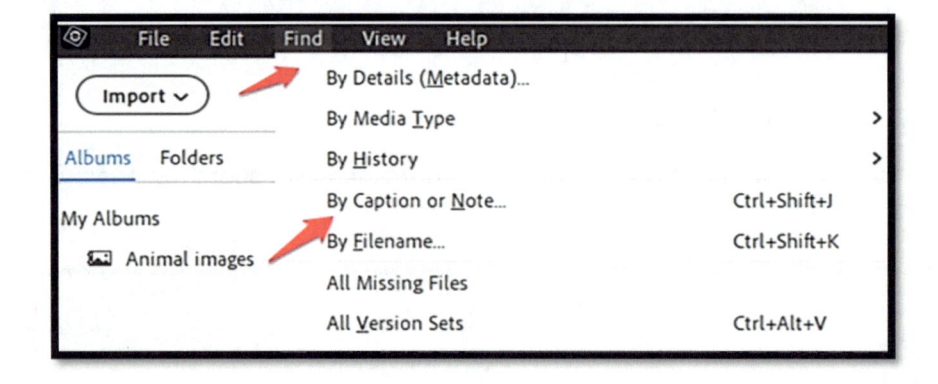

2. Enter the word you want to search in the Find by Caption or Dialog box. There are two options available in this dialog box.
   - **Match Only the Beginning of Words in Captions and Notes:** When matching only the beginning of words in captions and notes, you can use this feature if you are confident that the caption or note begins with the words entered in the text box.

- **Match Any Part of Any Word in Captions and Notes:** When uncertain about whether the word entered in the text box is at the beginning of the caption or note, use the option to match any part of any word in captions and notes.

3. Next, simply click on Ok.

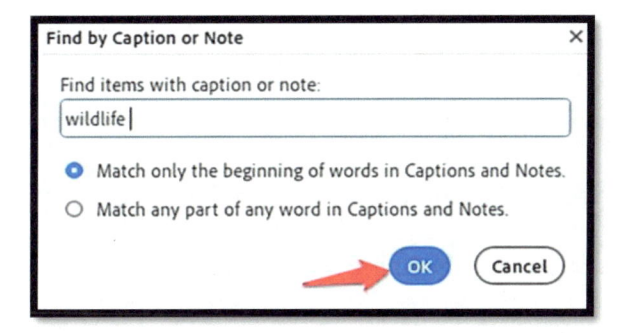

Searching by History

Begin your search for photos by using the Media Browser's activities as a reference. Some common examples are printing, emailing, and sharing. Choose an option from the History submenu once you have clicked on Find, History, and then History.

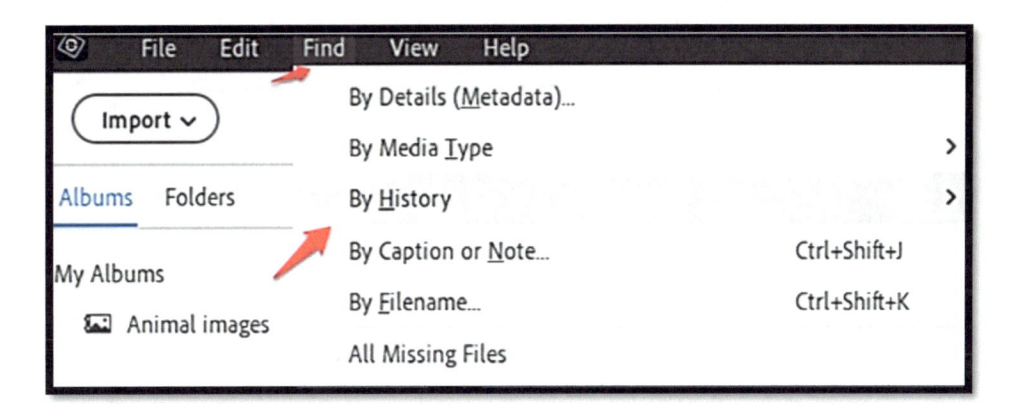

Searching by Metadata

Searching for photographs based on various criteria is made easier with metadata search. Metadata uses various criteria such as people, places, events, filename, file type, tags, albums, notes, authors, capture date, camera model, shutter speed, and F-stop.

Follow these steps to use the metadata search feature:

1. Navigate to Find and choose By Details (Metadata).

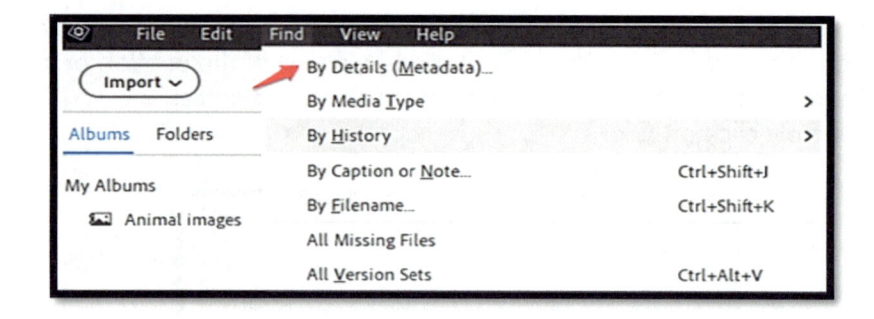

2. Make sure to choose either AND or OR in the Search Criteria under Search for Files which Match.
3. Choose the metadata type from the initial menu
4. Choose the range for the search from the second menu
5. When accessing the third menu, you have the option to either input or choose the metadata name you want to locate.
6. Click on the plus sign (+) at the right hand of the third menu to add metadata values to your search.
7. Click on the minus (-) sign at the right of the third menu to remove the metadata from the search.
8. Activate the Save This Search As Saved feature and enter the search.
9. Next, simply click on the Search button

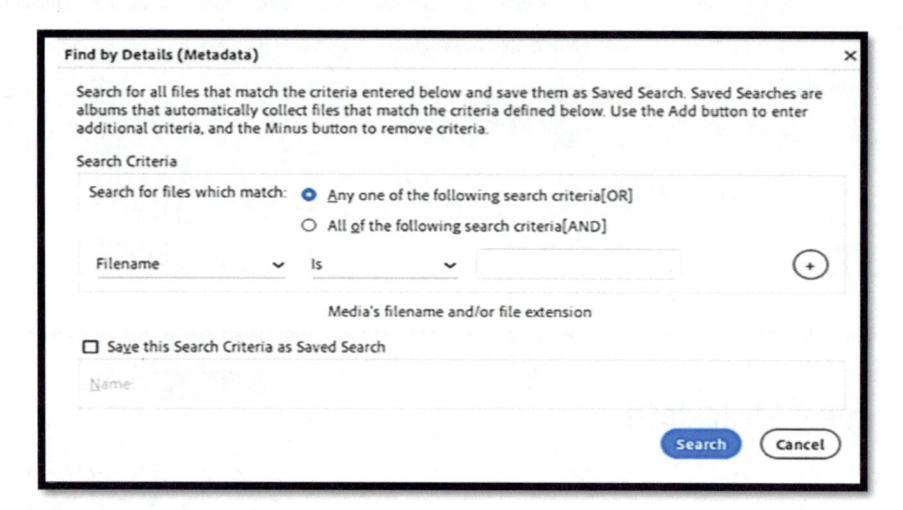

Searching Media Type

Use the media type to easily locate your photos. Head to Find, choose By Media Type and then pick one of the methods below to locate your photographs using the media file.

- **Photos**: This feature exclusively showcases images.

- **Audio**: This feature showcases an audio clip.
- **Project**: This section showcases various projects
- **Items with Audio Captions:** Displaying the photo along with the attached audio captions for the projects.

Searching by File Name

You can also locate images through filename searches. Follow these steps to search for photos.

- Head to the File menu and choose **Filename**.
- Make sure to input the file name in the Filename dialog box and proceed by clicking Ok

Searching for all missing files

This tool can help you locate any missing files in your creations or projects. Access the Missing Files option by going to find and selecting **All Files**.

Searching by All Version Set

When searching for images with the All-Version Set, the Organizer can display the best photos from each set. You have the flexibility to expand each set as needed. **Follow the steps below to use the All-Version Set:**
- Head to Find, then choose **All Version Sets**.
- To expand a version set, simply select **Version Set** and click on Expand Items In Version Set.

Searching by All Stacks

To access the All-Stacks option, navigate to the **Find menu** and select **All Stacks**.

Searching by Using Visual Searches

When looking for images through visual searches, the organizer uses details in the photo like color, shape, and objects to facilitate the search. **Follow the steps below to use the visual searches:**
- Navigate to Find and choose By Visual Searches.
  Next, select the By Virtual Searches Submenu

Searching for an Item with an Unspecified Date or Time

The Organizer can now showcase media files with unknown dates or times. **Follow the steps below to use this option:**
- Navigate to Find and select Items With Unknown Date Or Time

CHAPTER EIGHT

EDITING CAMERA IMAGES USING THE CAMERA EDITOR

What is the Camera Raw Editor?

The Camera Raw Editor plug-in included with Adobe Element enables efficient and high-quality image editing. This application enables you to import and improve raw photographs. Released in 2003, this program is compatible with Adobe Photoshop Elements, Adobe Photoshop, and Adobe Lightroom. The Camera Raw Editor converts the raw data from the camera into a final image. Camera Raw enables you to enhance photos through a range of editing options including cropping, sharpening, adjusting white balance, contrast, and color and tone range. The photo edits are non-destructive, allowing for easy undoing and preserving the original files. Whenever a raw file is opened, the Camera Raw Editor appears in a separate window. **Here's a guide on how to access the Camera Raw Editor in Adobe Photoshop Element.**

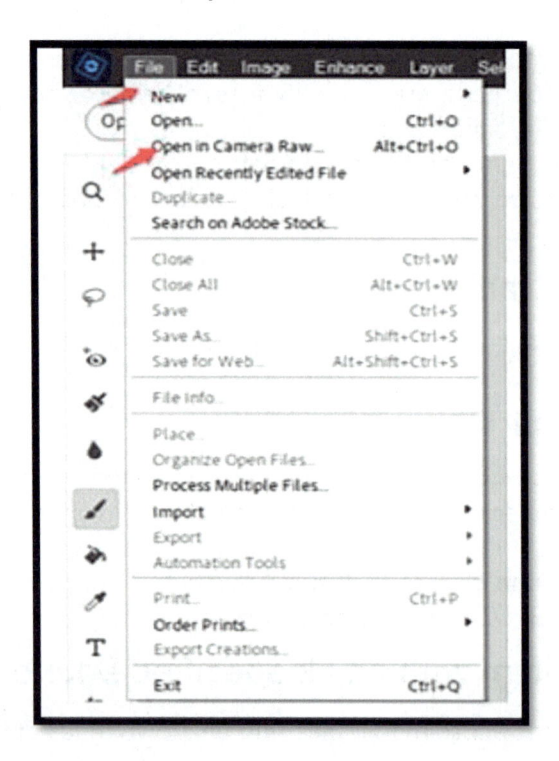

- Go to File and choose **Open with Camera Raw Editor**. Displayed on this page is the Camera Raw Editor

Exploring the Attributes of Raw File Formats

Raw files store images captured by the digital camera. Raw files, also referred to as digital negatives, consist of unedited data captured directly from the camera's image sensor. Due to the higher amount of data, Raw files tend to be larger than JPEG files. Raw files occupy more space on your hard disk or memory cards due to their larger size compared to JPEG files. You can adjust the highlights, brightness, shadows, and dark portions of an image separately in the raw data, a task that is not possible with the camera. Being able to retrieve image details from the Raw file that are not available in the JPEG file is a fascinating aspect.

Camera Raw files can be saved in various formats:

These are the file extensions commonly used by professional camera brands: Nikon (.NEF), Canon (.CRW), Sony (.ARW, SRF), Pentax (.PEF), Olympus (.ORF), Hasselblad (.3FR), and Panasonic (.RW2).

Exploring the Camera Raw Editor Window

Here, we will thoroughly cover the key features of the Camera Raw Editor in Adobe Elements, providing a comprehensive overview of the program.

Title Bar: The title bar displays the installed version of Camera Raw in your Element; Element 2024 uses version 15.5.

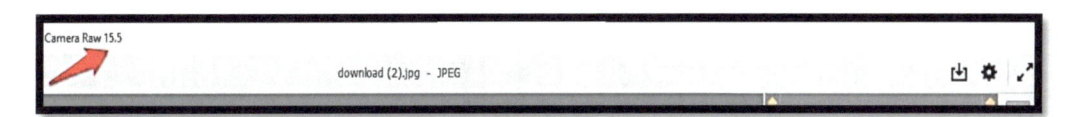

Convert and Save Image Button: Clicking on the Convert and Save Image Button will prompt the Save Options dialog box to appear, allowing you to save a copy of the camera raw image as DNG. Located at the upper right-hand corner of the Camera Raw Editor windows.

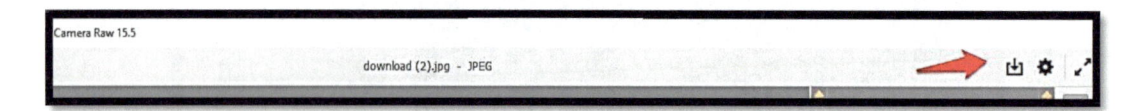

Toggle Screen Full Mode Button: Switch to Full-Screen Mode This button toggles between the full screen and a smaller version in the Camera Raw dialog box.

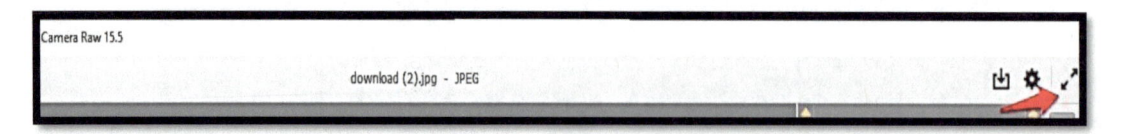

Open Preferences Dialog Button: Click on the button to access the Preferences Dialog. Open the Camera Raw Preferences dialog box

The Toolbar: Located at the far-right side of the Camera Raw dialog box is the Toolbar. It includes a range of tools for editing in the Camera Raw Editor. Starting from the top, there are options for Editing, Cropping & Rotating, Removing Red-Eye, and Additional Image Settings. Within the button, you'll find the Zoom and Hand tool toolbar in the Camera Raw dialog box.

Histogram: The histogram can be found in the upper right corner of the Camera Raw dialog box. Monitoring the tonal range of the raw file being edited is a key feature of this tool. Any modifications done in the Edit panel are automatically reflected in the histogram. The Shadow clipping warning and Highlight clipping warning are located in the upper left and right corners. The RGB can be found within the Histogram.

The Panels

The panels can be found below the histogram on the right side of the Camera Raw dialog. The Camera Raw Editor utilizes panels to perform various operations, similar to the panels in Elements. The panels in Camera Raw are conveniently located in one spot, which enhances usability.

Now, let's take a look at the panels in the Camera Raw Editor.

- **The Edit Panel:** The Edit Panel is utilized to make adjustments in the tab, which then automatically updates the Histogram of the current image. This feature uses the edit settings.
- **The Basic Panel:** The initial panel displayed is the Basic Panel, which includes essential features for editing Raw files. The panel includes control settings for color temperature and white balance, along with sliders for adjusting exposure, contrast, highlights, shadows, and white and black points. Located at the bottom of the Basic panel is the Clarity slider, which can be used to adjust the contrast in mid-tones. Lastly, the Vibrance and Saturation sliders are used to adjust color saturation.

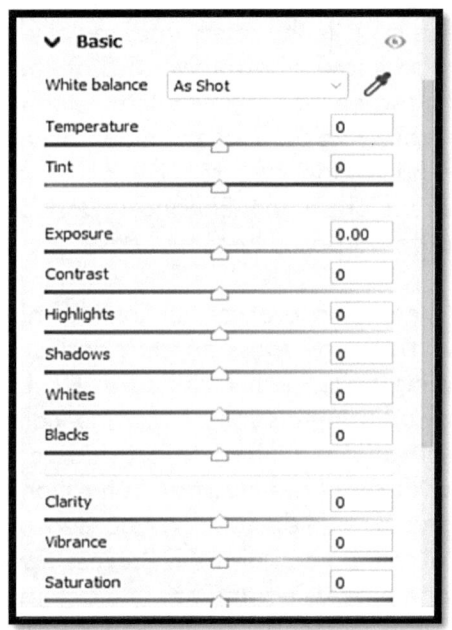

- **The Detail Panel:** The Detail panel is the third panel in the Camera Raw Editor. You can sharpen your images in the top half of the panel and reduce luminance or color noise in the bottom half.

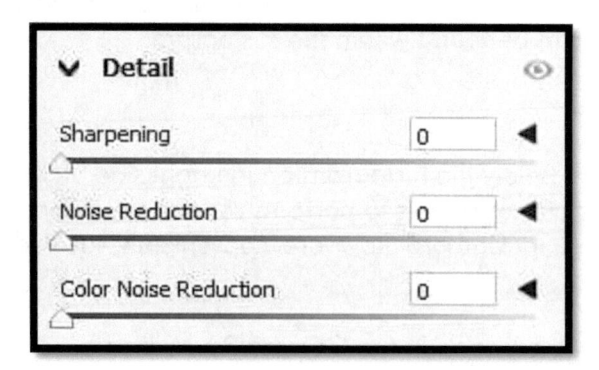

- **The Camera Calibration Panel:** Unlike previous versions, the Camera Calibration in Adobe Photoshop Elements 2024 is now labeled as The Calibration panel and boasts enhanced features. The Calibration panel contains five process versions. The latest release of Photoshop Elements 2024 is version 6.
- **Process Versions in the Calibration Panel:** When editing and outputting images in Camera Raw, the technique used is called Process Version. Access various options and settings in the Basic tab and make local adjustments based on the process version in use. There are a total of five process versions available in the calibration panel.
- **Process Version 6**: Version 6 is the latest one, initially introduced in Camera Raw 15.4 and now integrated into Camera Raw 15.5 of Photoshop Element 2024. This helps minimize banding when working with the Color Mixer and B&W.
- **Process Version 5:** Process Version 5 when editing new images in Camera Raw 11. Enhanced high ISO rendering in PV 5 reduces purple color casts that may appear in low-light shadow areas of photos. Enhanced Dehaze slider is now part of PV5. Adding haze for creative purposes becomes easy by moving the Dehaze slider to the left.
- **Process Version 4:** When using process version 4, images are edited for the first time in Camera Raw 10. Range Mask support and a more robust Auto Mask for improved noise handling have been included in PV 4. Images from PV 3 (2012) without any Auto Mask adjustments will be automatically updated to PV 4.
- **Version 3(2012):** This panel is utilized to provide solutions on how the camera captures color. At your disposal are Hue and Saturation sliders for all three primary colors: red, green, and blue. Additionally, you can use the Tint slider to adjust shadows. The panel at the top contains the Process option, enabling you to switch between different image processing engines in Camera Raw.

- **Process Version 2:** Camera Raw 6 automatically utilized Process Version 2 (2010) when editing images. When comparing the previous process version, PV 1, with PV 2, the latter provides improved sharpness and noise reduction.
- **Version 1(2003):** This version is 5. x and previous versions of Camera Raw's original processing engine.

To update a photo from the previous Process Versions to the current Process version 5(PV 5), you can do either of the following:

- Click on the **Update to Current Process button** located in the lower-right corner of the image preview.
- In the Camera Calibration tab, select **Process > Version 6(Current)**.
- When applying an older process version to a photo, navigate to the Camera Calibration tab and select the desired version from the available options.

Adjust Sharpness In-Camera Raw Files

The sharpness slider provides the edge definition you are looking for by adjusting the image's sharpness. This adjustment identifies pixels that differ from surrounding pixels based on the threshold you set and enhances the contrast of those pixels by the specified amount.

When applying sharpening to Raw file images, follow these steps:

- Make sure to zoom the preview image to at least 100%.
- Click on the Detail tab Adjust the Sharpness slider to increase or decrease the sharpening. When the slider is at zero, the sharpening is turned off. To achieve a more polished look, consider lowering the Sharpness slider.

Minimizing Noise in Camera Raw Images

The Detail tab in the Camera Raw dialog box features a slider to reduce image noise. Picture noise, a minor visible object, can lower the image quality. **There are two main types of image noise: chroma noise, which shows up as colorful objects in the image, and luminance noise, which creates a grainy look.**

- Zoom the preview image to at least 100% to reduce the image noise.
- Adjust the Luminance Smoothing slider to decrease grayscale noise and the Color Noise Reduction slider to minimize chroma noise.

Adobe Camera Raw Profile

Your profile dictates how tones and colors are displayed in Camera Raw images. The profile provides a foundation for initiating image transformations. To view the current Camera Raw profile, simply click on the **Edit button** located in the Toolbar next to the Camera Raw dialog box in Photoshop Elements. You can verify the Camera Raw profile by selecting it from the Profile drop-down menu in the Edit panel.

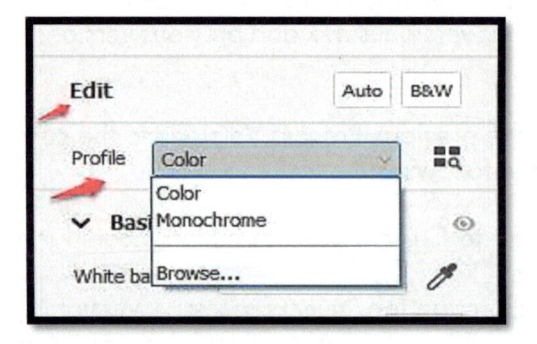

Note that the selected profile does not affect the editing values set by the sliders in the Basic and Detail panels. Thus, a profile can be applied either before or after making adjustments, without losing any adjustment values.

Applying Profile to your Image

Follow these steps to apply a profile to your image:

- Access the Edit Panel Camera Raw dialog box, and then select the **Profile drop-down menu** to see the available profiles. For access to additional profiles, simply click on **Browse**.
- Expand the profile group to see the profiles available in each group.
- Hover over a profile to preview its effect on the image, and then click to apply it.

Adding Profiles to Favorites

When adding a profile to Favorites choose the profile thumbnail and click on the star icon located at the top corner of the thumbnail.

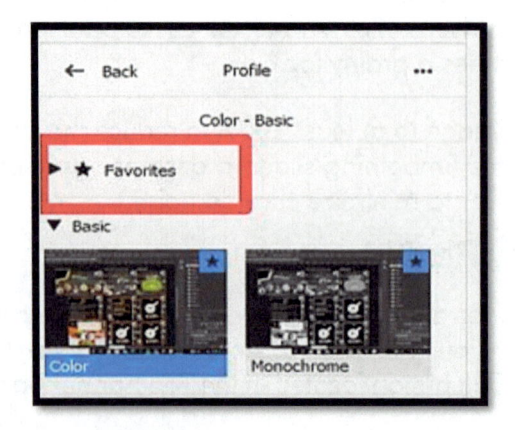

Creative Profiles for Raw and Non-Raw Photos

Creating a profile involves crafting a unique image or vibe. These profiles are compatible with a variety of file types, including TIFF, JPEGS, and raw images.

- **Artistic**: When aiming for a more intense color rendering in your photo with strong color shifts, consider using this option.
- **B & W**: For achieving the perfect tone shift in a black-and-white project, this profile is the most suitable option.
- **Modern**: This profile offers an impressive effect that complements modern photography styles.
- **Vintage**: This profile simulates the effects of a vintage photo Outlook

Creating Profiles for Raw Images

When editing a raw profile, the following profile groups will be displayed.

- **Adobe Raw:** Adobe Raw profile enhances the colors in images and provides a solid foundation for editing. This profile is automatically applied to the raw images when imported into the Camera Raw Editor.
- **Camera Matching:** This profile is shown according to the camera make or model of your raw image. Using the Camera Matching profile is most effective when you want your raw images to match what is displayed on the camera's screen.
- **Legacy**: This profile appears in the previous iteration of Adobe Camera Raw.

CHAPTER NINE
CREATING AND ADJUSTING SELECTIONS

Mastering Photoshop Elements Selections is a crucial skill that should not be overlooked.

Defining Selections

Choosing a selection involves identifying the specific part of the image you want to alter. After making a selection, you can then proceed to edit the chosen area. When creating a selection, you have the option to use either the selection commands or the selection tools. Every time a selection is made, a dotted outline called the selection border will appear. You can adjust, duplicate, or remove specific pixels from the image by using the selection boundary. Keep in mind that no actions can be performed outside the chosen area until it is deselected. You have the option to make multiple selections using the selection tools in Adobe Photoshop Element. Two common selection tools include the Magic Wand and Elliptical Marquee tools.

Crafting rectangular and elliptical selections

Developers constructed the Rectangular Marquee tool for creating square or rectangular selection borders. Follow these steps to select this option using this tool:

1. Head to the **Tools panel** and choose the **Rectangular Marquee tool**.
2. Make sure to check out the additional options of the marquee tools located in The Tool options at the footer panel.

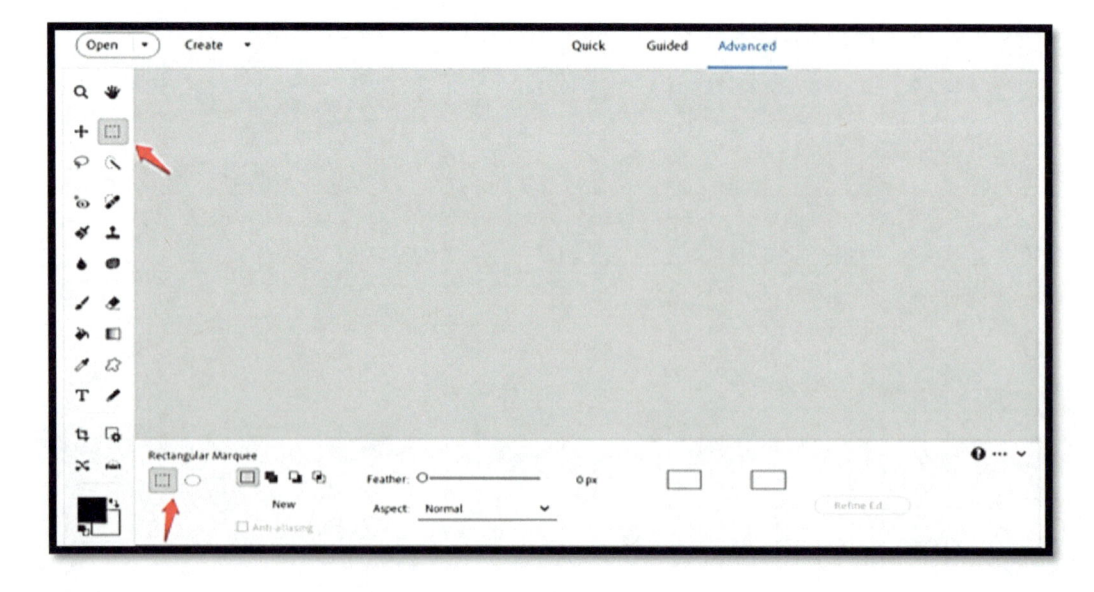

3. Place the mouse cursor on the spot where the corner of the image rectangle should be.
4. Drag the mouse from the area of the image you want to the opposite corner and then release the mouse for a rectangular selection to display on the image.

Master the Elliptical Marquee Tool

For creating elliptical or circular borders or selections, use the ellipse tool. Optimal objects for this tool include spherical items such as clocks, balloons, and similar objects.

Follow these steps to use the Elliptical marquee tool:

1. Once you've selected the Marquee tool, head over to the **Tool Options** located in the footer panel and choose the **Elliptical Marquee Tool**.

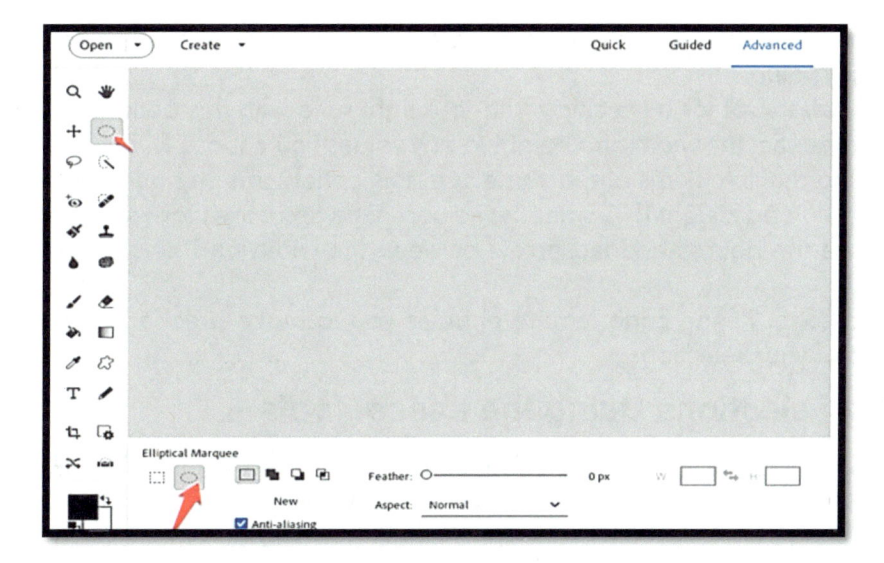

2. Position the cursor over the desired area, then click and drag it to select the object you want.

3. Next, let go of the mouse button.

Using the Marquee Tool

The Marquee tools offer a range of useful features for efficient use. Let's proceed with a rapid review of them.

- **Feather**: This option is designed to provide soft edges to the selected portion of the image. The adjustable slider value for the pixels, ranging from 0 to 250, indicates the level of softness. As the value increases, the edges gradually become more blurred.
- **Anti-Aliasing:** By excluding the softening application to the edge of the elliptical or irregular-shaped selection, this option helps prevent the photos' rough edges from appearing harsh.
- **Aspect**: This option includes the following settings:
  o **Normal**: The default setting allows you to adjust the size of a selection by dragging it to any value.
  o **Fixed Ratio**: Opt for a specific width-to-height ratio with this option.
  o **Fixed Size:** Set the width and height to any values you choose with this setting. When selecting multiple items of the same size, this option can be quite useful.
- **Width (W) and Height (H):** Enter the values in the text boxes for width (W) and height (H). Use the double-headed arrow between the width and height values to adjust them.
- **Refine Edge:** Refine Edge feature enables you to make precise adjustments to the edges of your selection.

Mastering Selections Using the Lasso Tools

With Photoshop Elements lasso tools; you can easily create freehand selections like curves or sections with straight edges for polygon selection forms.

Here are the categories:

- Lasso
- Polygonal
- Magnetic

Mastering the Lasso Tool

Use the Lasso tool to create selection borders on images or objects. Follow the steps outlined below to create a freehand selection.

1. Head to the Tools panel and choose the Lasso tool.
2. Place the mouse cursor over the object you want to select and then outline it.
3. After pressing the button, release it to finalize the selection.

Using the Polygonal Lasso Tool

This tool is used for drawing a straight-edged segment of a selection border. You can create multiple segments to form a selection border using this tool.

Follow the steps provided to use this tool effectively

1. Head to the Tools panel and choose the Polygon Lasso tool.
2. Click on a point to set the start of the first straight segment, then click again to set the end of the segment. Now you can proceed with another task.
3. Next, close the selection border.

Using the Magnetic Lasso Tool

When hovering your mouse over an object in a photo, the Magnetic Lasso Tool is used to create a selection border that reaches the edges of the object. This helps select objects with detailed edges against a high-contrast background.

Follow these steps to use the Magnetic Lasso Tool:

1. Head to the Tools Panel and choose the Magnetic Lasso tool.
2. Place the mouse cursor over the tools option and choose The Magnetic Lasso Tool.
3. Next, navigate your mouse cursor around the object and click where you want.
4. Once you have finished, return the mouse to the initial position and close the selection.

Mastering the Magic Wand

The main function of The Magic Wand tool is to select pixels within a similar color range or boundary with just one click. You can select the color range of tolerance using this tool. The tolerance value ranges between 0 and 255. When the tolerance range is set to 0, the selected area will have only one color. However, with a tolerance range of 255, all colors in the image will be selected.

Follow the steps provided to use The Magic Wand:

1. Head to the Tools panel and choose the Quick Selection tool.

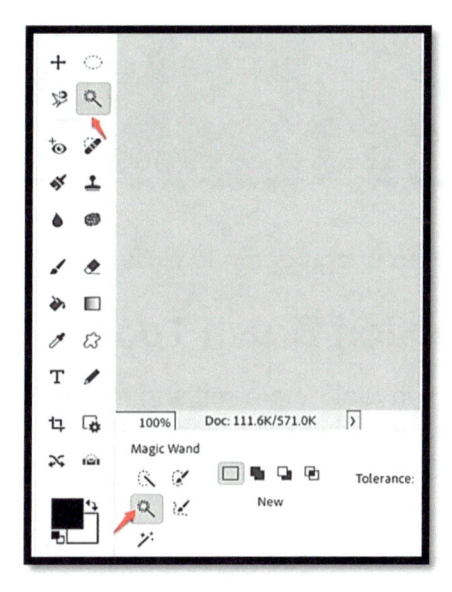

2. Choose the Magic Wand tool from the Tool options located in the footer panel
3. Choose a spot on your image using the default Tolerance setting.
4. Adjust the Tolerance setting in the Tool Options

Make sure to maximize the features listed in the Magic Wand before closing up.

- **Tolerance**: The tolerance value can range from 0 to 255. A lower value will select only one color in the area, while a higher value like 255 will select all colors in the image.
- **Sample All Layers**: Sampling all layers is most effective when working with multiple layers. Make sure to click on the option to select the pixels from the active layer using the Magic Wand tool.
- **Contiguous**: This feature enables the Magic Wand tool to select adjacent pixels. If it is not enabled, mining will not occur whether they are adjacent to each other or not.
- **Anti-aliasing**: The anti-aliasing feature softens the edges of the selection by one column of pixels.
- **Refine Edge**: Refine Edge enables you to eliminate any roughness from the edges by adjusting the Smooth slider.

5. Remember to click on the image again to close it.

Mastering the Selection Brush Tool

You can use a different selection tool before refining the selection by adding or removing pixels. There are two methods for making selections with these tools: painting over the area you want to choose in Selection mode or painting on the area you don't want to choose using a semi-opaque overlay in Mask mode.

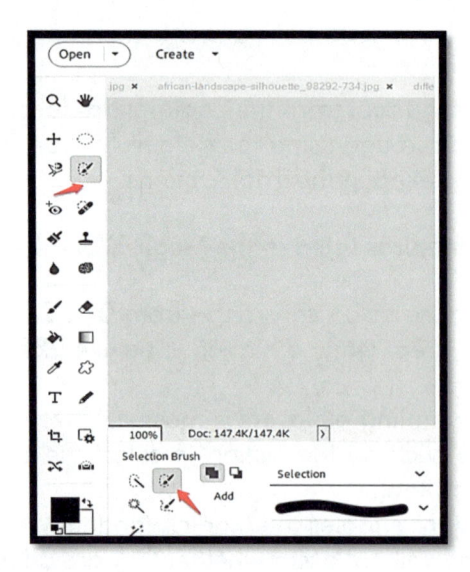

Follow these steps to use the Selection Brush tool:

1. Head to the Tools Panel and choose the Selection Brush tool.
2. Make sure to adjust the Selection Brush options in the Tool Option.

- **Mode**: This option allows you to select 'Selection' to paint over what you want to select, or **'Mask'** if you want to avoid painting over the part you don't want.
- **Brush Presets Picker**: Choose a brush from the presets drop-down list in this option.
- **Size**: You can adjust the brush size from 1 to 2,500 pixels. You have the option to manually input the value or adjust it using the slider.
- **Hardness**: Hardness can be adjusted to determine the brush tip's firmness, with a scale from 1 to 100 percent.

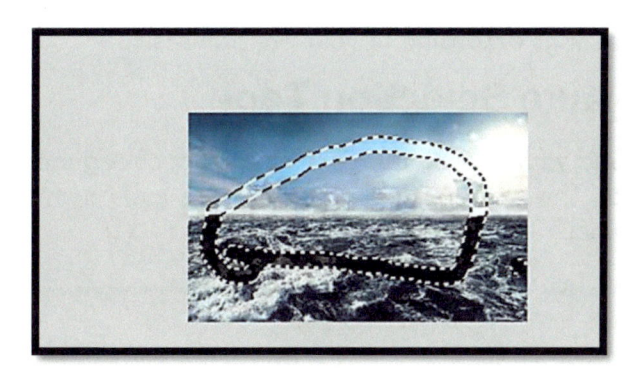

3. Next, proceed to paint the chosen area.

Mastering the Quick Selection Tool for Painting

Click on the region you want to select, and use the Quick Selection tools to make a precise selection based on texture and color similarities. One might liken the Quick Selection tool to a combination of the Brush, Magic Wand, and Lasso tools.

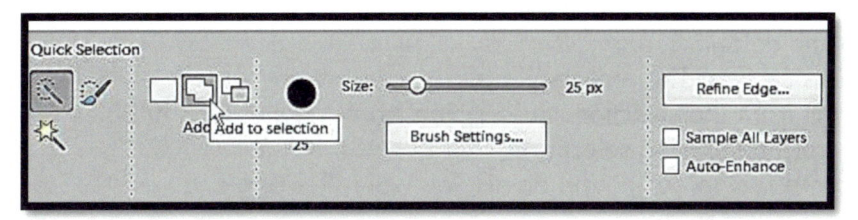

Here are the steps to use the Quick Selection tool:

1. Head to the Tools panel and choose the Quick Selection Brush tool.
2. Make sure to configure the settings in the Tool Options.
   - **New Selection**: Opting for the new selection enables you to initiate a new selection.
   - **Size**: You can select your preferred brush size by adjusting the diameter from 1 to 2,500 pixels.
   - **Brush Settings:** Adjust the brush settings to control the hardness, spacing, angle, and roundness of the Quick Selection Brush tool.

- **Sample All Layers:** Sampling all layers enables you to select from all layers in the image. Without choosing this option, you are limited to selecting only from the active layer.
- **Auto Enhance**: This feature assists Element in automatically enhancing the selection through an algorithm.
3. Paint the specific area of the image you desire. Feel free to make adjustments to your selections as needed.
4. For precise adjustments, access the Refine Edge option in the Tool Options and customize the settings according to your preferences.

Mastering the Auto Selection Tool

Creating a shape around your chosen image will automatically generate a selection using the Auto Selection Tool. The Auto Selection tool includes tools such as Rectangle, Ellipse, Lasso, and Polygon Lasso.

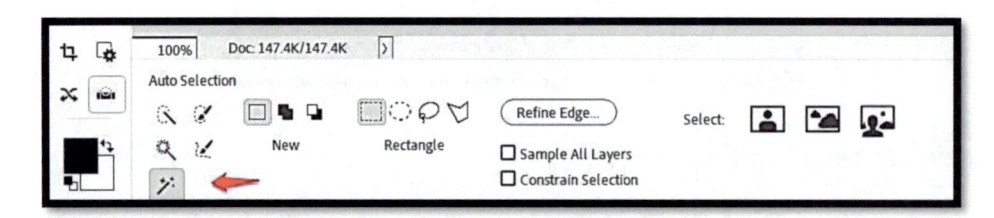

Follow the steps outlined below to use the Auto Selection tool:

1. Head to the Tools panel and choose the **Auto Selection Brush tool**.
2. Choose an option from the Tools Options bar.
- **New Selection:** Choose the **New Selection option** to create a new selection, which is set as the default.
- **Add to selection**: This feature enables you to expand the current selection.
- **Subtract from the selection**: Subtracting from the selection enables you to remove parts from an existing selection.
3. Choose a tool to outline the object you want (Rectangle, Ellipse, Lasso, or Polygon Lasso).
4. Outline the object you want to select in the photo.
5. You have the option to add, remove, or start a new selection to further refine it.
6. Make additional corrections and refine your selections by clicking on Refine Edge.

Mastering the Refine Selection Brush Tool

With the Refine Selection Brush Tool, you can easily detect edges in the image and adjust your selection accordingly.

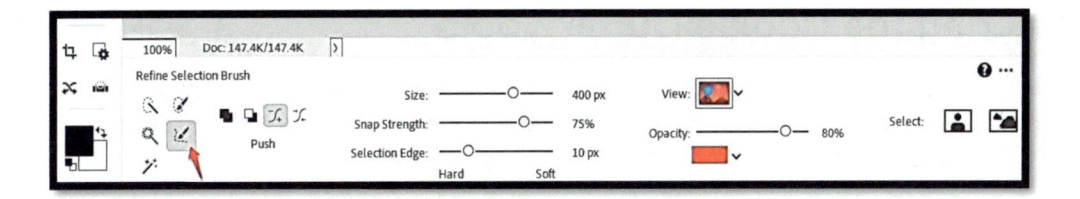

Follow these steps to use the Refine Selection Brush Tool:

1. Click on the Quick Selection tool and then proceed.
2. Opt for the Refine Selection Brush tool from the list of tools in the Tools Option, which also consists of the Quick Selection tool, Magic Wand, and Selection Brush.
3. Make sure to set the following parameters in the Tool Options:
- **Size**: Adjust the brush diameter size from 1 to 2,500 pixels using this slider option.
- **Snap Strength**: Adjust the snap strength of the slider from 0 to 100%.
- **Selection Edge**: The slider can be adjusted to control the hardness or softness of the edge.
- **Adding or subtracting**: This option allows you to either increase or decrease the selection.
- **Push**: By selecting the Push option, you can adjust the selection by moving the mouse cursor within the boundary of the outer circle of your cursor.
- **Smooth**: This feature allows you to refine the edges of the selection if they appear jagged.
- **View**: The option to view the selection is available. You have the option to view the selected object on a black or white background, or you can utilize the Overlay feature to view it against a red semi-opaque backdrop.
4. After that, perfect the selection using the Refine Selection Brush until it fits your requirements.

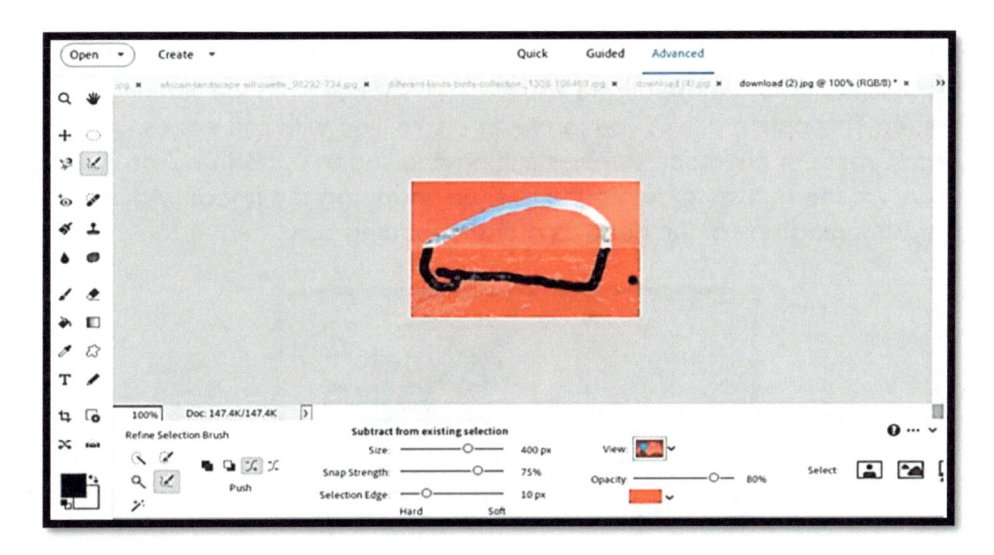

Mastering the Cookie Cutter Tools

The Cookie Cutter tool is used to eliminate any crooked elements in the image. To crop a picture into the desired shape, use the Cookie Cutter tool. For optimal results, consider using this tool to adjust the size and position of the bounding box.

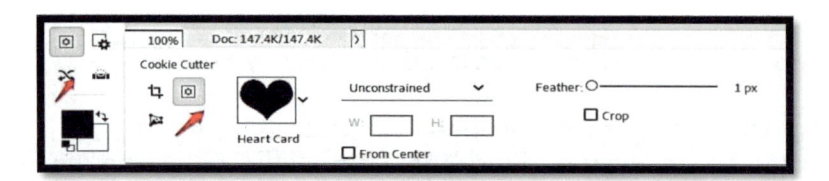

Here are the steps to use the cookie-cutter tool.

1. Head to the Tools panel and choose the Crop Tool.
2. Next, choose the **Cookie Cutter tool**, which is represented by a flower icon, located in the Tools Option
3. Make sure to adjust the desired settings in the Tool Options; the highlighted options are listed below:
- **Shape**: Choose a shape from the preset library in the Custom Shape picker. To view additional libraries, simply click on the Shape pop-up menu and choose from the available submenus.
- **Geometry Options:** These options enable you to create a shape with precise parameters.
- **Unconstrained:** Draw freely without any restrictions
- **Defined Proportions:** Ensuring consistent proportions by maintaining the height and width proportional.
- **Defined Size:** Used for cropping the image to its original fixed size of the selected shape.
- **Fixed Size:** Choose the fixed size option to input your preferred height and width.
- **From Center:** This feature allows you to draw shapes from the center.
- **Feather**: This option allows you to create a selection with soft edges.
- **Crop**: Cropping an image involves cutting it to shape using the Crop option.

Now you can use the mouse to create the desired shape on the image. Adjust the size of the shape by dragging one of the handles of the bounding box.

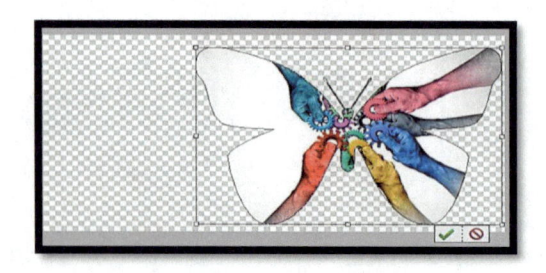

Make sure to press **Enter** to complete or use the comment button.

Mastering Eraser Tools

The Eraser tool in Photoshop Elements is a crucial feature that stands out among the other tools available. You can easily remove the image using the Eraser tools. Three categories make up the Eraser tools.

- The Regular Eraser Tool
- The Magic Eraser Tool
- The Background Eraser Tool

Eraser Tool

Erase your image to match the backdrop color using the Eraser Tool.

Here are the steps to use the Eraser tool:

1. Head to the Tools panel and select the Eraser tool button.
2. Choose your preferred background color from the Toolbox.
3. Choose the desired layer from the Layer menu.
4. Choose the desired eraser type from the Brush Preset Picker menu.
5. Adjust the eraser tip width using the Size slider.
6. Choose the optimal brush from the Type selection
7. Adjust the transparency level of the color by using the Opacity slider.
8. To delete using the existing settings, simply click and drag the image onto the current background color.

Background Eraser Tool

Easily remove or delete the background using the Background Eraser tool. This tool does not affect the foreground or anything on it. This tool eliminates the transparent background from a layer. Moreover, the tool expertly overlays photos onto a plain background. **Follow the steps outlined below to make use of this tool:**

1. Head to the Tools panel and select the Eraser tool button.
2. Choose the **Background Eraser Tool** from the Tools menu.
3. Use the Layer panel to choose the layer you want to erase

4. You have the option to set the following preferences in the Background Eraser Options.
   - **Brush Settings:** Customize the brush tip options including Size, Hardness, Spacing, Roundness, and Angle.
   - **Limits**: When selecting this option, you can choose between Discontiguous or Contiguous limits. Discontiguous eliminates all pixels of the same color throughout the image, whereas Contiguous eliminates only the adjacent pixels of the same color as the selected ones.
   - **Tolerance**: Adjust the tolerance setting to determine the required color similarity before deletion by Photoshop Elements.

5. When you choose the area you want to erase, the selected area will disappear.

Using the Magic Eraser Tool

When two neighboring pixels in an image require modification, consider using the Magic Eraser tool. When utilizing this tool on a background layer or a layer with locked transparency, you will observe that the transparent pixels will either adopt the background color or become transparent. Only pixels that are contiguous or have similar colors can be erased with this tool. When the background color of a photo is different from the subject, the Magic Eraser tool is very effective.

Follow these steps to use the Magic Eraser Tool:

1. Head to Tools Options and select the **Magic Eraser tool button** once you've chosen The Eraser Tool.
2. Configure the options in the Background Eraser Options as follows:
   - **Sample All Layers:** Sampling all layers enables you to erase colors by utilizing the combined data of all visible layers.
   - **Opacity:** Adjust the opacity of the erased pixels using the Opacity slider. At full opacity, the selected pixels are entirely erased, while lower opacity levels result in partial deletion of the pixels.

- **Anti-aliasing:** Anti-aliasing is used to generate a selection with smooth edges in the transparent area.
- **Contiguous:** This feature enables you to remove all pixels of the same color that are connected to the ones under the hot spot.
3. Once the settings are configured in the Tool Options, simply click on the pixel color in the image or layer to erase.

Using the Select Menu

Remember to locate the Select menu in the top menu on the Home Screen. When you choose the Select menu, the submenu will be displayed.

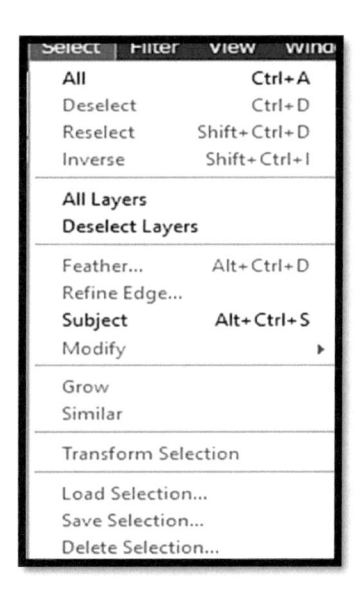

Choosing to Select All or Deselect All

- For selecting all the objects in an image, navigate to the Select option and choose All, or simply press Ctrl + A.
- Make sure to deselect all items in your image by going to the Select menu and choosing Deselect

Reselecting a Selection

To restore your previous selection, navigate to the **Select menu** and choose **Reselect**.

Reversing the Selection

- For the Inverse selection of your image, navigate to Select and choose Inverse

Feathering a Selection

- To create a feathered selection, navigate to the Select menu and enter the preferred pixel value between 0.2 and 250.

Saving and Loading Selection

You can easily access a saved selection for future use.

Follow these steps to save a selection:

1. Remember to go to the Select menu and then choose **Save Selection**.

2. When the Save Selection dialog box appears, choose **New Selection** and enter the name of your selection in the Name box

3. Next, simply click on OK.

4. Once you complete this step, you can reload the saved selection by navigating to the **Select menu** and selecting **Load Selection**. Then, choose from the options in the Selection drop-down menu.

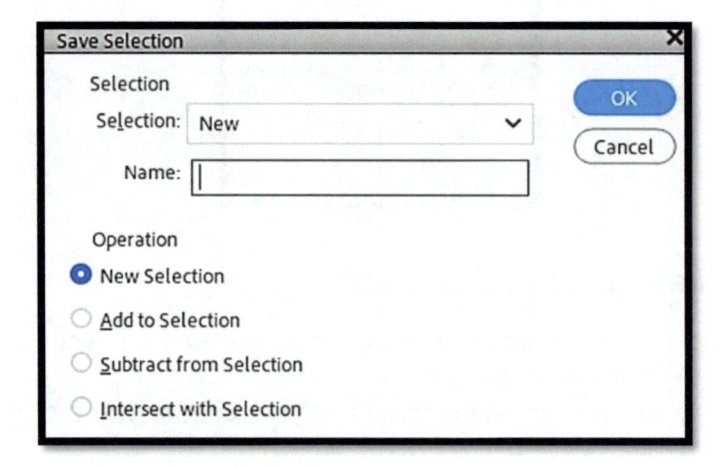

Refining the Edges of a Selection

You can fine-tune the edges of the selections made in your image using the Refine Edges feature. You can locate the Refine Edge option in tools like Lasso, Magic Wand, and Quick Selection tools.

Locating the Refine Edge tool:

1. Head to the **Select menu** and choose **Refine Edge** from the dropdown submenu.

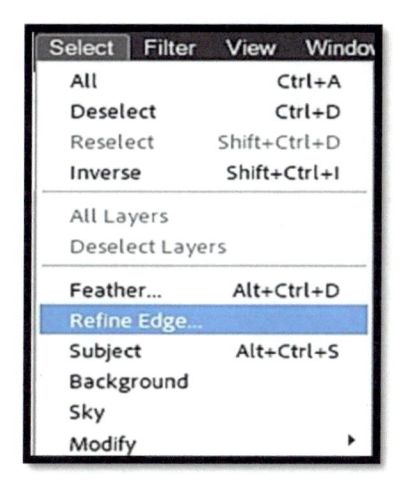

You can find the following options in the Refine Edge:

- **Select View Mode**: Pick a mode from the View pop-up menu. When in View mode, options include Marching Ants, Overlay, On Black and White, and Original.
- **Smart Radius**: Adjust the radius to achieve a smooth transition between soft and hard edges in the border region with the Smart Radius feature.
- **Radius**: Used to specify the size of the selection border for refinement. Using a small radius for sharp edges and a larger one for hard edges is recommended.
- **Smooth**: Used to minimize rough edges in the selection border for a polished look.
- **Feather**: Used for blurring the transition between the selection and the pixels. To achieve a gradually softer and more blurred edge, simply slide the slider to the right.
- **Contrast**: When the contrast is increased, the soft-edged transition around the selection border also increases.
- **Shift Edge:** Adjusting the Shift Edge option allows you to expand or reduce the chosen area within the image. Decreasing the selection border slightly helps to remove unwanted background colors from the selection.
- **Decontaminate Colors**: Replace the color fringe with the colors of the elements you have selected to decontaminate colors. The effectiveness of the color replacement depends on the smoothness of the edges chosen.
- **Amount**: Adjust the level of decontamination and fringe replacement using the amount set.
- **Output To**: When using Output To, you can decide whether the refined edge becomes a selection or mask on the current layer or creates a new layer or document.
- **Refine Radius Tool**: Refine Radius Tool is used to select the Paint Brush for making corrections on the border being refined.
- **Reasement Refinement Tool:** Use the Erasement Refinement Tool to eliminate any undesired refinements that have been applied, conveniently situated on the left-hand side.

- **Zoom Tool:** Used to zoom in on your image to review the impact of adjustments made in your settings
- **Hand Tool:** Use the hand tool to navigate your image and review any adjustments made in the settings.

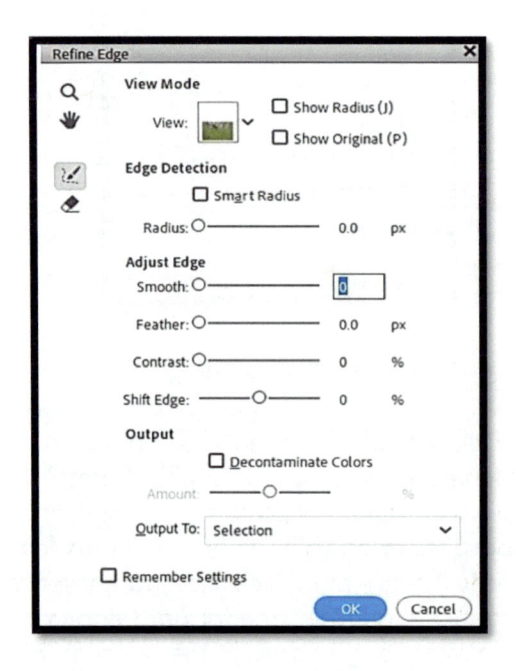

Mastering the Modify Commands

Discussing the Modify commands found in the Select sub-menu. While the Modify commands may not seem crucial, you never know when they might come in handy.

We will quickly review the updated commands:

- **Border**: This feature enables you to specify a region between 1 and 200 pixels inside the selection border.
- **Smooth**: Smooth out rough edges by entering a value between 1 to 100 pixels using this command.
- **Expand**: By using the expand command; you can adjust the dimensions of your selection by specifying a pixel value between 1 and 100.
- **Contract**: This command functions as the opposite of the Expand command. This function allows you to reduce your selection border by anywhere from 1 to 100 pixels.

CHAPTER TEN
WORKING WITH LAYERS

Here, we will focus extensively on layers, exploring their uses and the necessary tools and techniques for working with them. Keep in mind that layers allow for unlimited adjustments and modifications.

Recognizing Layers

Digitized versions of clear acetate sheets allow you to edit and add to images while preserving the original. Performing various operations on layers is similar to working with photos. This includes adjusting color and brightness, applying special effects, moving layer contents, adjusting opacity, blending values, and more. Layers can be easily added, removed, hidden, and rearranged. The layer panel houses the layers.

Overview of the Layer Panel

The Layers panel showcases a comprehensive list of all layers in the image, arranged from top to bottom and foreground to background. Head to Windows and locate Layers to access the layer panel. **Now, we will analyze each element in the layer panel as shown in the image below.**

1. **Create a New Layer**: Adding a new layer is done by selecting the option located at the top of the layer panel. For an additional layer, select **Layer > New** from the menu, and then click **Layer**.
2. **Create a New Group**: This option allows you to combine multiple layers into one.
3. **Fill/Adjustment Layer**: Adjustment Layers to easily incorporate patterns, gradients, and colors into a layer. Moreover, you can fine-tune the levels, hue, saturation, and brightness using this feature.
4. **Add Layer Mask**: You can show or conceal a particular part of a layer using the layer mask. The mask hidden within the layer appears in black, while the visible part is shown in white. Moreover, black pixels are concealed while white pixels are revealed in the thumbnails.
5. **Lock All Pixels**: Lock all layers to prevent editing by clicking on this button.
6. **Lock Transparent Pixels**: Each layer is considered transparent if it has no image pixels. Furthermore, transparent layers are not editable.
7. **Removing a Layer**: This feature enables you to delete a selected layer from the layer stack.
8. **Panel Options**: Panel Options include menu options like Rename Layer, Duplicate Layer, Delete Layer, Link Layers, Merge Visible, and Merge Down.
9. **Blend Modes**: Blend Modes determine how the colors of the image on one layer interact with the layer beneath it.

10. **Visibility**: To hide a layer, simply click on the small eye icon located on the left side of each layer. Just a reminder: changes made to this layer will remain hidden until you click on the eye icon.
11. **Link/Unlink Layers:** This option in the layer panel allows you to connect multiple layers so that any changes made to one layer will impact all linked layers.
12. **Background**: The lowest layer by default is the backdrop layer. When opening a picture or a new document, the background layer is consistently partially frozen.
13. **Standard Layer:** This layer showcases the pixel information for that specific layer.
14. **Adjustment Layer:** Adjustment layers are intended to affect the layer below them.
15. **Vector Layer:** This layer contains scalable data, like shapes.
16. **Text Layer:** This setting allows the layer to receive text content. The thumbnail for this layer is displayed as a T.

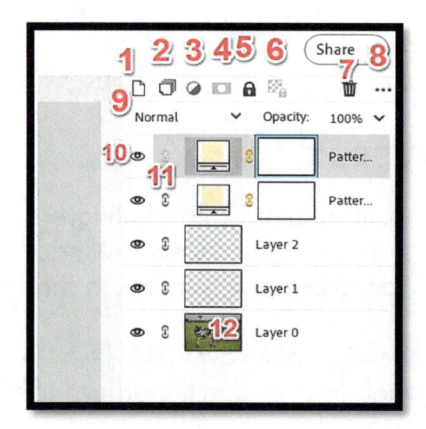

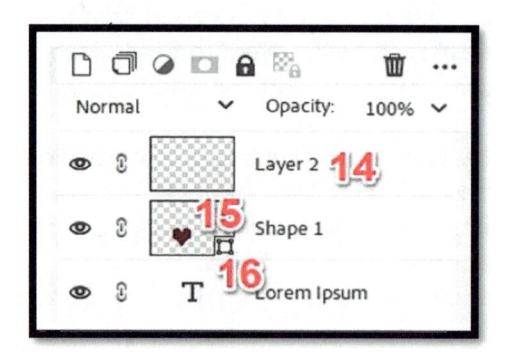

Mastering the Layer Menu

Certain commands are applicable in both the Layer menu and the Layer panels. Head to the menu bar and choose the Layer option to open the Layer menu.

- **Deleted Linked Layers and Hidden Layers:** Commands are available to delete linked layers or hidden layers from the display.

- **Layer Style:** Supervising the layer styles and special effects applied to the layers is done through the Layer Style command.
- **Arrange:** Use the Arrange command to adjust your layer stacking order with options like Back to Front and Send to Back.
- **Create Clipping Mask:** Use the Clipping Mask feature to create a mask using the bottommost layer for the one above it. Use the clipping mask when you want to fill a shape or type with various image layers.
- **Type:** This command is useful for managing the display of type layers.
- **Rename:** Use the command to easily change the name of the layer.
- **Simplify Layer:** This command transforms a type layer, shape layer, or fill layer into a standard image layer.
- **Merge and Flatten:** Combining and flattening layers involves merging them into a single layer. When flattening, all layers are merged into a single background.
- **Panel Options:** When chosen, you can showcase options and utilize the layer mask on the adjustments layers.

Mastering Various Types of Layers

Here, we will delve into the 5 different layers in Photoshop Element. It's important to note that creating image layers will require a significant amount of your time compared to other layers in Element.

The Image Layers

The Image Layer consists of the original photographs and any images imported into the document to occupy an Image layer. Follow these steps to create a new layer:

1. Make sure to navigate to the Window menu and select **Layers** to bring up the Layers panel.
2. Next, double-click on the Background layer within the Layers panel.
3. You can either rename the layer or keep the default name. Finally, click on OK to confirm.

Using the Adjustment Layer

These layers are used for fine-tuning an image's brightness, contrast, and saturation.

Here are the steps to use the Adjustment layers:

1. Make sure to navigate to the Window menu and select Layers to bring up the Layers panel.
2. Choose the image you wish to edit. Within the Layers panel, select **Create New Fill or Adjustment Layers**. When setting the options for the Adjustment layers, choose from the drop-down list.
   - **Level**: Adjust the tonal value in the image with the Level option.
   - **Brightness/Contrast:** The Brightness/Contrast option can lighten or darken the image.
   - **Hue/Saturation:** Adjusting Hue/Saturation can correct color deficiencies in the image while using a Gradient Map helps map pixels to selected gradient colors.
   - **Photo Filter**: This feature corrects the color balance and color temperature of the image.
   - **Invert**: Use the invert function to generate a photo with a negative effect by manipulating the brightness values of the image.
   - **Threshold**: Threshold is used to generate a monochrome image without gray, enabling you to identify the lightest and darkest areas of the image.
   - **Posterize**: This feature decreases the amount of brightness levels in the image, resulting in a flat, poster-like look for your picture. By selecting this option, the color palette is limited.

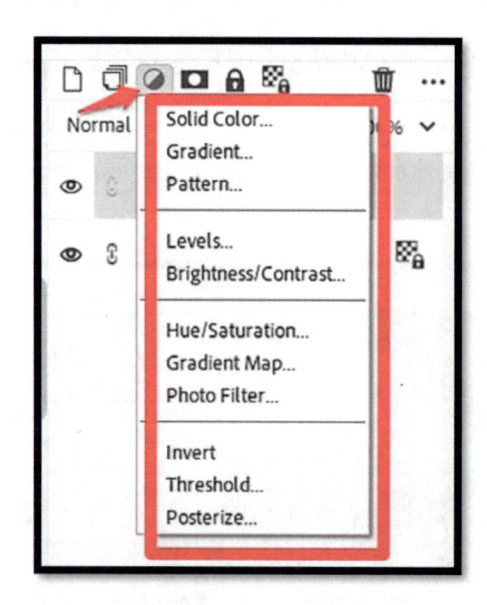

3. Next, simply click on OK. Knowing that a layer mask is automatically created whenever an Adjustment is made is crucial.

The Fill Layers

Easily enhance your image by applying a solid color, gradient, or pattern using fill layers. Fill layers come with layer masks just like adjustment layers.

Follow the steps provided to create a fill layer:

1. Open the image you want to edit. Click on **Create New Fill or Adjustment Layers** in the Layers panel.
2. Choose the options from the drop-down list:
- **Solid Color**: Here is where you select the color to add to the layer.
- **Gradient**: You can easily apply the gradient to your layer by choosing a preset gradient from the drop-down panel.
- **Pattern**: Pattern selection is made from the drop-down panel. You can also enter a value to adjust the pattern scale of the layer.

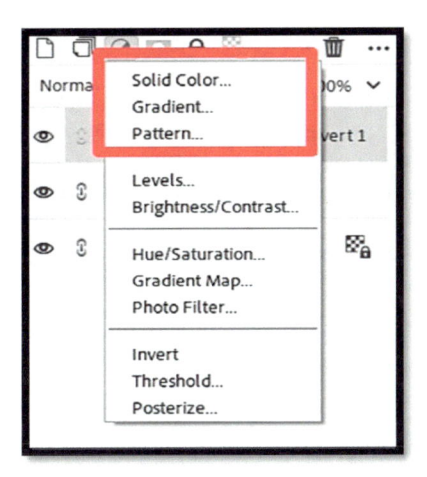

3. Click on the "OK" button.

The Shape Layer

The Shape layers help incorporate different shapes into an image. You can easily adjust the size of these forms and create sleek edges.

Here are the steps to effectively use the form layers:

1. Choose the Shape tools from the Tool panel.
2. Choose a shape from the Tool Option.

3. Click and drag the shape on the image to create a shape
4. When a layer is selected, the shape will be placed into it; otherwise, a new layer will be created automatically.

Text Layers

You have the option to add text to your photos using layers. The text in Photoshop Element is vector-based, allowing you to easily modify and resize it as needed.

1. Choose the Text tool from the Tool Panel.
    Click on a layer and start typing your text.
2. Once finished, click on the marker icon.
3. Make sure the text is on a blank layer that is selected.

Mastering the Fundamentals of Working with Layers

Creating a New Layer

Two main methods exist for creating layers in Photoshop Element:

Method One:

- Click on the option to create a new layer in the Layers panel, and the layer will be automatically generated with the default name "**Layer 1**."

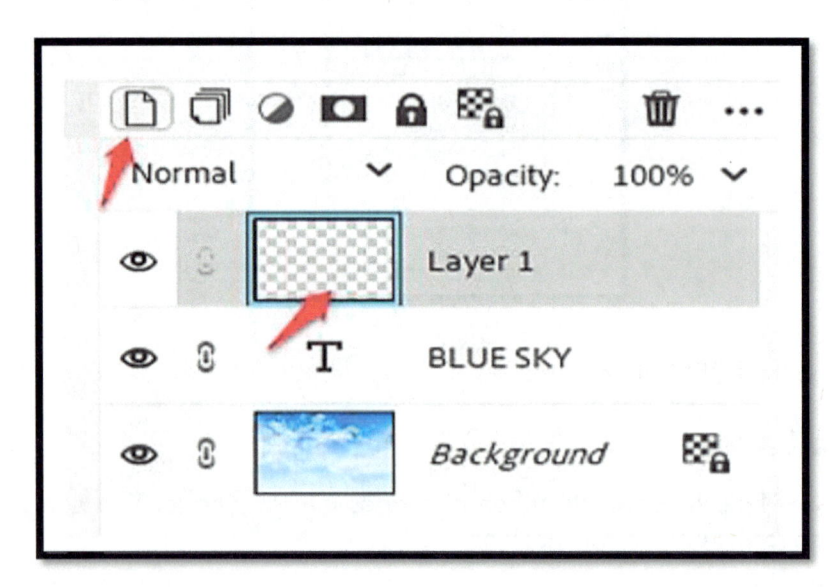

Method Two:

- Click on Layer in the Menu bar, then select **New** and click on Layer.

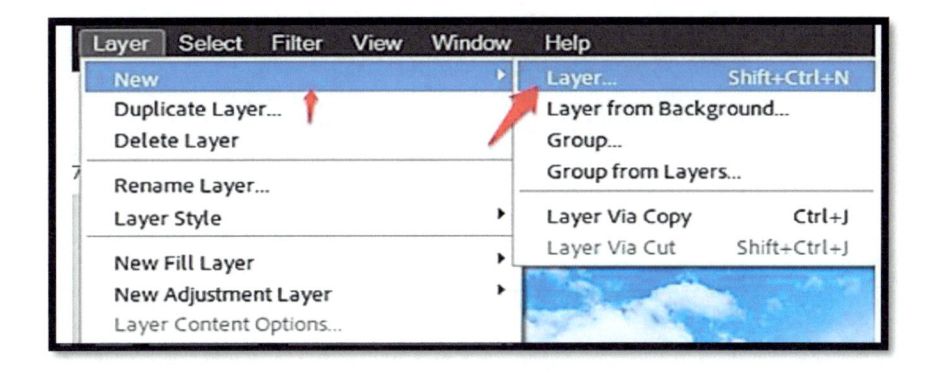

- Set the options provided below in the New Layer dialog box.

Name: provide the name for the new layer.
Color: Choose the desired color.
Mode: Select the mode from the drop-down list.
Opacity: Adjust the opacity using the slider. After clicking OK, the new layer will appear as a thumbnail on the left side of the layer panel.

Using Layer via Copy and Layer Via Cut

By using the Layer via copy and Layer via cut options in the layer menu command, a new layer can be created.

Access the Layer option from the menu bar:

- Choose **New** and then select **Layer via Copy** or **Layer Via Cut**.

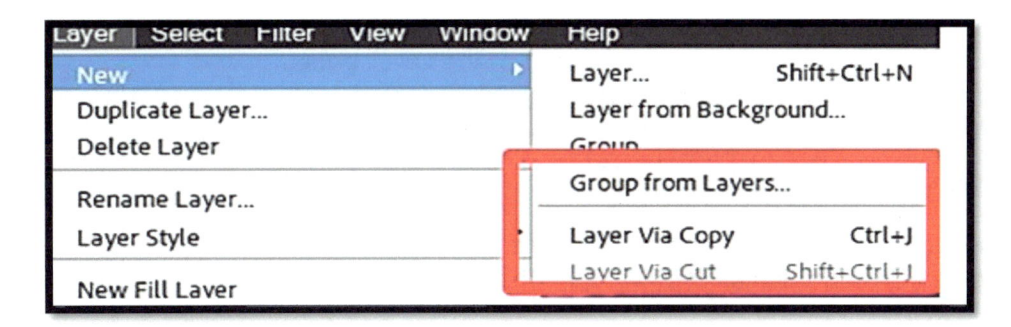

Duplicating Layers

You can duplicate your layers as many times as you want. Follow the steps provided to replicate layers.

- Once you've chosen Layer from the menu bar, simply select **Duplicate Layer**.

- Make sure to adjust the settings in the Duplicate layer dialog box before clicking OK.

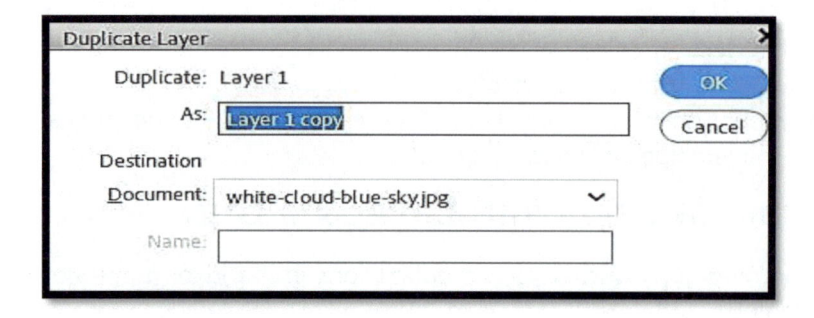

Dragging and Dropping Layers

Duplicating a layer can be done using the drag and drop command instead of copying and pasting. Follow these steps to complete this task.

1. Choose the layer you wish to move from the Layer panel.
2. Then, navigate to the Tool panel and pick the Move tool.
3. Move the item to your desired location by dragging and dropping it.

Transforming Layer

You can rotate or scale your photos using the Transform and Free Transform commands during layer transformations.

Follow these steps to transform a layer:

1. Choose the layer you want to transform.
   Navigate to **Image**, choose **Transform**, and then click **Free Transform**.
2. Your layer is enclosed by a bounding box.
3. Modify the bounding box by configuring the specified options:
   - **Size the contents accordingly**: For this task, simply drag the corner handle and make sure to maintain the proportions.

- **Constrain the proportions**: Use the Shift key when dragging
- **Rotate the content:** Rotate the content by moving the mouse cursor outside the corner handle, waiting for a curved arrow to appear, and then dragging.
- **Distort, skew, or apply perspective to the contents**: Manipulate, alter, or adjust the contents using distortion, skew, or perspective. To perform these options, simply right-click and choose the desired command from the context menu. You can find the scale and skew icons in the Tools Option menu, or input the transform values numerically.

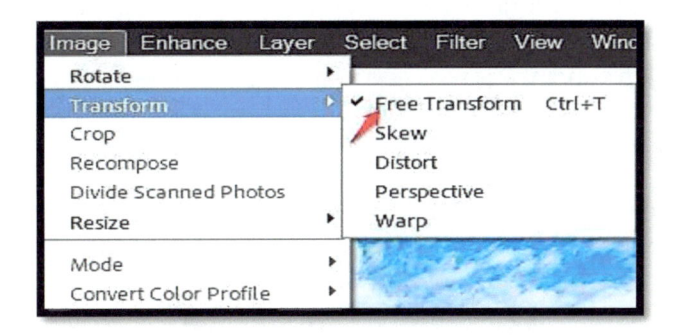

4. Once the layer is transformed to your liking, simply double-click inside the bounding box

Mastering the Layer Mask

The layer's visibility in the image is controlled by the layer mask, which is a resolution-dependent bitmap image. You can reveal or conceal part of an image by utilizing the layer mask. The mask's hidden portion appears in black within the layer, while the visible part is shown in white. Adjust the layer mask without altering the masked area or deleting any layer pixels. **Here are some of the uses of the layer mask.**
- Adding one layer on top of another and adjusting the layer mask to reveal or conceal the effects of the adjustment layer.

Applying a Layer Mask to an Image

Choose the specific image area for the layer mask and then simply click the **Add Layer Mask button** located in the Layer panel.

Additional Functions for Layer Masks

Here are some functions you can carry out using layer masks.

- Remember to use the Shift-click technique on a layer mask thumbnail in the Layers panel to hide it from view.

- Alt-click on the layer mask thumbnail in the Layers panel to show the mask without showing the image.
- Click on the link icon in the Layer panel to disconnect a layer from a layer mask.
- Drag the layer mask thumbnail to the trash icon in the Layers panel to delete a layer mask.

Flattening the Layers

To achieve a flat appearance, you need to delete the hidden layers and fill the visible area with white color. Reducing the file size is a crucial part of flattening the layer. When an image is flattened, all visible layers such as text, shape, fill, and adjustment layers are combined into a Background.

Follow these steps to use the Flatten option:

1. Make sure the visible layers are flattened by going to the Layer menu and selecting **Flatten Image**.

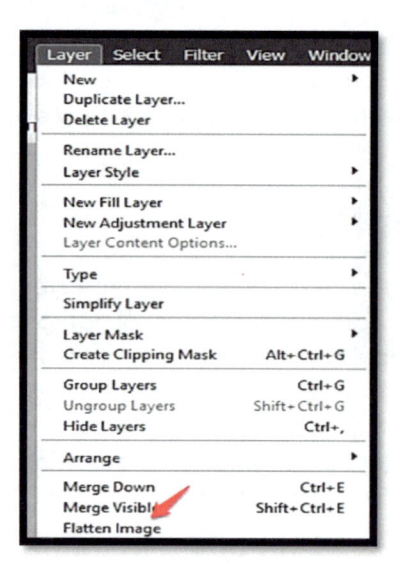

Merging the Layers

Combining all the layers into a single Background is possible through file merging. Consolidating visible, linked, or neighboring levels into a single layer can help optimize memory and storage usage.

To merge layers, follow these steps:

1. Select all layers to be merged.
2. From the Menu bar, go to Layer and then click on Merge Layers.

CHAPTER ELEVEN
SIMPLE IMAGE MAKEOVER

This section will teach you how to crop, straighten, and recompose photographs effortlessly. With detailed guidance, you will gain familiarity with various auto repair tools such as Auto Smart Tone, Auto Smart Fix, Auto Levels, and Auto Contrast.

Cropping Images

One of the essential skills in picture editing is mastering the art of cropping images. To establish a strong focal point and eliminate distracting backgrounds, consider cropping the image. One efficient method to crop an image is by using the Crop tool.

Mastering the Crop Tool

When using the Crop tool, follow the steps provided:

1. Head to the Tools panel and select the **Crop tool**. Specify the aspect ratio and resolution options in the Tool Options section.
- **No Restriction:** there are any restrictions, allowing you to cut your image to any size.
- **Photo Bin:** Use the Photo Ratio to maintain the original aspect of the image during cropping.
- **Preset Sizes:** Choose from preset sizes for common photographic dimensions.
- **Width (W) and Height (H):** You can select the desired dimensions for cropping an image.
- **Resolution selection**: Choose the desired resolution for your cropped image.
- **Pixels/ins Pixel/cm:** Choose the measurement units for Pixels/ins Pixel/cm.
- **Grid Overlay:** Use the grid overlay feature to properly frame your image before cropping. This choice consists of three parts: None, Grid, and Rule of Thirds.
2. Select the desired part of the image by dragging over it, and release the mouse when the crop marquee appears. Make sure the bounding box with handles is visible at the corners and size.
3. Finally, click on the **green Commit button**.

Using Selection Borders for Cropping

You can also use the selection border to crop an image. When cropping a picture with a selection border, the area outside the boundary is removed.

Below are the steps to crop an image with a selected border.

1. Select the **Straighten tool** from the Tool panel.
2. Select the desired settings from the Canvas Options available in the Tools section.
   - **Grow or Shrink:** This feature enables you to rotate the image and resize the canvas to match the image area.
   - **Remove Background:** Shape the background canvas out of the image by removing the background.

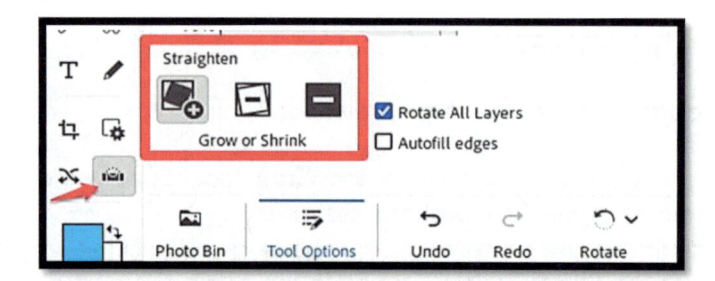

   - **Original Size:** Rotating the image without affecting the background canvas size.
3. Draw a line to your image indicating the new straight edge.

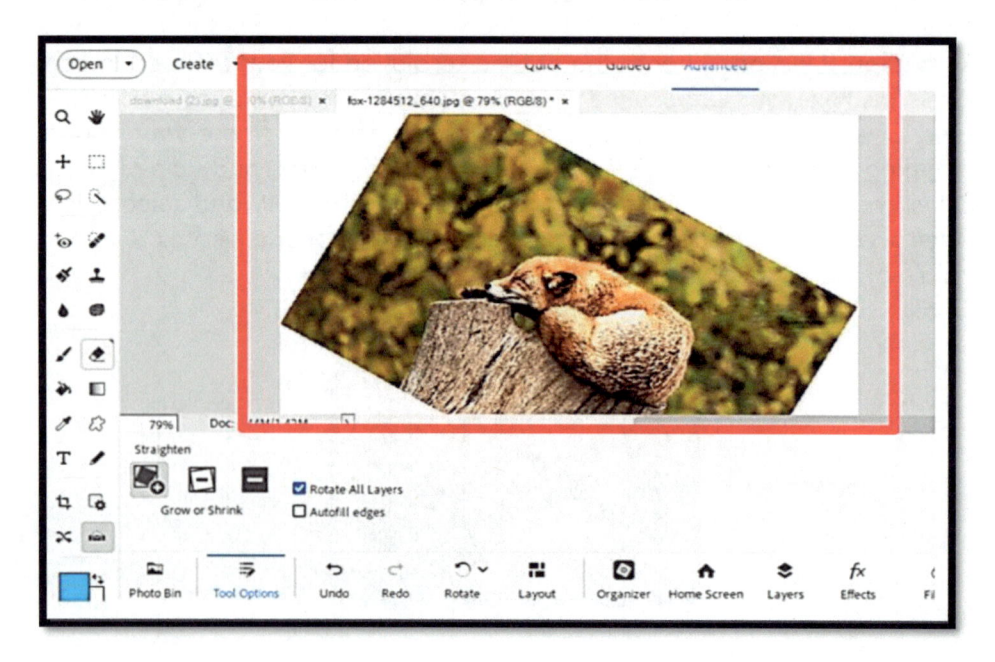

136

Recomposing images

You can resize your image using the Recompose tool without losing any important elements or content.

Follow the steps below to use the Recompose tool:

1. Choose the Recompose tool from the Tool panel.
2. Use the Mark for Protection Brush (the brush with a plus sign) in the Tool Options to carefully brush over the specific area of the image you want to keep.
3. Use the Mark for Protection Brush (the brush with a minus sign) in the Tool Options to brush over the area of the image you want to remove.

Adjust any settings in the Tool Options.

- **Threshold**: Adjust the Threshold slider to control the amount of recomposing displayed in the adjustment.
- **Preset Ratios**: Choose preset ratios to easily frame your image into specific dimensions.
- **Width and Height:** When resizing an image, you can adjust the width and height to your desired dimensions.
- **Highlight Skin Tones:** Ensure skin tones remain consistent when resizing.

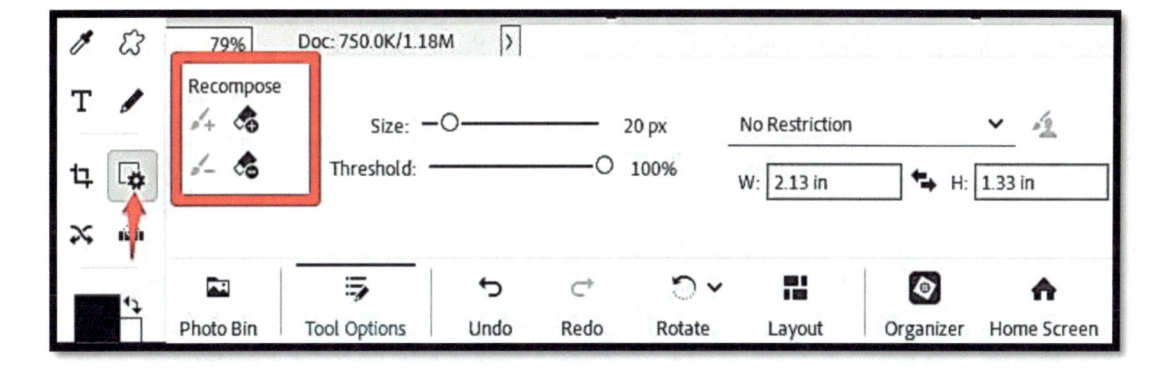

4. Adjust the size by dragging the corner or side handles, and then clicks the **Commit button** once you've finished editing.

Presenting One-Step Auto Fixes

Auto Fixes are efficient tools for swiftly adjusting lighting, contrast, and color to enhance the photo's appearance with just one menu command. Commands on the Enhance menu are accessible in both Advanced and Quick mode.

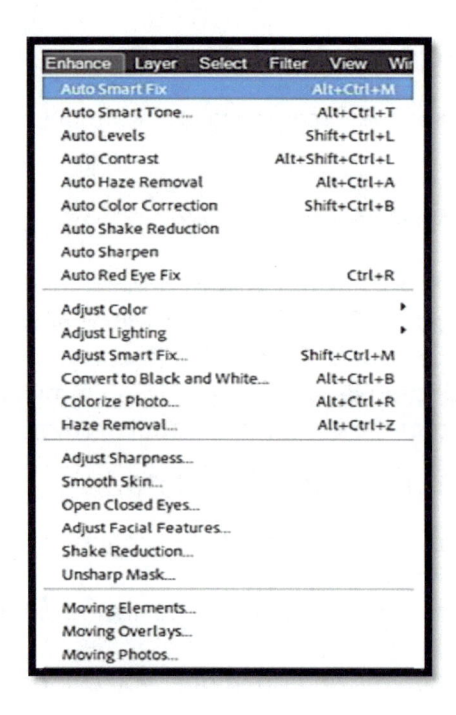

Auto Smart Fix

An effective tool for swiftly adjusting common issues such as contrast, color balance, and saturation is the Auto Smart Fix. Displayed below is the comparison of Auto Smart Fix's results before and after.

Auto Smart Tone

For adjusting the tonal values in your photo, the Auto Smart Tone auto-fix feature was created.

- When the image is open, choose Enhance and click on Auto Smart Tone.
- For optimal adjustment, position the controller in the center of the image.

- Click on the Learn from This Correction option in the lower-left corner of the dialog box.
- After completing the required adjustments, select OK.

Auto Level

The Auto Level feature fine-tunes both the hue and contrast of an image. This function enhances the contrast of the image by adjusting the darkest and lightest areas, converting them to black and white. Displayed below are the before-and-after results of Auto Levels.

Auto Contrast

Adjust an image's contrast without changing its color using the Auto Contrast function. This is most effective with slightly blurred images. Displayed below are the before-and-after results of Auto Contrast.

139

Auto Haze Removal

Clear haze and fog from your photos using Auto Haze Removal. If this command does not meet your needs, consider exploring the Haze Removal tool in the Tools panel. Here is a comparison of the results of Auto Haze Removal before and after.

Auto Color Correction

Enhancing an image's color and contrast by adjusting the shadows, highlights, and midtones can be achieved through Auto Color Correction. You can use this command to adjust the color balance in your image or remove any unwanted color casts. Here is a side-by-side comparison of the image with and without Auto Color Correction.

Auto Shake Reduction

Auto Shake Reduction was developed to reduce the blur caused by camera movement. When needed, this command proves to be quite helpful. Head over to Enhance and choose Shake Reduction for even more Shake Reduction benefits. Here is the Auto Shake before and after in the image below.

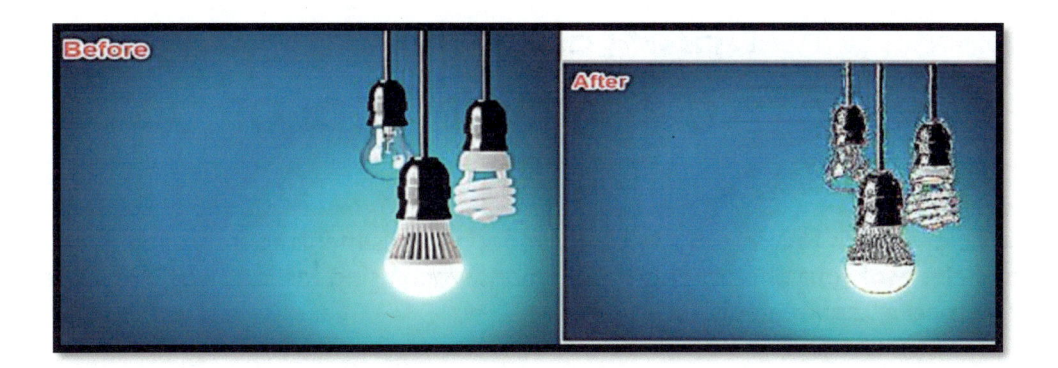

Auto Sharpen

Using the Auto Sharpen command helps improve pixel contrast, resulting in a sharper focus for the image. An over-sharpened image may look noisy and grainy.

Auto Red-Eye Fix

Identifying and correcting red-eye in an image is possible using the Auto Red Fix command. When an individual or animal gazes directly at the camera flash, it can result in a red-eye. If the Auto Red Eye feature is not working well, you can use the Red Eye tool in the Tools menu.

CHAPTER TWELVE
CORRECTING CONTRAST, COLOR, AND CLARITY

This particular section focuses on the use of manual adjustments to improve the contrast, color, and clarity of your photographs in situations when using fast and easy fixes does not meet your specific requirements.

Changing Colors

One of the objectives that each user of Element has is to alter the colors that are present in their picture. Within this area of the tutorial, you will also acquire the knowledge necessary to adjust the colors of photographs via the use of manual instructions.

Removing Colors Cast Automatically

There is a color cast that occurs when the color channels in the picture are not in balance with one another. The unfavorable look, which more often than not manifests itself as a strange color tint, is typically the result of the image's inadequate lighting. Fluorescence light is one of the key factors that play a role in the color cast that occurs in pictures. A command called Remove Color Cast was devised so that you could get rid of the cast and brings the color balance in your images back into equilibrium.

To use the Remove Color Cast, follow these steps in the appropriate order:

- To remove color cast, go to **Enhance** in the menu bar, select **Adjust Color**, and then navigate to **Remove Color Cast**.

Adjusting Lighting

Instead of making modifications to the vehicle, several basic methods may be used to enhance the lighting in photographs. The manual corrections are included in both the Advanced and Quick modes, which is the most important aspect. First, let's have a look at them.

Resolving Lighting Issues through Shadows and Highlights

You can quickly and simply alter areas of your images that are overexposed or underexposed by using the Shadows/Highlights commands. This command works very well with photographs that were shot in harsh lighting or from above. To use this command, you must follow these instructions.

- To adjust the lighting, choose the Enhance area of the menu bar and then select **Shadows/Highlight** from the list of options. After that, make sure the Preview check box is selected.

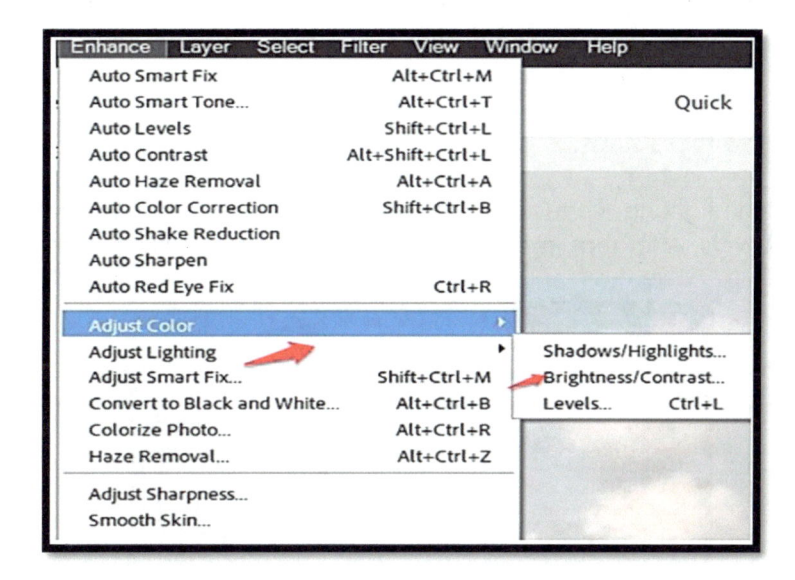

- If you want to adjust the amount of brightness and contrast adjustment, you may either move the sliders or enter a value in the Brightness and Contrast dialog box.

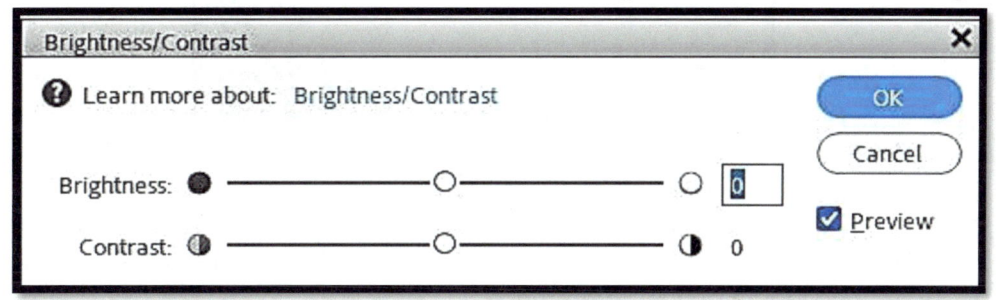

- Once you have completed the change, you should click on the OK button.

Working with the Levels

Through the use of the Level command, you have complete control over the eventual result. When compared to the Brightness/Contrast command, levels provide you the ability to modify up to 256 distinct tones and generate a completed output that seems to be much more natural.

To use Levels, follow these steps:

1. To adjust the lighting, choose the **Enhance** part of the menu bar and then proceed to select Levels. After that, make sure the Preview check box is selected.

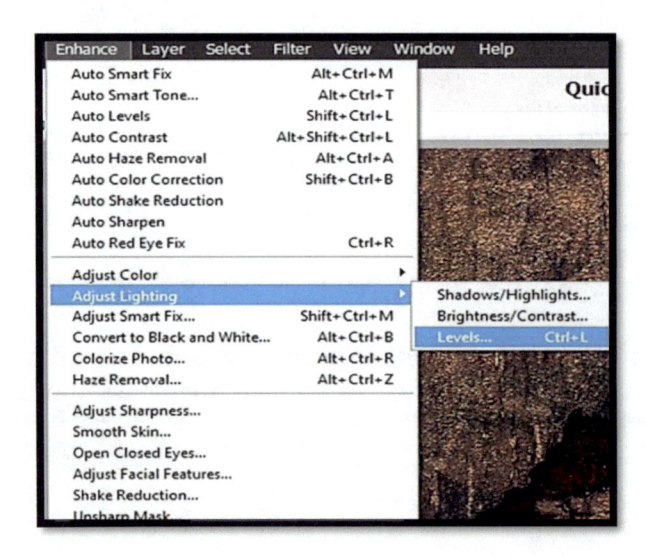

2. Choose the RGB option from the Channel menu.
3. You can adjust the values of the shadow and highlight by sliding the black and white Input Levels sliders or by entering the values into the first and third Input Levels text boxes depending on your preference.

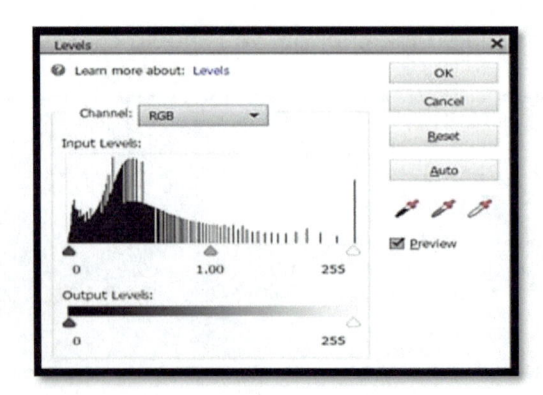

4. Click on the OK button.

Adjusting Color

One of the objectives that every user of Element has is to alter the colors that are present in their picture. During this portion of the textbook, you will also acquire the knowledge necessary to adjust the colors of photos via the use of manual instructions.

Removing Colors Cast Automatically

There is a color cast that occurs when the color channels in the picture are not in balance with one another. The unfavorable look, which more often than not manifests itself as a strange color tint, is typically the result of the image's inadequate lighting. Fluorescence light is one of the key factors that play a role in the color cast that occurs in pictures. A command called Remove Color Cast was devised so that you could get rid of the cast and brings the color balance in your images back into equilibrium.

To use the Remove Color Cast, follow these steps in the appropriate order:

1. Remove color cast by going to Enhance in the menu bar, selecting **Adjust Color**, and then clicking on **Remove Color Cast**.

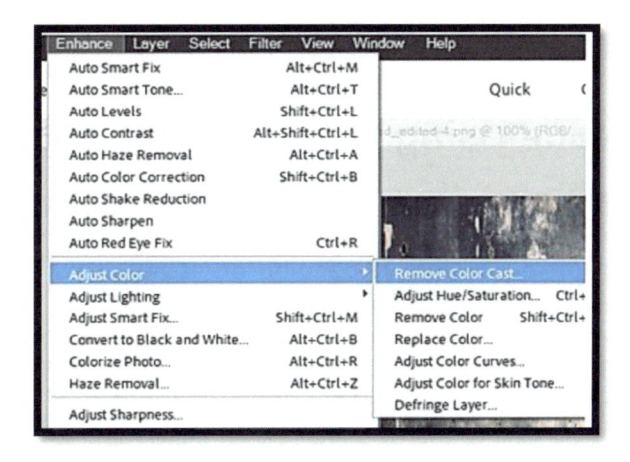

2. The command is executed in the Remove Color Cast dialog box when you click the Eyedropper tool into the picture at the location where it should be white, gray, or black. Due to the availability of this information, the colors are adjusted appropriately.

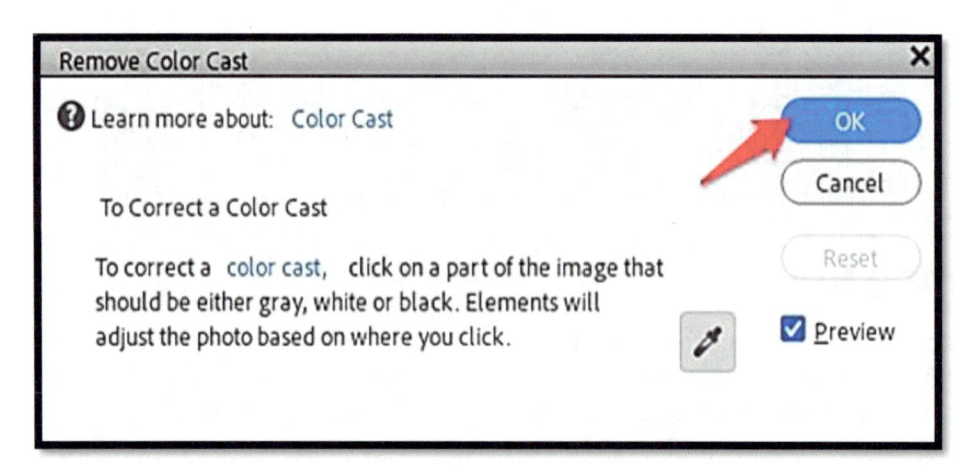

3. Click on the OK button to save the changes that you have made.

Adjustments Made Using Hue and Saturation

While the hue of your picture refers to the color, the saturation of your image corresponds to the intensity of the individual color. The Hue/Saturation command allows you to fine-tune or adjust the color of your picture depending on its hue, saturation, and brightness. This command is available throughout the editing process.

1. Go to the **Enhance option** on the menu bar, choose the **Adjust Color option**, and then proceed to click on the **Adjust Hue/Saturation option**.

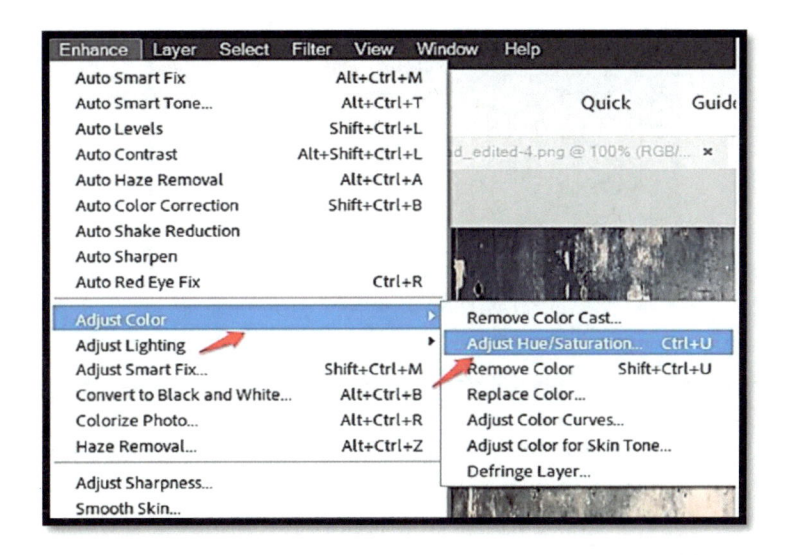

2. When you are in the Master option, choose any of the colors that you want to modify.
To modify the color, you can edit it by dragging the slider of the following settings.
   - **Hue**: This option allows you to shift the colors around the color wheel in either a clockwise or counterclockwise direction.
   - **Saturation**: The richness of the colors can be increased or decreased by using this option, which is called "saturation."
   - **Lightness**: The brightness values are increased by adding white, and the brightness values are decreased by adding black. This is referred to as the "lightness" feature.
3. If you want to modify the colors in the picture to a new color or a single color, you can choose the Colorize option.

4. After you have made the required modifications, click the OK button.

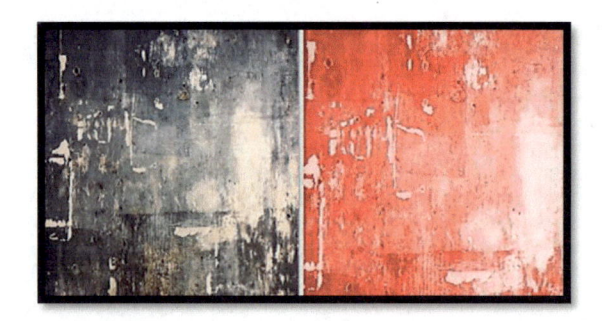

Eliminating Color with Remove Color Command

Element offers a basic approach for removing color from any photo, layer, or selection, which is useful if you want to minimize the amount of color that is removed. When the Remove Color command is used, there is a possibility that the picture will have a low contrast. To make use of the "**Remove Color**" command.

1. To remove the color from the picture, layer, or selection, you must first pick the desired item.
2. When you are ready, go to Enhance on the menu bar, choose **Adjust Color,** and then proceed to click on **Remove Color**.

Changing Colors Through the Use of Replace Color

Using the Replace Color command, you can alter a color that is present in your image. To make use of this command, you must first create a mask (for instructions on how to do this, go to the previous chapter), and then you must make exact adjustments to the hue and saturation of the colors that you have selected to get the effect that you want.

Follow these steps to make use of the command to replace the color:

1. To replace the color, go to the Enhance menu on the menu bar, pick Adjust Color, and then click on **Replace Color**.

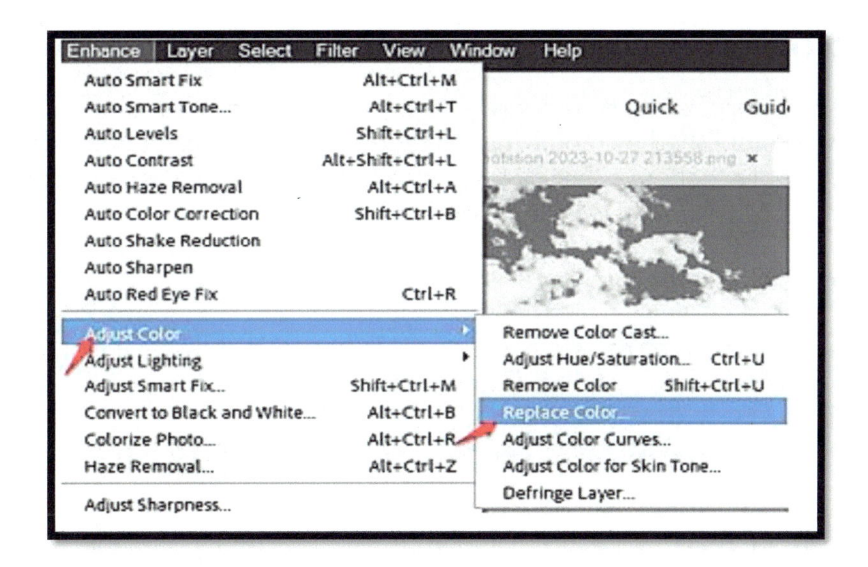

2. Select either the Selection or Image option from the Replace Color dialog box. Selecting the Selection option will expose the mask in the Preview area while selecting the Image option will reveal the actual image in the Preview area.
3. To choose the color that you want, be sure you select it in the picture or Preview box.
4. Use the Shift-click or the plus sign (+) Eyedropper tool to add other colors using the eyedropper tool.
5. To remove colors, you can either hit the Alt key or use the negative sign (-) Eyedropper tool.
6. By using the Fuzziness slider, you can add colors that are associated with the ones that you have chosen. Additionally, you have the option of adjusting, adding, or removing your pick by using the Fuzziness slider.
7. To alter the color, you may use the Hue slider. Use the Saturation slider to alter the level of color richness. By using the Lightness slider, you can either brighten or darken your picture.
8. When you have finished making the required modifications, do not forget to click on the OK button.

Using Color Curves to Make Corrections

The goal of the Color Curves command is to broaden the overall tonal range of color images. This is accomplished by modifying the highlights, shadows, and mid-tones in each color channel. Images that are either overexposed or have a dark backlight are the perfect candidates for this command given their characteristics.

How to use the Color Curves command:

- For the adjustment of color curves, go to **Enhance** in the menu bar, select **Adjust Color**, and then click on **Adjust Color Curves**.

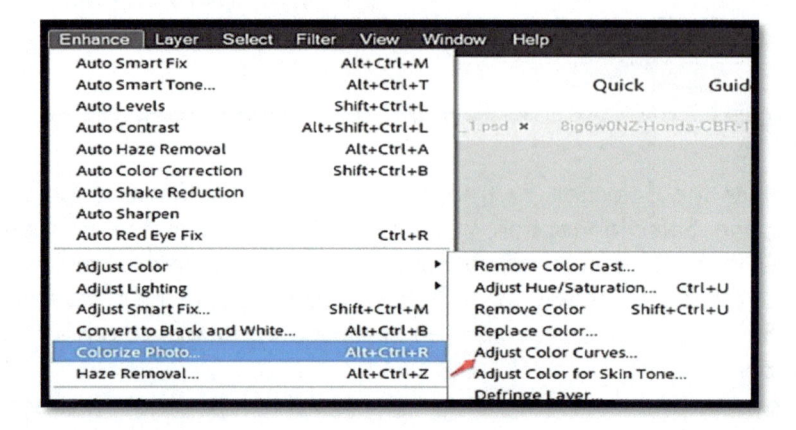

- Within the Adjust Color Curves section, choose the suitable curve adjustment styles from the area designated for selecting a style.
- For improved fine-tuning, it is recommended to use the sliders for adjusting the highlights, brightness, contrast, and shadows.
- If you are satisfied with the modification, you may proceed by clicking on the **OK button**.

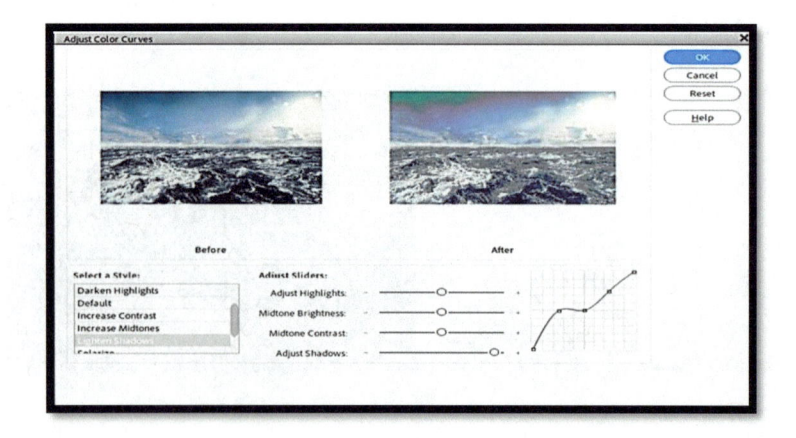

Changing People's Skin Tone

It is possible for a multitude of factors in your photographs or individuals to be the source of skin tones that seem unnatural. Elements has a command called Adjust Skin Tones, which may help the skin tone return to a more natural look with the use of this command. By using this command, you can alter either a selection or an entire layer. When you want to modify a piece of your picture that you do not want to change, you should use the selection tool to pick the region of the tool that you want to edit.

To make use of the Adjust Skin Tones command, follow these instructions on your computer:

1. The first step is to choose the layer or region of the skin that needs to be modified.
2. Move to the Enhance option on the menu bar, then select **Adjust Color**, and finally click on **Adjust Skin Tone**.
3. Navigate to the area of the skin that requires modification and click on it.

Set the settings that are shown below:
- **Tan**: To enhance or diminish the amount of brown pigment that is present in the skin.
   Brush: If you want to reduce the amount of redness in your skin, you can use a brush.
- **Temperature**: The temperature is used to alter the general hue of the skin, causing it to become warmer (right toward red) or cooler (left toward blue) as a result of the adjustment.

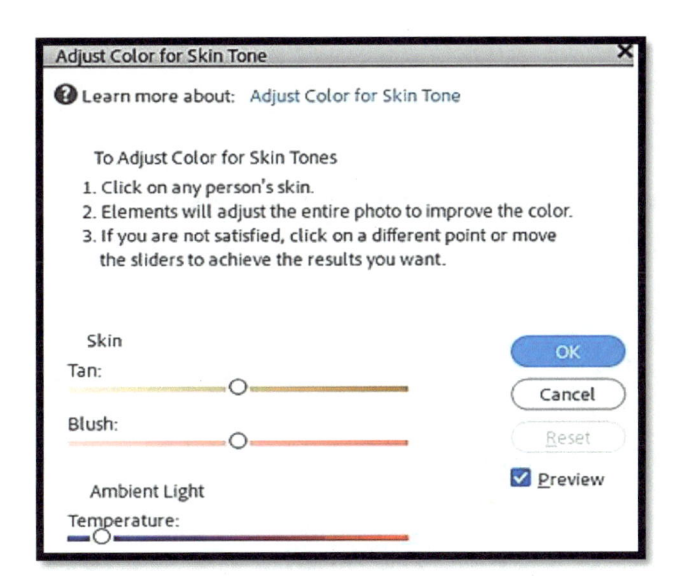

4. Once you have completed the necessary modifications, proceed to click on the OK button.

Defringing Layers

In the context of making, moving, or copying a selection, the word "**fringe**" refers to the region that is commonly seen because of these actions. In computer science, the term "**fringe**" refers to the collection of background pixels that surround your selection. When the Defringed layers command is executed, the colors of these unnecessary additional pixels are changed such that they are identical to the colors of neighboring pixels that do not contribute to the underlying color of the background.

If you want to use the Defringed Layers command, you will need to follow these methods:

- Either copy or paste a selection onto a new or existing layer, or you may drag and drop a selection into a new document.

Follow these steps:

- Navigate to **Enhance** in the menu bar, pick Adjust Color, and then click on **Defringing Layers**.

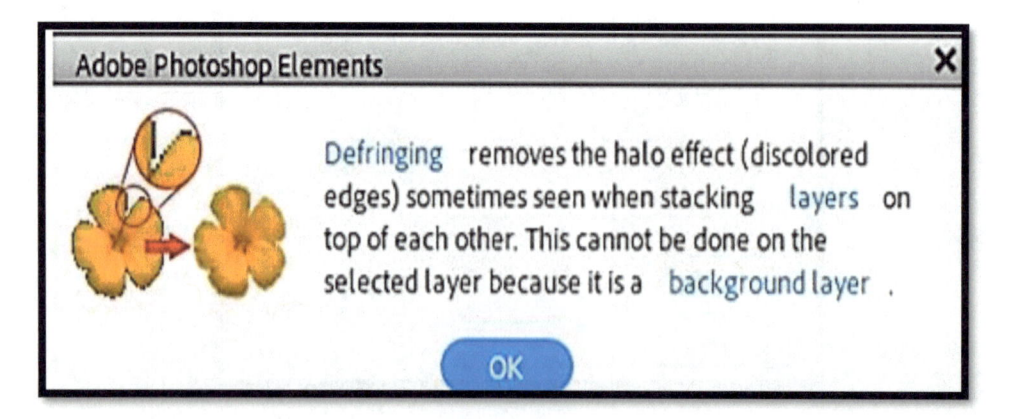

- Enter the value that corresponds to the number of pixels that you want to convert.
- Once you have completed the required modifications, choose the OK button.

Eliminating Haze

Make advantage of the Haze Removal tool to manually reduce the amount of haze and fog in your photograph. Both haze and fog may be produced when light interacts with particles in the air, such as dust, dirt, or other particles.

To use the Haze Removal Tools, follow the directions that are mentioned below:

1. Make sure to choose the picture that has to be modified.
2. Go to the Enhance option on the menu bar and choose the **Haze Removal option**. Be sure you specify the following parameters inside the Haze Removal dialog box.
   - **Haze Reduction**: This slider gives you the ability to decrease the amount of hazes that are present in the picture.
   - **Sensitivity**: This slider allows you to modify the degree to which the photos are affected by the Haze Removal.
   - **Before and After Toggle Button**: This button allows you to toggle between several perspectives of your picture, including the before and after views.

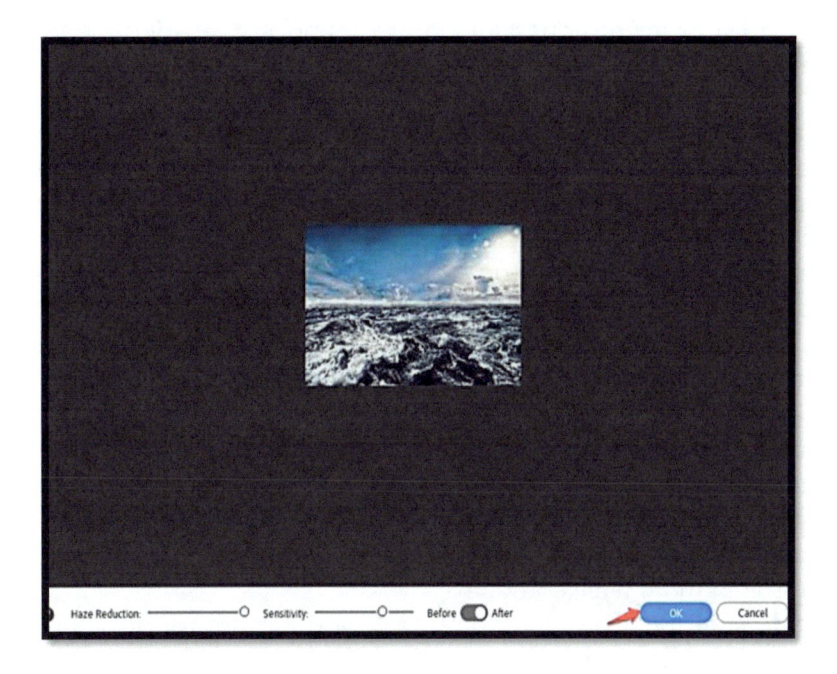

3. Once you have completed the necessary modifications, proceed to click on the OK button.

Changing the Color Temperature with a Photo Filter

Within your picture, you can make adjustments to the color temperature by using the Photo Filter Adjustment command.

To use this command, you must follow these instructions:

- Make sure to pick Adjustment from the Filter Menu, and then click on the **Photo Filter option**.
- The Preset filter can be selected from the drop-down list that is located beneath the Filter section of the dialog box.
- Choose the amount of color that will be applied to your picture by selecting the Density option.
- To prevent the picture filter from darkening your image, all you need to do is click on the **Preserve Luminosity button**.
- To proceed with the edits, click on the OK button after they have been finished.

How to Create a Color Map

By using the color mapper instructions, you may more easily modify the color values that are included in your picture. You can locate the color mapper command by going to the Filter menu and selecting Adjustments.

The following is a list of instructions that can be found in the Adjustments submenu for mapping colors:

- **Equalize**: The Equalize mapper is responsible for identifying the pixels in an image that are the brightest and darkest, and then assigning white and black values to those pixels. The remaining pixels are given values that are grayscale representations.
- **Gradient Map**: The Gradient Map feature allows you to set the color of the gradient you choose to correspond with the tonal range of a picture. As an example, colors such as orange, green, and purple are designated to serve as the shadow, highlight, and mid-tones, respectively.
- **Invert**: Invert can be used to invert all of the colors in your picture, transforming them into negative colors.
- **Posterize**: One of the commands that might help you reduce the brightness levels of your picture is called "**Posterize**." From 2 to 255, you have the option of selecting a value. Lower numbers result in pictures that are more similar to posters, whilst higher values result in more lifelike images.
- **Threshold**: With the Threshold command, you can transform your picture into a black-and-white rendering. All of the pixels that are brighter than the value that you provide are shown in white, while the pixels that are darker than the value that you indicate are shown in black.

Adjusting Clarity

All that is required of you is to make modifications to the contrast and color of your images. To give your images a more professional look, you need to be familiar with the process of modifying the quality of your photographs. As a consequence of this, we will learn a variety of techniques for adjusting the levels of clarity in your picture.

Elimination Noise, Artifacts, Dust, and Scratch

Due to the presence of sounds, artifacts, dust, and scratches, it is possible that your image may not provide the results that you want. To remove all of these undesirable components from your picture, you will need to go to the Filter menu and choose the **Noise option**. Among the various options available in the Noise submenu, the Add Noise option stands out as an outlier.

These options are as follows:

- **Despeckle**: By selecting the Despeckle option, you can reduce the contrast of your picture, eliminate any dust that may be present, and ensure that the edges remain intact.
- **Dust & Scratches**: This feature allows you to add blurs to your picture, which allows you to conceal any dust or scratches that may be present in your image. You may choose the size of the region you want to blur by using the Radius value that is included in this option. Additionally, the Threshold value in the option is used to establish the amount of contrast between pixels that must be present before they are blurred. This value comes into play when the option is set.
- **Median**: A median is a measure that is used to reduce the contrast that is present in the vicinity of dust spots. Make certain that the radius value, which represents the size of the region that has to be modified, is set.
- **Reduce Noise**: To eliminate luminance noise and artifacts from your photographs, you can use the Reduce Noise option. The luminance noise causes your picture to have an excessively grainy appearance. To lessen the amount of noise in your photographs, use the following settings under the heading "**Reduce noise**."
  - **Strength**: This is used to describe the amount of noise reduction that is being undertaken.
  - **Preserve features:** This option allows for a far larger proportion of the edges and features to be preserved, but it also reduces the amount of noise that is eliminated.
  - **Reduce Color Noise**: This function is designed to get rid of pixels that are randomly colored.
  - **Remove JPEG Artifact:** This function is to remove all of the blocks and halos that are seen during the JPEG compression process that are of poor quality.

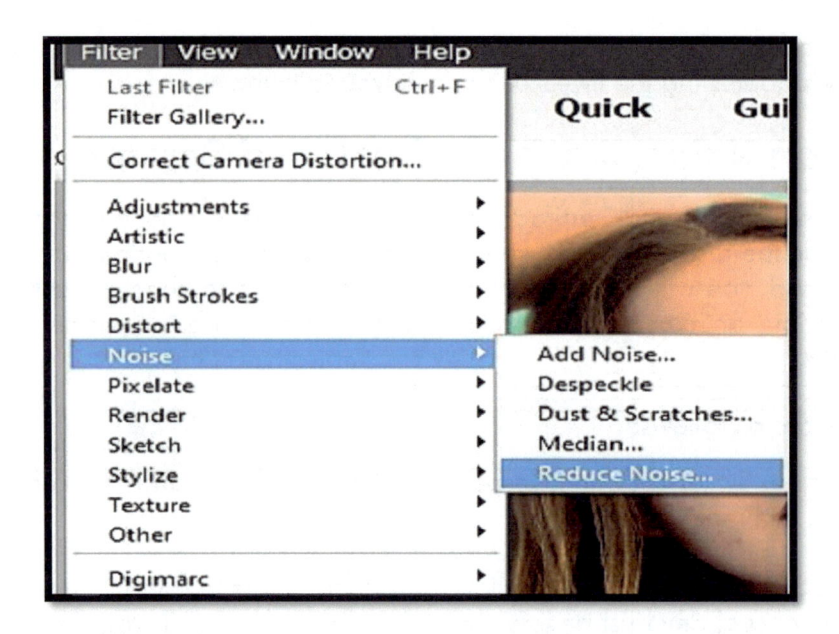

Blurring you Image

Adding a blur effect to photos is often accomplished with the use of the blur tool, which involves modifying the pixel values, contrast, and sharpness options. To resolve this problem, you will need to blur your picture before it becomes overly grainy. It may be necessary to blur the background of your shot to get rid of any distractions or even to make the foreground look more distinct and serve as the main point of the illustration. It is possible to get the blurring command by going to the Filter menu and selecting the Blur option.

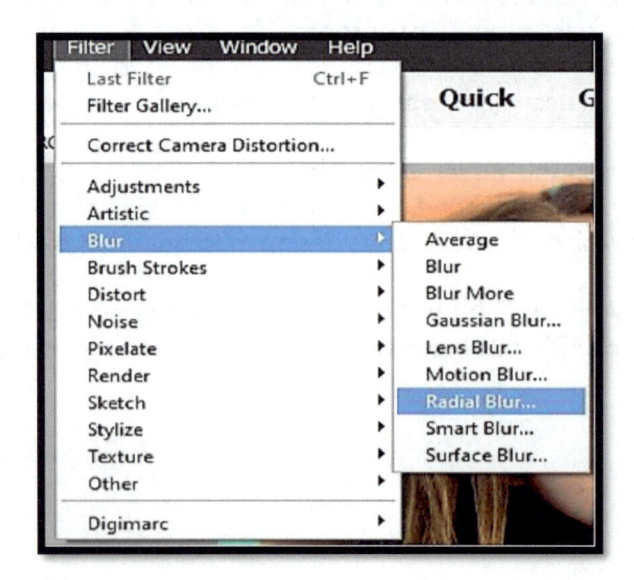

These are the instructions that are used for blurring:

- **Average**: This filter is a one-step filter that helps determine the average value of the image and covers the area that has that value. This is helpful in situations when you need to smooth out a portion of your picture that has an excessive amount of noise.
- **Blur**: Another one-step filter, Blur adds a predetermined degree of burning across the whole picture in a manner that is similar to the previous filter.
- **Blur More**: Blur more is a technique that is relatively comparable to blurring, but it yields effects that are superior to those achieved by blurring.
- **Gaussian Blur**: The Gaussian Blur is the most often used kind of blur because it allows for a significant level of control over the type and degree of blurring that is produced. This gives you access to a Radius parameter that gives you the ability to customize the amount of blur that you want.
- **Motion Blur**: This particular kind of blur enhances the visibility of the blurring caused by a moving object, allowing for the application of other filters. You must specify the distance and motion angle of the blur in this scenario.
- **Radial Blur**: It is recommended to use the Radial Blur effect to emphasize the blurring effect on moving objects. It is because of this that the circular blue appearance is created.
- **Smart Blur**: This feature gives you several alternatives to choose from, allowing you to choose how the blur should be applied. You must input the values for the radius and the threshold here. In addition, you are required to choose the mode that is shown below:
  - **Default**: This causes the whole picture or selection to become blurry.
  - **Edge Only**: This will only blur the edges of the photos, and the pixels that are blurred will be black and white.
  - **Overlay Edge**: Overlay Edge is another method that blurs the edges, but it only adds white to the pixels that have been blurred.
  - **Surface Blur**: Surface Blur is a technique that disregards the borders of a picture and focuses only on blurring the surface or interior of the image.
  - **Lens Blur**: Lens blur corresponds to the blurring that occurs when a photograph is taken using a camera, and this simulates that blurring. This filter comes with three features: faster, fuzzy focus distance, and invert. These functions are all included in the filter.

Sharpening for Better Focus

The sharpness of your images is yet another essential component that you need to take into consideration while working on them. Sharpening tools are designed with the main objective of enhancing the contrast between pixels that are near to one another. **The following are the two instructions for sharpening that will be emphasized:**

- Unsharp Mask
- Adjust Sharpness

Unsharp Mask

Using the Unsharp Mask filter, the photo is sharpened to a higher degree. Although this approach is most often shown with pictures that are projected for on-screen projection, it is effective for printed images. If you want to increase the quality of the printed images, you need to adjust the settings for the printed photos.

To use the Unsharp Mask, you must:

- Navigate to the **Enhance menu** and choose the **Adjust Sharpness option**.

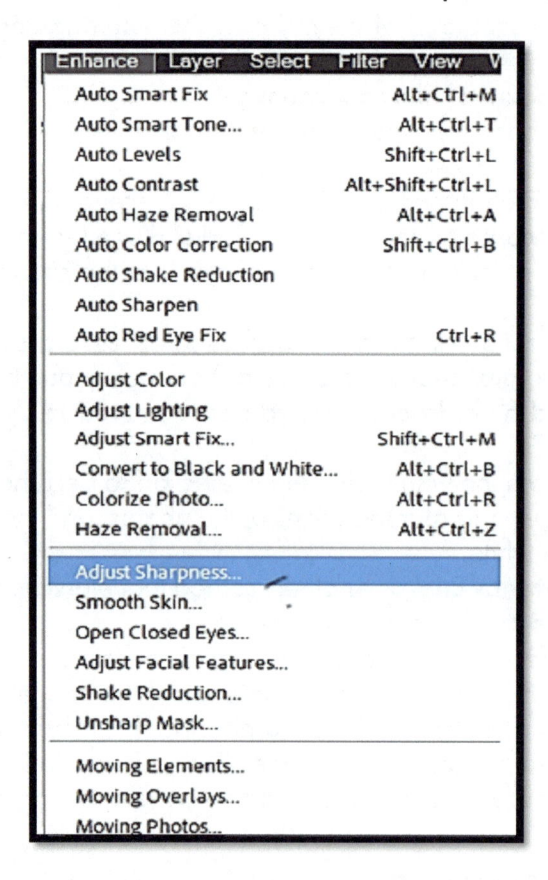

Within the Adjust Sharpness dialog box, ensure that the Preview checkbox is selected and proceed to configure the subsequent options.

- **Amount**: This identifies the volume of the edge sharpening, which may be anywhere from one to five hundred. When the value is higher, there is a greater degree of contrast between the edges.
- **Radius**: This gives the filter the ability to specify the width of the edges that it wants to sharpen, which may range from 0 to 500.

- **Preset**: The preset is where you will keep your sharpening settings so that you may reload them at a later time.
- **Remove**: On this screen, you will choose the sharpening algorithm that you want to use.
- **Angle**: When the Motion Blur algorithm is being used, the angle is used to identify the direction in which motion is occurring.
- **Shadows/Highlights:** This is the section of your picture where you can regulate the amount of sharpening that is applied to the shadows and highlights of your digital photo.

Click on the **OK button**.

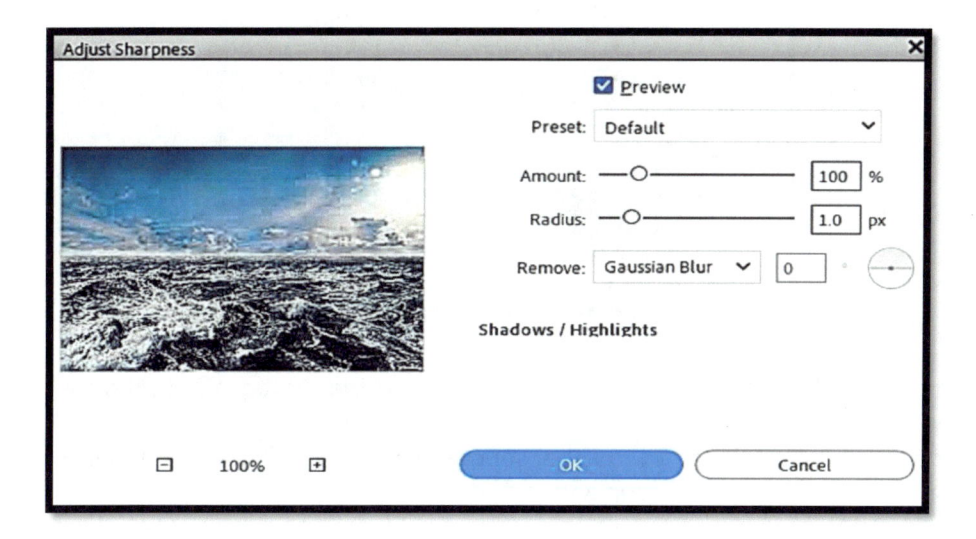

Open Closed Eyes

Through the use of the open-closed eyes command, you can apply a specific group of eyes to a face inside an image if the Element can recognize the eyes that are included within a face. Because of this, it is easy to make adjustments to closed eyes inside a photograph and to recreate a set of eyes that are the same from one photograph to another. When the two pictures are more similar to one another, the eye replacement is successful.

To make use of the Open Closed Eyes command, follow the procedures that are mentioned below.

1. Launch the picture that you want to use.
2. Access the Enhance menu and choose the **Open Closed Eyes option**.
3. To apply the source picture, just click on it.
4. Once you have completed everything, proceed to click on the OK button.

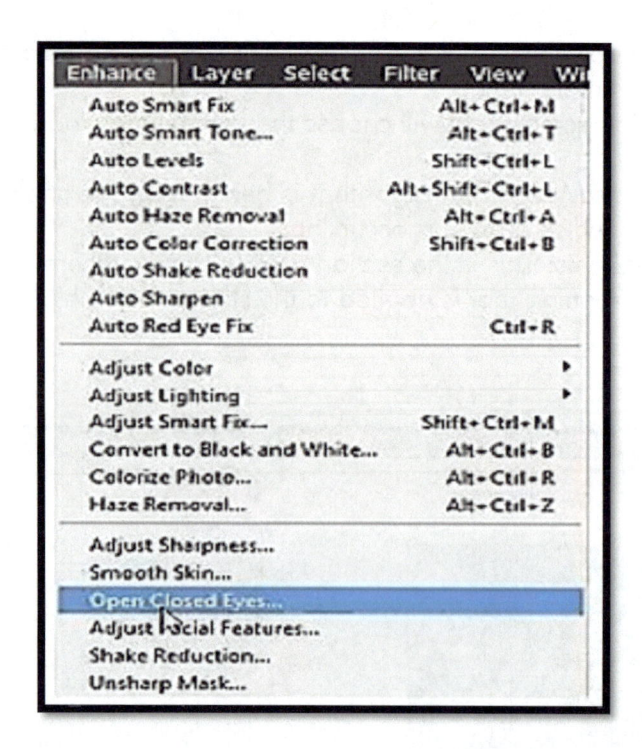

5. The affected region is surrounded by a circle in the dialog box that appears when you open your eyes.
6. Choose a photo to serve as the source picture for the eyes, either from your computer or from your organizer.

Colorizing a Photo

When you use the Colorize Photo command, you have the option of manually coloring a certain region of the image or automatically coloring the whole image.

Use the Colorize Photo command by carrying out the steps that are detailed below.

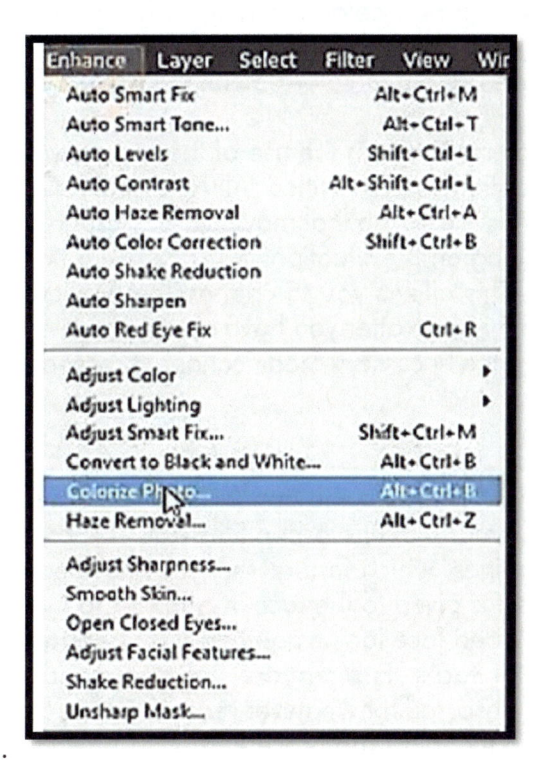

1. Click on the Enhance menu and then choose the **Colorize Photo option**.
2. Make sure that the following settings are selected in the Colorize Photo box.
- **Zoom Tool**: This tool is used to zoom in and out of the picture.
- **Hand Tool**: When necessary, you can use the Hand Tool to pan in the photos.
- **Colorize Panel**: One of the panels is called the Colorize panel, and it gives you the ability to adjust the colors of your photographs.
- **The Toggle Switch**: This switch allows you to go from the automated button to the manual button.

To manually colorize your picture, you will need to click the toggle button and then specify the following parameters: You can pick the selection tool that you want to use by clicking on either the Selection tool or the Magic Wand tool.

- **New**: If you want to create a new selection, you can use this.
- **Add**: To add a new selection to an existing selection, use the "**Add**" command.
- **Subtract**: To remove anything from a selection that already exists.
- **Tolerance**: To specify the necessary parameters for the selection tool that you chose, you will need to use the tolerance setting.

- **Droplet Tool:** This tool is used to add droplets to each color to mark the current color to colorize with a new color. Droplets may be added inside the selection for this purpose.
- **Color palette:** Make use of the color palette to alter the color of the region that has been picked.
- **All Application Colors:** Through the use of the sliders, you are also able to choose a color from this option, which is titled "**All Application Colors**."
- **Display Droplet:** This is a switch that may be used to toggle the display of the choices on and off depending on the situation.
- **Before and After**: This allows you to change the preview between the before and after versions of the image after you have applied a colorization effect.

Once you have completed the necessary modifications, proceed to click on the OK button.

Smoothing Skin

You may quickly and efficiently reduce the appearance of wrinkles in the skin of a face by using the Smooth Skin command in Photoshop Element. This command works by reducing the sharpness of the skin lines, which in turn reduces the appearance of wrinkles. To do this, a minor blurring effect is given to the face in addition to the fact that doing so aids in making the skin of the selected face look smoother. It is important to keep in mind that this command is exclusively for faces. Furthermore, the command cannot be used with this picture if the face is partly obscured for whatever reason. **To use the Smooth Skin command, follow the steps outlined in the following procedure:**

1. Open the image you want to work on.
2. Make sure to choose **Smooth Skin** from the Enhance menu option.

3. The region that is going to be impacted is encircled by a circle in the Smooth Skin dialog box on the computer.
4. By using the Smoothness slider, you may apply the desired level of smoothness to the picture of your choice.
5. If you want to see what the Smooth effect looks like before and after you apply it, you can use the Before and After toggle button.
6. Once the modifications have been completed, you have the option to click on the OK button to leave and save the changes.

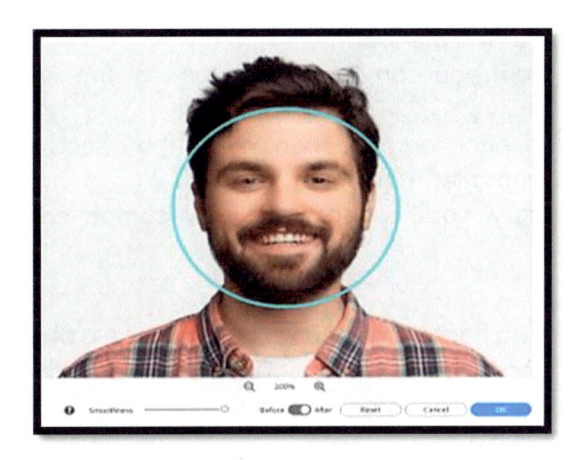

Adjusting Facial Features

Through the use of the Adjust Facial Features command in Photoshop Element, it is possible to make adjustments to the lips, eyes, nose, and face of a person in a picture. Should the face be partly obscured, the order will not be able to be executed with this picture.

To use this command, adhere to the guidelines that are mentioned below:

- From the Enhance menu, choose the option to adjust the facial features.
- Use the slider that is located in the Adjust Facial Features dialog box to make adjustments to the facial features including the eyes, nose, lip, chin, and skin of the face.
- Once all the necessary modifications have been completed, proceed to click on the OK button.

Reducing Shake

If you want to get rid of the blur or shaking that occurs while you are holding your camera or phone while taking a photo, manually change an image by utilizing the Wobble Reduction tool. Using this option allows you to manually modify the picture if you do not like the results that the Auto Shake produces.

For instructions on how to use the Shake Reduction command, see the following steps:

- Choose the image that you want to modify.
- Access the Enhance menu and choose the **Shake Reduction option**.
- The dialog box for Shake Reduction will appear, and it will show a selection box over the picture you are working with.
- To adjust the size of the selection box, you can modify it by clicking and dragging the resizing handles on the box.
- By using the Sensitivity slider, you may make adjustments to the level of sharpness that will be applied to the picture.
- To add another area, you can take advantage of the Add another Shake area feature.
- Use the Before and After toggle button to see the effects of the Shake Reduction effect both before and after it has been applied.
- Once all the necessary modifications have been completed, proceed to click OK.

Moving Photos

Through the use of the Moving Photos command, you can take a photo while simultaneously providing a simple pan, zoom, or rotate option. To transform the image into a moving picture, you may export it as an animated gif picture.

It is possible to create a moving picture by following the methods that are mentioned below.

- To transform a moving shot into a still image, open the photo in the shot Editor.
- Navigate to the **Enhance menu** and choose the **Moving Photos option**.
- The window for moving photos is presented at this location.
- The Zoom tool and the Hand tool are located on the right-hand side of the screen. These tools allow you to zoom and pan the preview picture that displays as required.
- While applying the Motion Effects, you will be able to see the preview of the effect being applied to the photo. Motion Effects are shown in the pane that may be scrolled, which is located on the right side of the window.
- The 3D Effect toggle button, located at the bottom of the screen, may be used to turn the 3D Effect on or off.
- You can repeat the effect preview by clicking the play button that appears below the previous picture. This will allow you to do so after you have played an effect.
- The picture can be exported as an animated gif by clicking on the Export button and then following the steps that are provided.

Moving Elements

Adobe Photoshop Elements has received several updates, one of which is this function. It is a function that was not accessible in the prior edition of the program, and it gives you the ability to provide motion to objects that are contained inside a static picture.

Making moving parts can be accomplished by following the steps below:

1. When you want to make changes to a picture, you need to first open the photo.
2. Navigate to the **Enhance menu** and choose the **Moving Elements option**.
3. To add motion to a specific region, you can choose to use a brush, a rapid selection tool, or an auto selection tool to choose from the available options.
4. It is recommended that you click on the **Arrow pointer** and then move your mouse pointer in the direction that you want the motion to proceed inside the region that you have chosen for change.
5. Drag the speed slider until you are done with the degree of speed that the element is moving at. This will allow you to choose the speed of the element's motion.
6. To see your preview, you can do so by clicking on the **play button**.
7. When you are done with the changes you have made, you can then export your file by clicking on the **Export button**.
8. You have the option to export your file as either a GIF file or an MP4 Video file.
9. Select the **Save button**.

Moving Overlays

Using the Moving Overlay Command, you can include animations into your shot as an overlay. Overlays, Graphics, and Frames are the three kinds of animated components that may be found in the Moving Overlay Command Centre. **Following the steps outlined below will allow you to apply the Moving Overlays to your photo:**

- To edit a picture, open the picture Editor and choose the photo you want to adjust.
- From the Enhance menu, choose **Moving Overlays** to start the process.

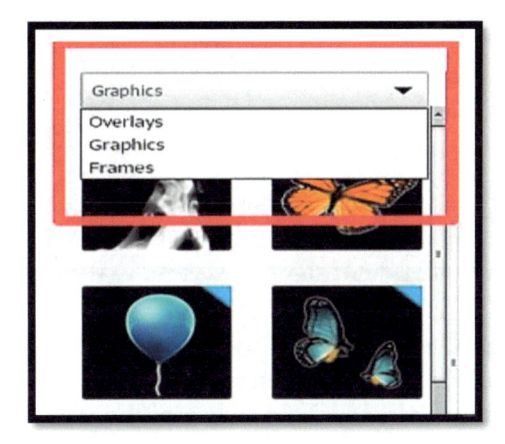

- The Moving Overlays window is presented at this particular location.
- On the right-hand side of the screen, you will see the option to choose the kind of Overlay Animations that you would want to add to your picture. These animations include Overlays, Graphics, and Frames.

- By selecting the Protect Subject option, you will be able to spare the subject of your photograph from being altered by the overlay change.

- To change the opacity of the animations that have been introduced, use the Opacity Slider.

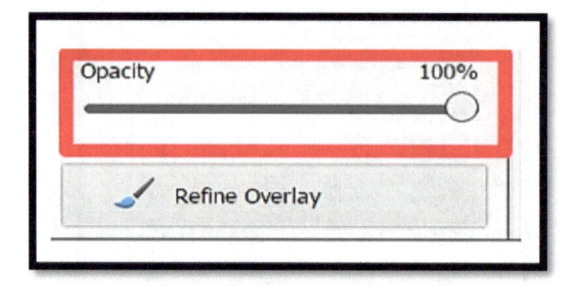

- Applying the **Refine Overlay button** allows you to adjust the location of your animation overlay to suit your preferences.
- Click on the **Play button** to receive a preview of the alterations you have made.
- The picture can be exported as an animated gif by clicking on the **Export button** and then following the steps that are provided. After that, choose the **Save button**.

Working Intelligently with the Smart Brush Tools

Smart Brush Tool

The Smart Brush tool allows you to choose to apply many different effects to your picture by allowing you to brush over it. There are a variety of fifty different preset effects available for use. This tool includes effects that may be used to produce and enhance details, as well as change color and tones, among other things. In addition to lipstick, tan, contrast between clouds, infrared, impressionist, and a variety of color tints, these effects also include many more.

Take advantage of the Smart Brush tool by following the instructions that are provided below.

- To access the Smart Brush tool, go to the Toolbar and pick it.
- Navigate to the Preset menu to choose the effects that you want to apply, such as the Nature effects and the Photographic effects.
- Adjust the characteristics of the shrub by navigating to the Brush Settings drop-down window.
- The icons for New, Add, and Remove Selection may be used to create selections, add selections, and remove selections, respectively.
- Refine the region that you have picked in your picture by using the Refine Edge tool.
- To fine-tune the adjustment in your picture, you can make use of the Adjustment layer.
- Once you have completed the necessary modifications, proceed to click on the **OK** button.

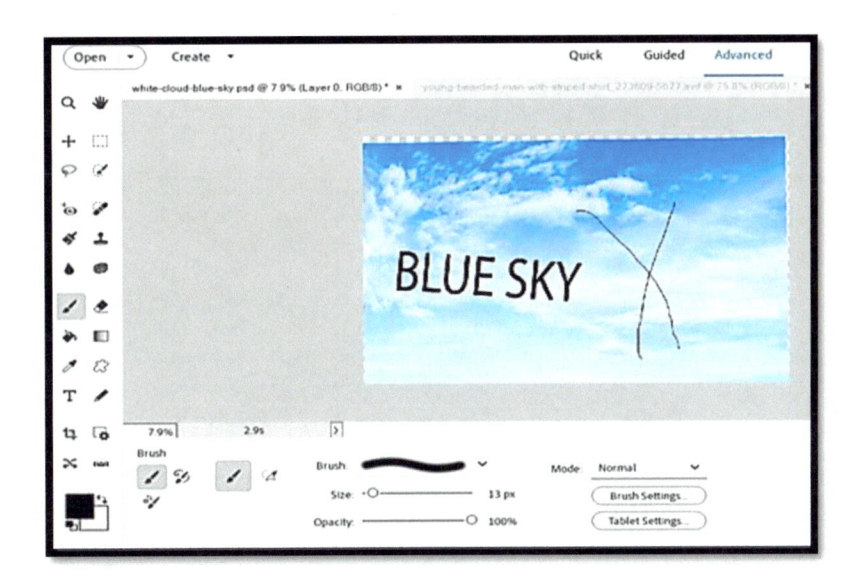

The Detail Smart Brush Tool

There is a tool called the Detail Smart Brush that is comparable to the Smart Brush tool. The main difference is that the Detail Smart Brush tool gives you greater control over the choices you make and allows you to paint alterations straight into the picture.

To take advantage of the Detail Smart Brush tool, the following processes need to be followed:

- To access the Smart Brush tool, go to the Toolbar and pick it.
- Choose the effects you want to apply by going to the Preset menu.
- Adjust the characteristics of the shrub by navigating to the Brush Settings drop-down window.
- Refine the region that you have picked in your picture by using the Refine Edge tool.
- To fine-tune the adjustment in your picture, use the Adjustment layer.
- Once you have completed the necessary modifications, proceed to click on the OK button.

CHAPTER THIRTEEN
TIPS AND TRICKS ON PHOTOSHOP ELEMENTS

Here, we will go over several tips and tricks for working with the Photoshop Element. Several pointers and strategies are being presented to promote a culture around the use of the Photoshop Element. Now let's examine some tips and methods with Photoshop Element.

Viewing an Image in Two Windows

You can choose between two alternate versions of a picture with the Photoshop Element. This feature might come in handy when you need to enlarge a picture to carry out some intricate tasks. When the picture is zoomed in, you may not be able to see how your adjustments have affected it. **To see your picture in two distinct windows, go to the View menu and pick New Window.**

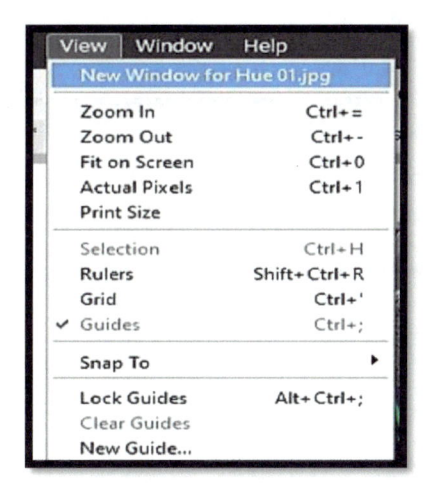

When the aforementioned methods are followed, the picture ultimately appears in two windows.

Saving your Selections with your Photos

The store Selection feature allows you to store every selection you've made while working on your picture. This command gives you access to whatever option you need in the future.

To save a selection, adhere to the below-listed methods.

- Select and then press **Save Selection**.

- Select **New Selection** in the Save Selection dialog box that appears, and then enter the name of your selection in the Name field.

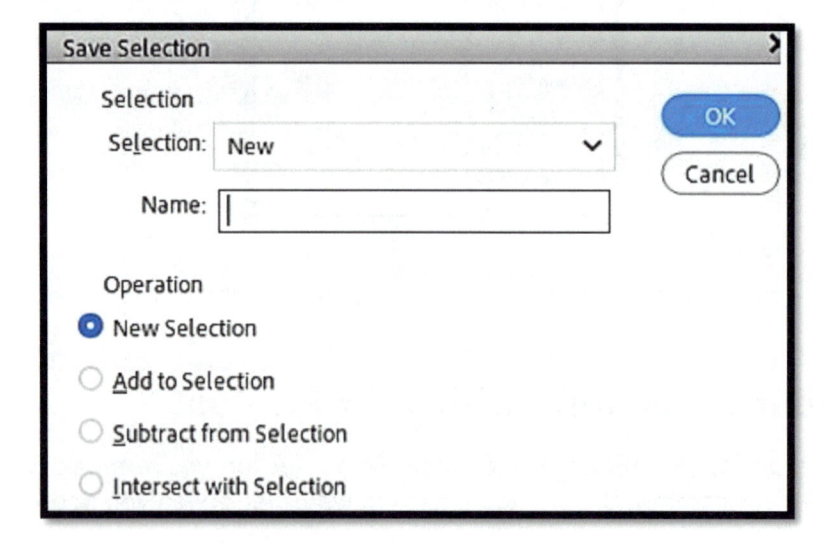

- Next, choose "**OK**."
- When you're done, go to **Select**, click **Load Selection**, and then choose an item from the Selection drop-down menu to load the previously stored selection once again.

Resetting a Dialog Box without Closing It

You should know by now that most of Photoshop Elements adjustment options are found in the dialog box. While making modifications to the dialog box, you may need to dismiss it and open it again to get started. This time, all you have to do is click the Reset button. Still, dialog windows do not always display the Reset option. All you have to do in these situations is hold down the Alt key until the **Cancel button** turns into the **Reset button**.

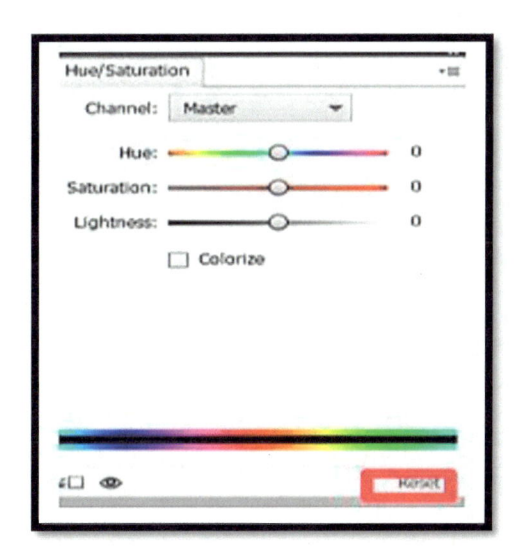

Changing the Ruler Unit of Measurement

There are several measurement units available for the Photoshop Element, such as pixels, inches, millimeters, centimeters, points, picas, and percentages. Before adjusting the unit of measurement, make sure the ruler is displayed. If not, choose Ruler from the View option on the option bar. Once the ruler is shown at the top and left of your picture, you can right-click anywhere on it to bring up a pop-up menu where you may choose the desired unit of measurement.

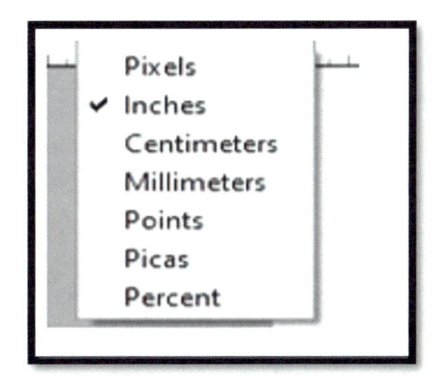

Having Access to Additional Dialog Box Options

Did you know that you have access to additional choices even while the dialog box is being used? All you have to do is choose View from the menu when your dialog box appears. You can utilize the entirely black commands in the View menu, but not the gray ones. Under the Window menu in the dialog box, there are more options accessible. Furthermore, all black instructions can be accessed, but gray commands cannot.

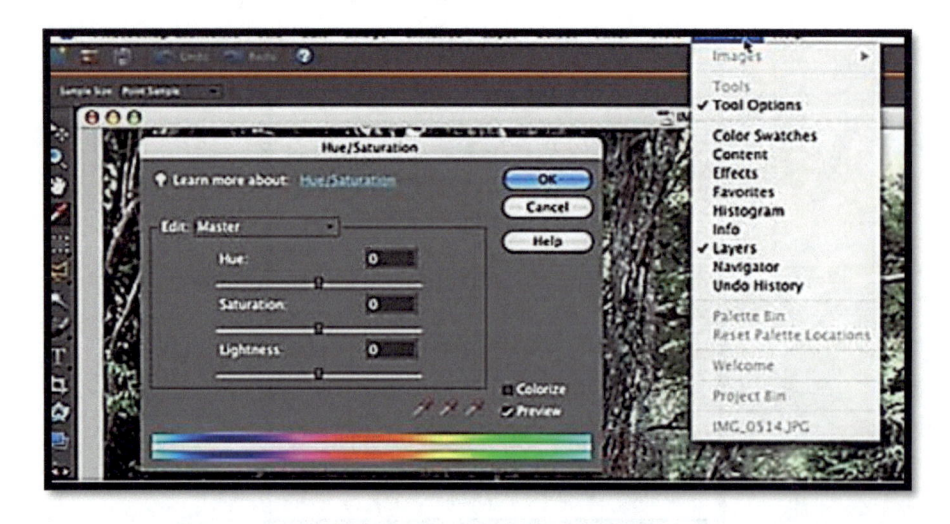

Viewing Additional Files in the Recently Edited List

Like the History panel, you can see the list of the last 10 files you opened. Choose **Recently Edited File** from the File menu to see these files.

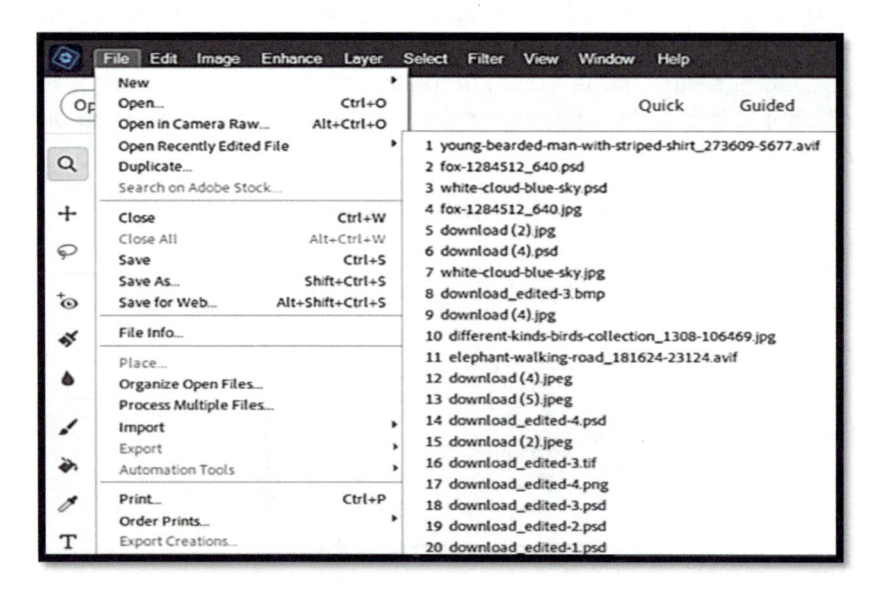

By heading to the Photoshop Elements Edit menu, choosing Preferences, and then clicking on Saving Files, you can also examine up to 30 files. From there, you can modify the figure to your liking.

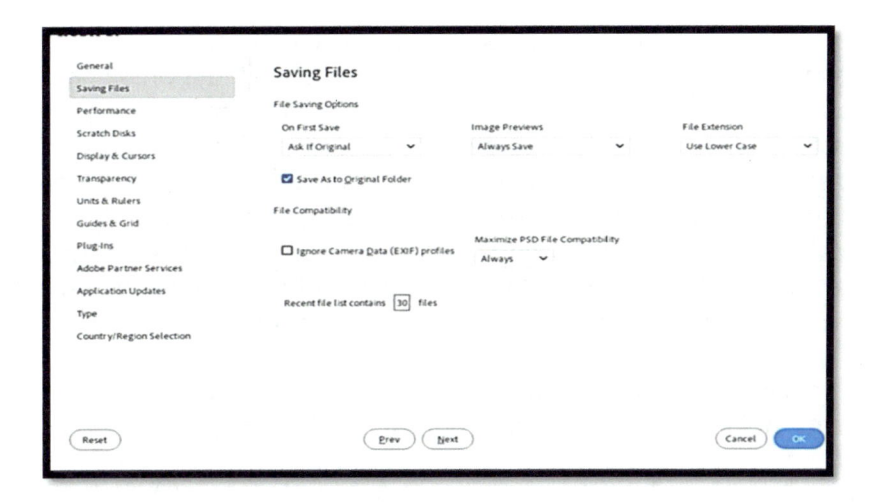

Creating Fin Pieces

How to Create an Organizer Slideshow

If you have photos in your organizer and look at the home page, Elements has probably already created a video for you. The Auto Creations tool is to blame for this. With Elements, creating a video is fast and simple. With this edition, you may create a show using a larger choice of themes. Much like the previous iterations, putting together a performance that is at least decent is simple and fast.

Save and Export: Rename the file and save it using the option located on the right side of the video screen. The "**Export**" option over there allows you to upload the video straight to Vimeo or YouTube or to a folder on your computer (like "**Export to Local Disk**").

Here's how to quickly construct a simple but impactful slideshow in a matter of minutes:

- Select the images that you want to use. Selecting horizontally oriented photos is the greatest option because of how the video will be kept.
- In the Organizer, create an album dedicated to the photos from your presentation.

The best course of action is this:
- Select every image. Later on, you can add or delete the photos.

Choose the photos you want to use from the Organizer. You can either choose **Slideshow** from the Create menu in the top left corner of the page, or you can click the **Slideshow button** at the bottom of the page.

- **Immediate feedback**: Almost immediately, a preview of the video is displayed. The amount of time it takes to load may vary depending on how many photographs you've contributed. It acts on its own accord after it is formed. If you have any objections to the music or theme, you may change them by using the little button located at the top left of the screen to pause the slideshow. Eleven themes and eleven music tracks are now available for selection without breaking any copyright regulations. This option also allows you to add other images, movies, or audio if necessary. You may rotate or remove any photo by using the right-click menu. You may also add text slides or subtitles by checking a little box. It's a wonderful touch as the slideshow plays since these words move into the picture.
- **Copyright Warning**: Make sure the slideshow video is free of images, audio, and videos that you do not own before releasing it into the public domain. Numerous free music and images are available on the internet for you to download.

Download without worrying about copyright concerns and use for personal or professional projects. It seems that after you master one project, it will be much simpler to complete the others since the majority of the Elements' project-based capabilities are either partially automated or powered by Adobe Sensei (AI). Now let's see how easy it is to create schedules and cards.

How to Create a Photo Calendar

A calendar is a thoughtful gift for friends, family, and even the workplace. It's also a fantastic opportunity to showcase your photographic abilities, and creating a calendar has never been simpler. In this instance, Adobe has condensed several really difficult picture tasks into a simple, one-click procedure.

Overall, it functions quite well.

- Organize your work and create a calendar picture book using the Extra tools and features. For the majority of artistic endeavors in Elements, this is an excellent concept.
- In the Organizer's upper right corner, choose **Photo Calendar** from the Create drop-down menu. Then, explore the variety of calendar layouts available in the following step.
- Select a medium for your work.
- Select a style from the 31 options, enter the start month and year, and click OK. Verify that the option to "**Auto Fill with Selected Images**" is not selected. It is simple to reposition the images on the appropriate pages at a later time. You may have to wait while the templates for that style are downloaded from Adobe.
- Go to the front cover first if it isn't there already on the main screen. If you take the time to organize the photographs that correspond with the calendar into an album, you can discover the images in the Photo Bin at the bottom of the page. Grab the image, click, and hold it, then firmly insert it into the gray gaps. It organically twists

and resizes to take the form of the photo template for that particular calendar design.

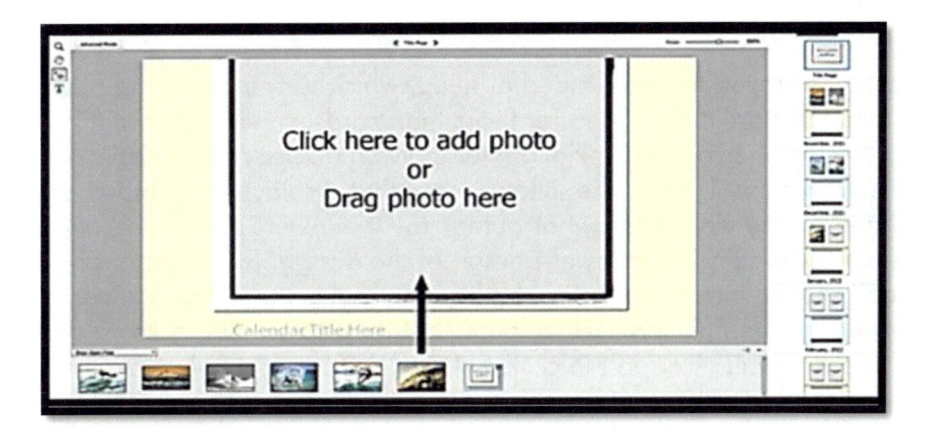

- When you double-click on the text box, type your title and description. If everything you typed seems correct, click the green "**OK**" button. Return to the page, double-click the text to make it active again, and correct any errors.
- The click, hold, and push procedure should be repeated for the remaining monthly photos.
- **Customize**: Changing the number of photos on a page or their arrangement is a simple process when you enter the Layouts panel in the Advanced or Basic window.
- Double-click the image in the panel once you're there to use a new design. It's easy. You may use a single image or all of them for this. In Advanced mode, you can even learn how to modify the attributes of each layer separately.
- When you're finished creating the calendar, save the file so that it can be printed. A standard photo inkjet printer can be used to produce this. With a cover page, it has 12 pages total. After that, you can have it spiral-bound at an office supply shop so that it's ready to be sent to loved ones.

How to Create a Greeting Card

Making a welcome card follows almost the same processes as creating a calendar, except you only need to create one page as opposed to twelve.

You can adjust the size and positioning of the photos using the menu.

- Create an Organizer Album with a few photos to use as a Christmas card.
- Depending on how many images you want on the card, choose one, two, or three from this album. Next, choose the Greeting **Card** from the Create menu.
- Select a look from the little design possibilities that show up. Click OK after that. After a brief download, you may drag & drop an image from the Photo Bin into the card design. On the Greeting Card page, take note of the menu located on the

right side. It allows you to alter the design's aesthetic and the quantity of images utilized.

Working Tips

This specific tool is limited to single-sided printing, which is one of my main issues with it. Most of the templates are more suited for flyers than cards, so we suppose this is probably because not everyone has a home inkjet printer that can duplex print, or print on both sides of the paper. As previously said, the little window that displays the various card kinds is really small and, in my view, somewhat outdated. If we were to use this, we would just include one or two images in the lower portion of the design. In this manner, nothing will be on the back and the picture will be on the front when it is printed and folded in half. Use matte printer paper. It's not only well-colored, but it's also simple to score flat and fold. Certain glossy sheets feel nicer and thicker, but they are considerably more difficult to fold correctly. Before folding, either trim the spine with a dull knife or use an expert card-bending tool, which is often available at a craft store.

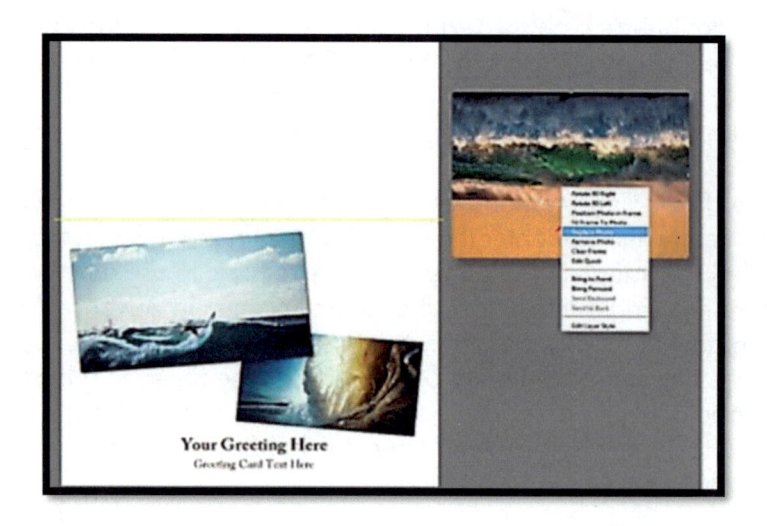

After downloading the selected design, reposition the images on the card to see whether they were there by mistake. To do this, right-click on the image, choose **Replace Photo or Delete,** and locate an Alternative. Position the photo stands so they will look their best. Keep in mind to focus on the yellow fold line located in the center when printing them at home. If you want to fold an Adobe Designs page in half, it might be difficult since the photographs span the whole width of the page. Take note that the double-headed arrow becomes a spinning arrow when you move the mouse near any picture's borders. This implies that you may adjust the image's rotational value by clicking, holding, and dragging it. Before continuing, make sure your photo moved successfully by clicking the green "**check**" button. Conserve. When you save one of these projects, a unique file type (.pse) is created. This kind of file allows you to store text, images, clip art, and color. Photoshop files cannot be read by Elements; only PSE files can. The only other file that can be saved in this format is a PDF, which is universally readable.

How to Create a Photo Collage

The Create button is located in the top left corner of the screen in both the Editor and the Organizer. With your photos, you may create beautiful pages that you can distribute as digital files or print off. Elements offer a wide variety of pre-made themes, but you may customize every aspect of them to create projects that are entirely your own. In Create, you may create a picture collage page. This kind of page displays one or more images, either with or without a backdrop that has a theme. Elements instantly provide you with a simple design and recommended picture locations. In addition to adding or removing photographs, you may alter the backdrop, frame styles, and other elements.

How to make a collage of photos

Select or open a few photographs in the Organizer or Editor. While it's not required, Elements may instantly add your pre-selected photos to the collage. Elements will notify you that all of your open files will be immediately saved before they create your collage if you alter photographs without saving them. Before beginning a new Create project, be sure to close the files after making any modifications you don't want to retain.

- Go to **Photo Collage > Create**.
- If you begin in the Organizer, Elements will direct you to the Editor so you may create the collage. Don't let the Photo Collage window's initial modest size deter you. After making your choices and selecting OK, the Editor box will reappear.
- Select a page size from the options on the left side of the Photo Collage box.
- This is a print-at-home project if you're wondering what the "**Print locally**" option above the size selections signifies. On some of the other projects, such as picture albums that you can print online, you'll notice "**Shutterfly**" above the list of products that you may purchase from them.
- If you create a collage and don't like the way it appears in the orientation you choose, it may be simpler to start again with a fresh file in Advanced mode. This is because you can't just shift the collage sizes to go from portrait to landscape or vice versa. You can do whatever you can do here and there. The main distinction is that you don't begin with a project that is preplanned; thus, you must add everything to the project rather than altering existing elements.

Choose a theme in the middle of the Photo Collage Window

Themes allow you to coordinate the frames, backgrounds, and sometimes even text styles with your images. When you click on the image of a theme to pick it, a larger view of your selection appears on the right side of the window. It makes no difference if you don't like any of the preset styles—you can change any aspect of the Create window. Simply choose the theme that you find least appealing. You may not see any more choices if you choose the Basic theme while creating your first collage. It's OK.

Specify whether you want Elements to add your photos to the collage automatically

In the Photo Collage box, make sure the "**Autofill with Selected Images**" option is checked at the bottom. The images you selected before will be included automatically from the Organizer or Photo Bin when Elements creates the collage. If you did not pick a picture beforehand, it adds the one that is now chosen in the Editor. If you wish to choose which shots go where, this option shouldn't be ticked.

Click OK after you've made your choices.

Elements return you to the main Create window while you're there and begins assembling the collage. The college is shown in the editing section. If you choose your photographs ahead of time and leave the Autofill option selected, Elements will automatically frame the pictures for you. It adds a layer to every image in the collage. If you didn't choose any photographs or didn't select enough to fill all the spaces, you see the phrase "**Click here to add a photo or Drag a photo here**" within each empty frame. That's OK, however, since you can add photos. Now let's go to work using what Adobe refers to as "**Basic mode.**"

Select a layout

Elements presents you with several more choices after completing the collage. Beneath the Create box, there's a Pages button. When you click this button, the photo for that page appears alone since a collage only has one page. (If the project had several pages, such as a photo book, here is where you would flip between images of the various pages.) If you're satisfied with the example that Elements provides, there's no need to make any modifications. What happens if the Layouts button under the Create panel is clicked? This will provide a list of several styles arranged according to the number of photographs they can accommodate. To test a different plan, double-click its image or drag it into the collage in the viewing area. If you don't like it, remove it (Ctrl+Z/⌘ -Z) and try another one. A tip for using a small number of photographs is to scroll down the Create panel until you find a layout that uses just one or two images. The superfluous picture frames in the Basic layout will be swiftly removed by doing this. You may remove the excess frames by double-clicking.

Adjust the images

In case you have not yet chosen any photographs for this project, just drag and drop a picture from the Photo Bin onto an object. Click on the "**Photo Bin**" button under the sample area if you are unable to view the Photo Bin. Alternatively, you can click on the blank frame in the collage containing placeholder text, and then choose a picture using the menu box

that appears. No matter how you added the photos, you may edit them once they're in the collage in a few different ways. **Here are a few simple adjustments you can make:**
The Move tool's box should encircle a frame when you click on it. (To see the Move Tool's settings, click the Tool settings box underneath the sample area.) You can use the **Move tool** to arrange your photos in the desired sequence, whether you want them to match or spread apart. Once a frame has been selected in the collage, click the **Graphics button** under the Create panel to alter its design. Next, double-click or drag the chosen frame to the panel's picture.

Customize the collage

Drag a picture from your collage by clicking on it to reposition it. Alternatively, you may drag artwork from the panel onto your collage by clicking the Graphics icon below the Create panel. These are vector graphics; therefore resizing them won't affect their quality. You may also add text by clicking where you want to add text and then clicking the T on the left side of the viewing area. If you go to Advanced mode, you may adjust the smoothness of your image and apply effects over the whole page.

Complete the collage

After you're finished, consider these alternatives for what to do next:
Click **Save** at the bottom of the Create area. By doing this, the Save As box will appear, allowing you to name and save the project. It must be saved as a PSE file, which can only be used for Create projects, or as a PDF file. However, you may click Close at the bottom of the Create section if you decide to change your mind about your college. Next, instruct Elements not to save your file when it prompts you to. These instructions will walk you through sharing a collage created in a standard image format, such as a TIFF or JPEG. Save your collage whenever you're finished, but to ensure that you don't lose anything in the event of a crash, you may want to click the **Save option** often while working. Your photo may be printed from Create in the same way as any other file. To print, click the Print button located at the bottom of the Elements window, or press Ctrl+P or ⌘ + P. For example, you might send your collage to a provider that prints only JPG files, or you could share it with individuals who cannot view PSE files. Next, choose File, followed by Export Creations. You may then save your collage as a JPEG, TIFF, or PDF file in the window that opens. Select the desired kind from the drop-down menu. Next, choose where to store it by clicking the **Browse option**.

Adjusting Photos and Frames

Elements offer a plethora of options for modifying the images in a collage:
- **Turn a photo within its frame.** Right-click or control-click a picture, choose Rotate 90 Right or Rotate 90 Left to turn it 90 degrees clockwise or counterclockwise.
- **Modify an image's appearance inside its frame.** Right-click (or control-click) a picture to choose "**Position Photo in Frame**".

- **Take a picture out of the collage.** By holding down or right-clicking on the picture, choose "**Clear Photo**". Click to choose the picture, then use Backspace or Delete to remove the gap and frame.
- **Take the picture's frame off**. Holding down on the image or performing a right-click will choose **Clear Frame**.
- **Adjust a frame's size**. A frame may be adjusted before or after a picture is added. Single-click a vacant space in the frame (not the placeholder text) to display the adjusting handles. Next, adjust the frame's size by dragging one of the corner handles. These handles may also be used to turn frames.
- **To fit a picture, resize a frame**. To change the order of the frame and picture, right-click or control-click the image, then choose Fit Frame to picture.
- **Modify an image**. Elements will instantly transfer the image to "**Quick Fix**," where you may make any last-minute adjustments when you press and hold the picture and choose "**Edit Quick**." For some reason, this statement is grayed out in various file types. (In other words, collages cannot be created with it.) The "**Back to Creations**" button is located in the preview area's top left corner. When you're done making changes, click it.
- **Add image**. Simply drag a frame from the Graphics part of the Create panel to a vacant area in the collage, then click within the frame to add a picture. To see it, you would need to click Graphics underneath the panel. The new frame may replace the old one if you approach it too closely. If so, undo your previous actions by pressing Ctrl+Z/⌘ -Z, and then gently drag back to the empty area. You may also drag an image from the Photo Bin into the collage.
- **Modify a frame's layer style**. The majority of the frames in the Create panel now have layer styles applied to them. In the collage, click and hold a frame, then use the right-click menu to choose Edit Layer Style. This will allow you to adjust elements such as the drop shadow's size inside the frame.
- **To improve a picture, use a filter**. With the "**Advanced**" setting of all the Elements' effects, you can easily create the appearance of brushed or rubber-stamped surfaces. However, before you apply effects to the image, you must first simplify its layer.

How to Create a Photo Book

Using elements, you can create pages in various sizes to use in photo books that can be printed and bound, making them excellent presents. Go to Create first, followed by a Photo Book. There are many sizes available. The sizes on the Photo Book window's left side. Clicking on one causes the information about that size to appear on the right-hand side, as shown below. The majority of picture books are available for purchase online, but you may also print an 8.5 by 11-inch (really 11 by 8.5-inch) photo book at home. If you'd like, you may even print any Create creation from home using your printer. If you know how long you want the book to be, Photo Book offers a box at the bottom where you may enter the desired page count. You cannot delete pages to make the total fewer than 20, since Shutterfly's photo books start with 20 pages because it is the minimum quantity you may purchase (the most Shutterfly will produce is 100 pages plus the title page). Choose "print locally" for an 11" x 8.5" size if you wish to create a 4- or 10-page book.

If the number in the box at the bottom of the Photo Book window changes one day, don't be alarmed. Shutterfly may adjust the minimum page count required for photo books. Compiling a photo book has similarities to creating a collage. The Pages panel in the Create section now has pages that you may go through, which is the sole difference. Click the Pages button to see it under the Create panel. Click on it to work on an alternate two-page spread. To navigate between pages, use the buttons located above the sample area. The double-page spreads that appear while the book is open are shown to you by Elements. Since most photo books have the front cover taken off, the title page is the first page. Navigate to the Pages panel and choose the thumbnail of the two-page spread you want to duplicate to add pages to your picture book. Next, choose the **Add Page button** located at the panel's top. A double-page spread cannot be reduced to one page. Click the garbage button after clicking on its image to get rid of it. Take care that the minimum page count for books produced by Shutterfly is not exceeded. Pages may be rearranged by dragging their pictures inside the panel. Once you've finished creating the book, you can click Save or Print at the bottom of the Elements box, just as with a collage. If you choose one of Shutterfly's choices in the Photo Book window, you may also purchase the book immediately. A purchase button is located underneath the viewing area. After downloading the file as a PDF, which is almost universally compatible, purchase the book from another publisher.

To save a photo book, click the **Save option**. To edit the book again later, use the Photo Project Format (PSE) option. After making all the necessary changes, you may also save it as a PDF file. Also available to you is the **Export option**. For photo book files, there is an icon in the Photo Bin and Organizer that resembles a stack of pages. It cannot be opened to see individual pages as previous Elements versions did. You don't even need to use Elements' picture Book function to make a photo book. Simply open your web browser, go to the Shutterfly website, and upload your photos. After that, the business will publish them in a photo book manner. This technique also works with other photo-printing websites, such as Lulu.com and MyPublisher.com. Ordering books is possible for Mac users via iPhoto and, when the new Photos program is released, probably as well.

How to Create a Photo Reel

- Go to **File** > **Open** to see the images you want to use for the Photo Reel. It should be noted that a Photo Reel requires a minimum of two images.
- Press "**Create**" and then "**Photo Reel**."
- All of the selected images' frames will be shown in the Timeline. You may drag and drop the photographs to reposition them.
- Add additional images to the Timeline by choosing the Add media from the Computer or Organizer option in the Layout panel.

- Select a picture arrangement from the arrangement panel that complies with the requirements of the social network you want to use. Standard settings for Instagram, Facebook, YouTube, TikTok, Snapchat, Twitter, and Threads are available in the Layout box.

Tapping on the time shown on the picture clip allows you to adjust the time that each photo frame in the picture Reel displays. To have the same time display in every photo, check the box next to Apply to All. Click the three-dot button above the photos to adjust additional parameters for each picture frame. To add the phrases you want to your photos, use the Type tool. To better fit your requirements, you can change the text's typeface, tracking, style, size, color, heading, alignment, and other elements.

Use one of the two methods below to add the desired effect to your photos:

- Choose the desired Effects image and apply it just to the selected image.
- Choose "**Apply to all photos**" to apply the desired effect to every picture.
- To reverse the impact that has already been applied, choose **No effect**. Adjust the intensity of the effects using the strength scale located in the Effects tab.
- To choose the desired drawings, click on any image in the drawings section.
- By selecting **Export > Save**, you can export the Photo Reel as an MP4 or GIF file.

How to Create a Quote Prints

Choose to begin without selecting a picture, choose a photo from the Organizer, or open a photo in the Picture Editor. The Organizer or the Photo Editor are the two ways to access the Create drop-down menu. Next, choose **Quote** Graphic. The designs that you may choose from are shown on the first screen. You can begin from new without using a design with one alternative.

Select a template to work with. Immediately after, a list of configured sizes and sharing places appears on the screen. Among other things, you can create an Instagram post, a Facebook cover, a Twitter post, or a Pinterest post. If you would rather not post it to a social media platform, you can open one of the preset sizes in the Photo Editor.

You can reach the Background/Effects panel by selecting an option in the second panel. The default is the background panel, where you may select from different backdrop patterns and colors. You can select from an enormous variety of different types of effects when you click the Effects panel. To insert a new image, access the Photo Bin in the Photo Editor and drag it onto the document. Remember to click the Save button located at the bottom of the Background and Effects boxes once you have finished.

Print each item separately using your local printer

You have the option to print your photos using your home or office printer.

- Choose the photos you want to print from the Organizer section.
- Click on "**Create**" followed by "**Photo Prints**."
- Select a local printer. (Mac OS) Printing is done through Photo Editor in Elements
- Organizer. Ensure that Photoshop Elements is open before proceeding.
- Select the options you wish to print and then click on the Print button.

Print a Picture Package or Contact Sheet using your local printer

Preview a group of images by displaying thumbnail images on a single page using a contact sheet. **When using Windows, Choose one of the following options:**
- Choose "**Create**," then select "**Photo Print**," and finally click on "**Contact Sheet**." It launches the area in the Elements Organizer.
- Choose Contact Sheet as the print type in the Print menu box by navigating to **File > Print**.
- Select the desired options in the Print window box.
- Click on the **Print option**.

When Using a Mac,
- Choosing **File > Contact Sheet** II is the best option.
- Choose the desired options in the Contact Sheet dialog box and then select OK.
- A contact sheet has been generated and will open in the Photo Editor workspace.
- Click on "**File**" and then select "**Print**."
- Select the desired options in the Print window box.
- Click on the **Print option**.

Print a Picture Package

By using a picture package, you have the option to print multiple copies of the same photo on a single page.
For Windows:
Choose one of the following options:
- Choose "**Create**" > "**Photo Print**" > "**Contact Sheet**." It launches the area in the Elements Organizer.
- Choose **Picture Package** as the print type in the Print menu box by navigating to **File > Print**.

- Select the desired options in the Print window box.
- Click on the **Print option**.

On Mac:
- Select **File > Picture Package** from the menu.
- Select the desired options in the Picture Package dialog box and then click OK.
- The contact sheet is created and opened in Photo Edit or Workspace.
- Click on "**File**" and then select "**Print**."
- Select the desired options in the Print window box.
- Click on the **Print option**.

How to Create a Video Story

Create a compelling narrative using your photos and videos. Utilize the Video Story option in the Create menu to showcase your photos and videos of an event, such as a wedding, in a story format. The process is structured in a step-by-step format for easy navigation. You will be expertly guided through the process of categorizing your assets into sections and incorporating commentary, notes, music, and other elements. Transform your video story into an incredible experience by selecting a mood from pre-set options such as Sentimental and Classic.

Create a Video Story

Here are the steps to create a video story:
- Select **Create** and then **Video Story. Or**
- Access the home screen in Premiere Elements and select **Make your Video Story**.
- Elements guide you through creating a video story. You can view the tips by using the left and right keys.
- Once you've finished reading the tips, simply click on "**Skip**" to return to creating your video story.
- Exit the Video Story process to return to the main area of the app.
- To view the tips again, simply close and reopen the app.
- Choose a category to start creating the video story. To assign a general theme to your video story, simply click on "**General**." If the theme is not available on the computer, an Online Content Download will appear showing content being downloaded for that theme.
- To switch between styles, simply click the left and right buttons.
- Access movies and photos on your timeline by selecting the media option or clicking the Get Started button.
- Using the Media from My Timeline option imports all the videos and photos from your timeline into the story asset view in the Video Story workflow.
- To include story images, select a media source from the list of import options. Here are the media sites available for adding pictures, movies, and music videos. To import content from one of these sources, simply click on the provided link:
- Use Elements Organizer to import movies and pictures.

- You have the option to import videos from FLIP cameras, AVCHD cameras, or other memory or disk drives.
- Import photos from digital cameras, phones, or removable drives.
- Import files such as movies, photos, and music from your computer's hard drive using the Files and Folders feature.
- Select the file in the Add Media box and then click on "**Open**."
- Click on a video to view a brief clip. Select a file by clicking on it, and then delete it to remove it from the story contents. Select all the clips by pressing Ctrl + A, then delete them from the chosen story asset. The file remains in its original location without being deleted.
- Proceed to the next step. All the files in Story Assets are provided for creating the Story Overview.
- Organize your pictures and movies by placing them into chapters for a more structured display. This story consists of several chapters.
- Systematically organize your collection of videos and photos to structure and oversee your video narrative in a chapter-based format.

Within the Story Overview view, the following are some more activities that may be completed:

- A simple click on the "**Add Media**" button located inside the Story Assets pane will allow you to import more movies and photos.
- **Title of the Story and Credits**: Use the video titled "**Story Title**" at the beginning of the chapter, and the video titled "**Story Credits**" at the end. The addition of several video clips to other chapters is permitted; however, only one clip may be included in each chapter that has the Story Title and Story Credits elements.

Effects Collage

The wonderful thing about this Guided Edit function, which can be found under **Guided Edit > Fun > Effects Collage**, is that it can apply this collage and coloring effect to your photo in a matter of seconds. It is quite unlikely that the majority of us would be able to do it by hand since it would take us more than an hour to do so. A tedious human operation may be transformed into a quick and simple automated function that performs well thanks to the many clever tiny effects that are available in Elements. After opening your image, choose the Effects Collage option from the **Guided Edit > Fun menu**, and then select either a two-, three-, or four-panel effect. After that, choose a color effect by clicking the **Style tab** and selecting it. It is really easy. Adjust the most recent item you did and experiment with a new mixture if it does not come out the way you had hoped it would. You may reduce the intensity of the effect by repositioning the Opacity tool if you feel it is necessary to do so.

CHAPTER FOURTEEN
SHARE YOUR PHOTOS AND VIDEOS

Share your Photos via email

Instead of saving your image from Elements and then opening your email software (like Outlook or Apple Mail) and choosing the photo to attach, you can use Elements to instantly send photographs over email with just one click. This is a far more convenient method.

When sending a photo or piece of artwork by email, be sure to follow these steps:

- Make a selection in the Organizer of the photographs that you want to send to a friend. Within the Share box, choose the Email Attachments option. When you attempt to send photographs by email for the very first time, Elements will launch the Organizer Preferences panel and prompt you to configure your email account configuration. After you have typed in what you want to say in the boxes, click the OK button.
- Convert Photos to JPEGs is a checkbox that has to be checked. Once you have selected a quality option for the file, go to the next step. At the bottom of the screen, there is a box labeled "**Estimated Size**." Move the Quality scale, and then look at the file size that is shown there. Before you send the picture by email, you may need to make adjustments to the file size by using the Image Size dialog box.

Add recipients

In the next panel, you will find choices for inserting a message as well as adding recipients from an Address Book from your address book. You can do this without adding any individuals from your Address Book. It is possible that the Select Receivers box does not have any receivers that are indicated. Within the new message box of your email application, you can manually add the email addresses of the recipients. Push the button labeled "**Next**." First, the photo(s) are resized to fit the dimensions of the output screen. In a short amount of time, Elements will complete the sample process. After that, the photographs will be attached to a new email message that will be sent using your regular email application. Using Elements, the material is included in a whole new email message. You must switch to your email app to either see the message or send the letter. It is important to verify that the information that is included in the To, Subject, and Attach fields is accurate. Following that, you should hit the **Send button**. Through default settings, Elements will make use of your primary email client, which may or may not be the email tool that you use. The Preferences box may be opened by pressing the Ctrl+K (or Command+K on a Mac) in combination. Changing the default email app may be done by going to the Organizer and clicking on Email in the left column.

This will allow you to make the change. Within the Sharing options, there is a menu that allows you to choose the email program that you would want Elements to use. It is possible to use Elements with web-based email applications. Photos may be sent using the email application you are currently using, regardless of whether you use Yahoo!, Gmail, or other accounts of your choosing. If you choose "**Other**" in the Email Preferences interface, you will be required to provide the port number and SMTP server that you use. If you want assistance in configuring email for accounts that are not included in Email Preferences, you should get assistance from your Internet service provider (ISP).

Share your Photos on Flickr

Through the media view, choose the images that you want to share with others.

Take one of the following actions:

- Choose **Flickr** from the Share menu.
- Enter your login information.
- Submit your images to the website by following the directions that appear on the screen.
- Make sure that the Elements Organizer is configured to share emails.
- To access the email from Elements Organizer, choose **Preferences** > **Email**.
- Make sure you press "**New**." What is the name of your account? Choose a name that will assist you in locating your page at a later time.
- Make your selection from the list of service providers that are already present.
- On the page asking you to set up your email account, you will need to provide your name, email address, and password for the email address.
- When the procedure is successful, elements will display an approval notice before you click "**Verify**."

Share your Video on Vimeo

Before using this service, you must first ensure that you have effectively registered with Vimeo.

Choose the videos that you would want to share.

Take one of the following actions:

- Choose **Vimeo** from the Share menu.
- Enter your login information.
- Submit your images to this website by following the directions that appear on the screen.

Share your Video on YouTube

With the help of Elements Organizer, you will have no trouble uploading your videos to YouTube. To upload videos to YouTube, you will need to have a YouTube account. If you have a Gmail account, you may use it to verify your identity and log in to YouTube. You should familiarize yourself with YouTube's guidelines for sharing videos before uploading one to the platform. Before uploading your video to YouTube, check that it is the appropriate size, duration, and style.

- Take a movie clip from the Elements Organizer and choose it.
- To access YouTube, click on the **Share button**.
- If you share a video for the very first time, you will be required to sign in to your Google account.
- Following that, you will be prompted to provide permission before sharing your videos.
- There is a window that displays YouTube.
- Follow the instructions below to enter the information into the YouTube box, and then click the "**Upload**" button. The information that you provide will make it simple for users to locate your video when they are searching for it.
- Assign a title to your film and write a brief caption for it.
- Include tags that explain the title of your movie. For example, if the video is about your vacation to Paris, you may include tags such as France, Paris, June, Eiffel Tower, and similar.
- Choose a category that corresponds to the subject matter of your video.
- Select whether your video is accessible to anybody by clicking on the "**Public**" or "**Private**" buttons. Your video will only be seen by you and anyone else who is authorized to view it. Your channel, search results, playlists, and/or any other location does not include the video in question.
- You will be informed that the upload is currently taking place by the appearance of the progress box.
- Visit YouTube.
- Create a new window for the YouTube website, and then input your login credentials when it appears.
- To choose Videos, click on your User ID, which is located at the very top of the window in the browser. The video that you submitted should be shown in the "My Videos and Playlists" area of the website.

Troubleshooting Elements 2024

When it comes to capturing photos, things do not always go according to plan. For this reason, we make use of Photoshop Elements to make adjustments to aspects such as color, frame, and picture clarity. However, there is still the possibility that the software may malfunction. Although Adobe does an excellent job of ensuring that Photoshop Elements is secure and reliable, there are still instances in which issues have arisen. This is because practically everything operating in this industry is either altered or replaced every couple of months. In this section, you can discover the answers to some of the most typical imaging concerns, such as problems with the catalog, missing files, and bad color results.

Problems with saving files

There are a lot of photographers who, every once in a while, end up losing their whole collections of photographs. Not only is it unpleasant for me as a teacher, but it is also sad for them since they have no clue what took place or where things can be found! However, several things may be done to prevent a catastrophe of this kind. First, when you are prompted to click OK, you shouldn't simply do that. You should take a minute to look at the Save or Save As box to determine the location where your essential files will be stored. Nevertheless, Elements will always save a file in the same location that it was opened, so if you have saved anything and suddenly discover that you are unable to locate it, you should search in the folder that it was saved in the first place. If you accessed the vacation photo in Organizer (let's suppose it originated from the Vacations folder), made modifications to it, and then saved it (using the **File > Save or Ctrl/Cmd + S**) command, where did the photo go? After that, it was moved back to the Vacations folder, which is a decent place to start looking for anything. On the Save As menu, you will have the option to save the modified version back into the Organizer again. On the off chance that you want to get the most out of this file reader, it is highly recommended that you constantly keep this checked. There are also occasions when elements irritate me since they force me to save things as copies, which is something that I often do not want to do. Even though I would only ever use the most current version of the photo, I would like it if the application would update the file whenever it was modified. This would save me from having five or six versions of the same picture available. To prevent folks who aren't paying attention all the time from doing what I just said, which is to overwrite files, Adobe included this as a safety feature in their software.

Adjusting dates to accommodate a variety of time zones

The date setting on your camera must be accurate for an image search to be successful. The Elements search will return incorrect results. After all, it will be looking for a different date if you do not specify the right date because it will be searching for a different date. Remember that you may still go back in time, even if you forget to set the date on your camera correctly. When you go to a different time zone, your searches will likewise be all over the area that you are looking for. It makes no difference whether you are traveling north or south; traveling from east to west may cause any search query to be thrown off or incorrect. Photoshop Elements allows users to modify the information included inside a photo file to alter the date that the file was created.

How to carry it out:
- Select the files in the Organizer that include dates that you want to change. This is the first step. In the second step, right-click on the images, and then select "**Adjust Date and Time of Selected Items**" from the option that comes from the context menu.

- Open the dialog box that allows you to adjust the date and time of the items that have been selected.
- Change the time zones by a certain number of hours.
- The Time Zone Adjust screen will appear, and you will need to choose either the Ahead or Back option to determine the time difference.
- Instead of images of family members waving you off at the airport the day before you flew to Hawaii, you should now be able to access pictures of the breathtaking sunsets you captured while you were there.

Finding files that have been lost or disconnected

Included in the Elements Organizer is a box that may be checked in the File>Save As window. If you do this, Elements will save all of your updated files as well as all of your original files in the Organizer where they were saved. Observations? That is true, but we are all aware that in the real world, things do not always go as planned. It is not uncommon for photographs to get corrupted, misplaced, or just vanishes. If you are unable to locate photographs that you believed you had saved and put into Elements' organizer, the following are some options that you may use. Within the Media area of Organizer, you could discover one or two files that have been lost daily. It has come to my attention that Elements is highly effective at locating these misplaced files. As long as it has time (that is, you do not finish the search early) and the file is still there (that is, the image has not been deleted or modified), it will allow you to look for other files.

Check the Organizer: It is possible that the photo was loaded into the Organizer, but for some reason, it has vanished since then. If this is the situation, you will nonetheless be able to discover its little symbol in the primary Organizer window, even if it is nothing more than a question mark. Even if the original photo is no longer there, Elements is aware of the name of the file and immediately begins searching for it. When you double-click on the image of the file, you will be presented with the following screen in Elements Organizer: Searching for a file that has been lost. It may take a few minutes or perhaps longer, but the file that was lost will be located as long as it was not deleted.

To instruct the Organizer that you want to make the photo full-size, double-click on it. This will make the picture full-size. If it has lost its connection to the source file, this Search panel will become visible. Elements will locate the file that you have lost if you wait for a sufficient amount of time and the original is still there on your system. Due to its ability to locate deleted data, an element is among the most effective applications for modifying photographs. Even if you are aware of the location where a file was relocated, if Elements is unable to locate and reconnect a missing file, you can try selecting **File > Reconnect > All Missing Files...** Or, you may just relocate the file to the correct location and then try again. Are you looking for a picture? Examine the route in the Keyword/Info panel, which is located on the right side of the main Organizer window, to determine where it ought to be or where it was initially before it became disoriented. First things first, check to see that the Information tab is available. After that, check for the link to the location in the section labeled "General Notes."

Restoring your catalog

The collection is stored on the hard disk of a computer that is set to the default setting. On the other hand, it is possible to store it on any disk, even one that may be deleted. You have to make backups of your catalogs regularly. When doing this, it is recommended that you use a portable drive or even the cloud. Using the same disk that you use to run Elements as a backup is not a reliable method of data protection. Never let your books go lost. There should always be a copy saved on a separate disk. I am aware that backing up may seem to be a tedious process; but, believe me when I say that you only need to experience the loss of everything once to comprehend the significance of the seemingly little act of backing up. This might be due to a virus, a malfunctioning system, or something else entirely. How therefore do we go about restoring a collection if we lose data? The first thing you should do is check to see whether the computer has any viruses or other problems. It would be a waste of time to avoid placing your information in danger once again if the computer is not resolved. Bringing back the catalog is a simple process. Simply launch the Organizer and connect the disk that contains the backup copy to the computer. As a result, you will be presented with two fields: first, locate the backup file. Next, transfer it to the location where you want it to be restored, and then click "**Restore**." If you only want to restore the catalog to the state it was in when it was first loaded, check the box next to the **Restore Original Folder Structure option.**

Liquify Filter

Individuals who shoot photographs of people for a living, such as fashion photographers, wedding photographers, and anybody else, will find this filter to be an excellent tool. Through the use of Liquify, you can transform your digital file into a liquid pool of pixels. After that, these pixels may be moved about in the same manner as wet oil paints. The initial intention was to alter the appearance of models by reducing the size of their features, repairing damaged noses, and increasing the size of their eyes. On the other hand, Liquify provides you with a great deal of control over the whole image, regardless of whether it is a face or a body. The excellent Adjust Facial Features tool that is located in the Enhance menu performs a terrific job.

Amateur family photographers may also use this tool to muck up their family photographs. By using this filter, you can perform the following:

- Reduce or enlarge the size of the nose.
- Make adjustments to the contours of your ears, chins, stomachs, thighs, and waists.
- Transform the expressions.
- Shift the reality

Included on its toolbar are:

- **Wrap tool**: In many ways, the Warp tool is comparable to the Smudge brush; nevertheless, it is superior.
- **Twirl Counter Clockwise**: This feature allows you to turn the dots in a counterclockwise direction by holding down the mouse button or dragging as you move the mouse.
- **Pucker**: While you are holding down the mouse button or dragging it, the Pucker tool will pull pixels closer to the center of the brush area.
- **Bloat**: In the process of bloating, pixels are shifted out from the center of the brush area as you continue to hold down the mouse button or drag.
- **Shift Pixels**: The motion of pixels across the stroke direction is referred to as "shifting pixels." Pixels can be moved to the left or right by dragging them. It is possible to press Alt- on macOS. To shift pixels to the right, drag (or use the Option-drag shortcut).
- **Reconstruct**: Reconstruct is a command that erases part or all of the modifications that you have made. If you go to **Advanced > Tool > Distort > Liquify**, you will find this wonderful tool, which you can use.

Resolution Problems: Adding Pixels

In some circumstances, the photos that you are required to utilize could not be of a quality that is enough for the task that you have in mind. Imagine, for example, that you are in the process of putting together a picture book for your family and that you discover very quickly that some of the older photographs that were scanned from the originals are too tiny. It is impossible to make the visuals larger than a matchbox without the risk of their becoming blurry. You are in luck since Photoshop Elements has a fantastic feature known as "resampling" that enables you to alter the size of image files by incrementing or decreasing the number of pixels. However, it is important to bear in mind that the output quality of the resampled file is directly proportional to the size of the source file. As an example, if the source is a little photo with a resolution of 2 megapixels that was obtained from the internet, you can only increase the size of the picture by around 5 percent before the quality begins to decrease, which means that it will seem lighter.

However, if the original photograph was shot with a camera that has a resolution of 20 megapixels or above, you will most likely be able to double or even quadruple the size of the photograph while still obtaining a clean and crisp image. When you resample the file, you can add almost any expansion number; however, the results are not always guaranteed. You should be aware that this alters the size of the file, which provides you with information on whether or not the photo will be able to fit on the page. In this particular instance, the width of the picture increased from 400 pixels to 1,600 pixels, which resulted in the image's file size increasing from 0.75 MB to 4.6 MB. It is preferable to the alternative of having to reduce the size of the file to that of a postage stamp, even though the new file does not seem to be crisp since a large number of extra pixels were added to an original that had a low resolution. It is important to keep in mind that you may also enhance the image by working to correct any blurriness that may have been generated by the resampling process.

Frequently Asked Questions

Frequently Asked Questions Regarding Adobe Photoshop Elements

Adobe Photoshop Elements is a strong image editing program that was developed for individuals who wish to improve their photographs without having to deal with the complexities of professional-grade tools such as Adobe Photoshop. Even though it has an intuitive user interface, not only novice users but even more experienced users could have questions about its features, operation, and application. Within the scope of this all-encompassing tutorial, we will endeavor to answer a few of the commonly asked inquiries (FAQs) about Adobe Photoshop Elements.

What are Adobe Photoshop Elements?

The Adobe Photoshop Elements software is a simplified version of the Adobe Photoshop program that provides users with a broad variety of tools and capabilities for editing, organizing, and sharing digital photographic pictures. Hobbyists, amateur photographers, and members of small enterprises who want significant editing skills but do not want to deal with the complexities of professional software are the target audience for this product.

Which of Adobe Photoshop Elements' major features are the most advantageous?

Adobe Photoshop Elements comes with a wide range of tools that are specifically designed to facilitate the editing, organizing, and sharing of images.

Among the most important features are:

- Guided Edits are editing tools that provide a step-by-step learning experience for adding effects and improving photographs.
- The term "**automatic editing**" refers to the automated features that automatically fix exposure, and color balance, and reduce red-eye.
- The Magic Wand, Quick Selection, and Selection Brush are all examples of selection tools. These tools are used to make certain choices with great accuracy.
- Offering support for layers, which allow for the independent organization and manipulation of various aspects of a picture?
- A broad variety of filters and effects may be applied to photographs to make creative modifications.
- Text Tools are tools that allow you to add text to photographs and format it as you want it.
- It is possible to apply modifications to many photographs at the same time using a process known as batch editing.
- Tools for organizing and managing picture collections, including labeling, rating, and keyword search. Also known as "**organizational tools**."

What are the main differences between Adobe Photoshop and Adobe Photoshop Elements?

Although Adobe Photoshop Elements and Adobe Photoshop have numerous similarities, there are several significant differences between the two:

- **Complexity**: In comparison to Photoshop Elements, Adobe Photoshop is a more complicated piece of software as it is designed for professional use and has a steeper learning curve as well as more complex capabilities.
- **Price**: When it comes to pricing, Adobe Photoshop is offered via a subscription-based approach as part of Adobe Creative Cloud, but Photoshop Elements may be purchased without the need for a membership of any kind.
- **Feature Set:** The feature set of Adobe Photoshop contains sophisticated capabilities that are designed specifically for professional photographers and graphic designers. These features include support for CMYK color mode, advanced compositing, and 3D modeling, all of which are not accessible in Photoshop Elements due to certain limitations.
- **Target Audience**: The Adobe Photoshop software is designed for professionals and expert users, whilst the Photoshop Elements software is geared for amateur photographers, hobbyists, and small companies.

To what extent are Adobe Photoshop Elements suitable for usage in professional settings?

It is possible to use Adobe Photoshop Elements for some forms of professional work, such as small-scale graphic design projects, social networking graphics, and basic picture editing chores, even though it was originally developed for amateur photographers and photographers who are just starting in the field. On the other hand, Adobe Photoshop or another professional-grade program can be better appropriate for tasks that are more complicated and intricate.

What are Guided Edits in Adobe Photoshop Elements?

Guided Edits are a collection of lessons and tools that are included in Adobe Photoshop Elements. These tools and tutorials are designed to guide users through a variety of editing methods and effects. These guided lessons cover a broad variety of subjects, ranging from fundamental editing techniques like cropping and scaling to more sophisticated methods such as making double exposures and adding creative effects. The goal of Guided Edits is to facilitate the learning of new editing methods and the effortless attainment of outcomes that seem to have been edited by professionals.

When it comes to removing backgrounds from photos, is it possible to use Adobe Photoshop Elements?

Adobe Photoshop Elements does come equipped with tools that may be used to remove backgrounds from photographs. It is possible to erase backgrounds from photographs of varied degrees of intricacy by using the Magic Eraser and Background Eraser tools throughout the editing process. Furthermore, when it comes to eliminating backgrounds from photographs, the Select Subject and Select and Mask tools may assist users in making exact choices and refining boundaries.

Which steps should I take to install Adobe Photoshop Elements?

You can buy and download Adobe Photoshop Elements either directly from the Adobe website or via approved resellers. After the program has been bought, customers can download it and then install it on their computer by following the instructions that appear on the screen. In addition, Adobe provides consumers with trial copies of Photoshop Elements that they may test out before making a purchase.

Does Adobe Photoshop Elements include apps for both Windows and Mac operating systems?

Adobe Photoshop Elements is indeed not only compatible with Windows but also with Mac operating systems. Users can install and make use of the program on the platform of their choice since it is compatible with the most recent versions of each operating system, including macOS and Windows.

To edit raw pictures, is it possible to use Adobe Photoshop Elements?

Without a doubt, Adobe Photoshop Elements is equipped with the capability to edit raw photos. The program can read and edit raw files from a broad variety of digital cameras. This gives users the ability to make modifications to exposure, color balance, and other settings straight from the raw picture data. In addition, Adobe Photoshop Elements is equipped with automatic functions that aid in the enhancement of raw photographs. These features include the Auto Smart Tone and Auto Curves adjustments.

What are some ways that I may study Adobe Photoshop Elements?

For those interested in studying Adobe Photoshop Elements, there are a variety of materials accessible to them, such as video courses, books, and online tutorials. On its website, Adobe provides customers with a wide range of lessons and tools, including video tutorials, step-by-step instructions, and community forums where users may ask questions and exchange advice with one another. In addition, there are a great number of educational platforms and websites that are not affiliated with Adobe Photoshop Elements that provide users of varying ability levels with lessons and courses relevant to Adobe Photoshop Elements.

Can I use plugins from third-party developers with Adobe Photoshop Elements?

There is a possibility that Adobe Photoshop Elements is compatible with third-party plugins, which enables users to enhance the capabilities of the program by adding more features and effects. Plugins and extensions for Photoshop Elements are available from a wide variety of third-party developers. These extensions and plugins provide many creative effects and filters, as well as sophisticated editing features. Users can install plugins by downloading them from the developer's website and then following the instructions that are given for the installation process.

In Adobe Photoshop Elements, what are the steps I need to take to resize images?

The following actions need to be taken to resize a picture in Adobe Photoshop Elements:

- In Photoshop Elements, resize the picture you wish to work with by opening it.
- Choose "**Image**" from the menu that is located on the top toolbar.
- Make your selection from the dropdown menu by selecting "**Resize**" and then "**Image Size.**"

- The width and height of the picture may be customized by entering the required values in the picture Size dialog box. It is possible to set the dimensions in pixels, inches, or any other unit of measurement.
- The "**Constrain Proportions**" option must be selected to ensure that the image's aspect ratio is preserved.
- To apply the adjustments and resize the picture, click the "**OK**" button.

What are the capabilities of Adobe Photoshop Elements for creating panoramas?

There is a function called Photomerge Panorama that is included in Adobe Photoshop Elements. This capability enables users to create panoramic photos by stitching together numerous shots.

In Photoshop Elements, the following steps need to be taken to generate a panorama:

- The panorama can be created by opening Photoshop Elements and selecting the photographs that you want to use.
- Proceed to the "**Enhance**" menu and choose "**Photomerge**" followed by "**Photomerge Panorama**."
- In the Photomerge Panorama dialog box, choose the photographs that you want to combine, and then select the layout option that you want to use (Auto, Perspective, Cylindrical, Spherical, or Collage).
- Simply clicking the "OK" button will allow Photoshop Elements to automatically build the panorama by stitching the many photographs together.
- After you have generated the panorama, you can use the editing tools that are included in Photoshop Elements to make further edits and refinements to it.

To what extent is it possible to produce picture slideshows using Adobe Photoshop Elements?

Users can create dynamic picture slideshows with transitions, music, and text overlays by using the Slideshow function that is included in Adobe Photoshop Elements.

In Photoshop Elements, the following steps need to be taken to make a slideshow:

- To add the photos to the slideshow, open Photoshop Elements and select the images you want to include.
- Navigate to the "**Create**" tab, and then choose "**Slideshow**" from the menu that appears under it.
- Change the slideshow settings in the Slideshow dialog box. These choices include the layout, length, transitions, music, and text overlays.
- It is possible to preview the slideshow and make any required edits by clicking the "**Preview**" button.

- Click the "**Save**" button whenever you are pleased with the slideshow. You can then export it as a video file or burn it to a DVD so that it may be shared with others.

Is it possible to immediately share the modified photos that I have created using Adobe Photoshop Elements?

Adobe Photoshop Elements does come with built-in sharing capabilities that enable users to share their modified photographs straight from inside the program itself. Users can build PDF slideshows that they can then share with their friends and family, as well as share photographs via email, social media, or online galleries. In addition, Photoshop Elements is compatible with Adobe's Creative Cloud services, which enables users to quickly share their photographs with others and synchronize them across all of their devices.

CONCLUSION

When it comes to editing, organizing, and sharing photographs, Adobe Photoshop Elements is a tool that is both powerful and simple to use. Within the scope of this tutorial, we have covered a wide range of topics that are essential to the use of Photoshop Elements, ranging from fundamental editing tools to more complex ones. Components, including instructions on how to trim, resize, alter colors, apply filters, and enhance photographs. Having a firm foundation from which to begin researching and developing their photographs is provided to users who are familiar with the usage of these tools. In addition to that, we discussed the procedures for organizing items in Photoshop Elements, as well as the significance of cataloging and tagging photographs to make them simple to locate. If you use albums, tags, and keywording, you will be able to locate certain photographs within a vast collection in a much more expedient and straightforward manner. We also investigated the sharing options that are available in Photoshop Elements. These options allow users to share photographs via email or social media, as well as print them directly from inside the software. The process of sharing edited or curated photographs with family, friends, or a larger audience is simplified as a result of this. Be creative, put in the effort to practice, and familiarize yourself with all of Photoshop Elements' many features and functionalities if you want to become proficient in this program. Through further exploration and use of its capabilities, users have the opportunity to enhance their picture editing skills, better the efficiency with which they organize their collections, and make it simpler for them to share their visual tales. Keeping up with the most recent features and functionalities in Photoshop Elements may make the experience even more enjoyable by providing users with new tools and techniques to express their creativity. This is because Adobe is constantly updating its program. In the end, Photoshop Elements is an excellent tool that is suitable for both novice and seasoned photographers simultaneously. If you want to get the most out of your digital photographs and cultivate a greater appreciation for the art of photography, this program provides you with all of the tools you want.

INDEX

"

"**Create**" has been added next to the Open button, 7

1

100 percent or less, 41
176 unique styles available in the Styles section, 62

2

2024 upgrade adds, 3
25 megabytes in size, 11

3

3D Effect slider, 11

6

64-bit versions only, 14
6th Generation Intel processor, 14
6th Generation Intel processor or newer, 14

8

8 gigabytes of RAM, 14

A

a guide to help you choose from the available options, 2
a person, 6, 163
a phone based on integrated GPS data, 6
A platform for sharing photos, 24
A platform where users can easily create stunning portfolio websites, 24
a scenery, 6
A tab on the Effects panel, 12
a very welcome addition, 3
a wide range of tools, 1, 193
ability to alter the selection view, 9
ability to perform preset actions, 9
above the taskbar, 63
access many of the most often required modifications, 7
access previously opened photos or create new files., 48
Access project files, 20
access the contextual menu, 52, 53
Access the File menu, 2
Access the official Adobe Elements website, 50
access the System Menu Button, 48
Access the **Undo or Redo button** in the Taskbar., 27
access the web address of Elements, 7
access to a wide variety of stuff, 9
access to several tools, 5
access varying menu commands, 52
accessing online content., 14, 15
accessing the real editor, 4
accurately capture the halftone., 71
ACDSee are two examples of competitors, 6
ACR, 9
Actions, 63, 64
add a touch of flair to your films, 11
Add Event, 75
Add Location, 75
add photographs to a face tag., 7
Add recipients, 186
add the photos to the slideshow, 197
Adding captions to the media file., 87
Adding Icons to Tags, 78
Adding media to Auto Creations, 19
Adding New Events, 81
adding or applying to foreground images, 63
adding or removing pixels, 43, 114
Adding pictures to the organizer, 68
Adding Pixels, 192
Adding Profiles to Favorites, 106
addition of peek-through and pattern overlays, 4
additional checkboxes, 12
Additional Information, 63
additional options, 39, 64, 108
additional purchases, 12
additional tools created by Adobe for use in comparable scenarios, 30
Additional type-related options, 59
Additional upgrades that have been released over the last several years, 4
adds new capabilities, 3
Adjust any settings, 137

199

Adjust Sharpness, 105, 157, 158
Adjust Sharpness In-Camera Raw Files, 105
Adjust text attributes in the Type Preferences section, 67
adjust the aspect ratio of a picture., 4
Adjust the images, 178
adjust the image's dimensions, 40
Adjust the Luminance Smoothing slider, 105
adjust the perspective of the image, 60
adjust the position of a picture, 61
Adjust the statistics number, 29
Adjust the Threshold slider to control, 137
Adjust the Threshold slider to control the amount of recomposing displayed in the adjustment., 137
Adjust your photo by cropping it or using Smart Fix., 23
adjusting brightness and color,, 21
adjusting brightness,, 21
Adjusting Clarity, 154
Adjusting Color, 145
Adjusting Facial Features, 163
Adjusting Lighting, 142
Adjusting Photos, 7, 179
adjusting similar pixels, 58
adjusting the color using features like enhanced color, 65
adjusting the distance of the motion., 11
adjusting the Quality Slider., 35
Adjustment, 23, 62, 125, 126, 128, 129, 153, 154, 167, 168
Adjustments, 21, 63, 146, 154
adjustments from your devices, 3
Adjustments panel, 21
administrative privileges, 15
Adobe Camera Raw Profile, 105
Adobe Creative Cloud's online storage, 4
Adobe Element on the Adobe website, 31
Adobe is constantly updating its program, 198
Adobe Lightroom and official Photoshop, 4
Adobe Partner Services, 67
Adobe Photoshop Element Software application, 14
Adobe Photoshop Elements, 1, 2, 14, 15, 44, 100, 104, 164, 193, 194, 195, 196, 197, 198
ADOBE PHOTOSHOP ELEMENTS, 2
Adobe Photoshop Elements 2024 is the newest version, 1

Adobe Photoshop Elements does come with built-in sharing capabilities, 198
Adobe Photoshop Elements is a tool, 198
Adobe Photoshop Elements is a versatile graphic editing software developed by the Adobe software community,, 1
Adobe Photoshop Elements is offered as a one-time purchase, 1
Adobe Raw, 107
Adobe Stock, 2, 4, 9
Adobe's online storage, 7
Adobe's Photoshop and Lightroom,, 3
Advanced, 12, 13, 21, 22, 39, 48, 53, 54, 56, 58, 60, 62, 137, 142, 175, 177, 179, 180, 192
advanced functions, 14
Advanced Tools, 12
Albums, 24, 74, 81
Align your text horizontally, 2
All of the photographs, 9
all picture data, 39
All the panels such as Layers, 50
Allow Me to Choose, 47
allow users to blur or erase a backdrop, 4
allow users to share photographs, 198
allowing users to easily organize, 1
allowing you to replicate objects, 56
alter colors, 198
Always Optimize Colors for Computer Screen, 46
Always Optimize for Printing, 46
amazing functionality, 8
AMD equivalent with SSE4.1 support., 14
An Internet connection is necessary for product activation, 14, 15
analyze colors, 45
analyze each pane and its specific functions, 66
Animation, 40
animation may be saved in either format., 10
annual subscription fee, 3
another application, 38
Another comparable alternative is ACDSee Photo Studio, 3
Anti-aliasing, 113, 121
antivirus programs, 15
Any kind of generative artificial intelligence (AI),, 3
appealing to photographers, 1
Apple silicon M1 processor, 14
application already has a plethora of picture tools, 3
application cannot be installed on a volume, 15

application installation, 14
application searches, 7
application searches for a variety of factors, 7
Application Updates, 67
applications for video editing and other features, 3
apply filters, 198
applying a filter, 62
Applying Profile to your Image, 106
applying sharpening to Raw file images, 105
appropriate ones., 53
arcs, 14
arrange images, 68, 73
Artifacts, 155
artificial intelligence, 4, 8, 12
artificial intelligence and transforms still images into animated GIFs, 4
Artistic, 8, 12, 107
artistic style transfers, 12
As a Copy, 33
Auto Color Correction, 140
Auto Contrast, 135, 139
Auto Creation at Work, 80
Auto Creations, 5, 19, 80, 173
Auto Creations are located at the bottom of the Home Screen, 19
Auto Curate for a search, 7
Auto Curating Images, 80
Auto Haze Removal, 140
Auto Level, 139
Auto Red-Eye Fix, 141
Auto Selection tool, 12, 116
Auto Shake Reduction, 140
Auto Sharpen, 141
Auto Smart Tone, 135, 138, 196
auto-curation, 5
automated sharpening process on photographs, 14
Automatic Colorization,, 4
automatically recognizes a human, 11
available in the Menu Bar section, 48

B

backdrop color, 63, 119
Background, 4, 13, 58, 119, 120, 126, 127, 134, 136, 183, 195
Backing up Your Catalog, 90
Backing up your photos and files, 92
Backup Catalog Structure, 90

Baseline Optimized, 35
BASIC IMAGE EDITING, 41
BASIC IMAGE EDITING CONCEPTS, 41
Basic Requirement, 14
Basics Edit, 65
Be creative, 198
Be sure to click on the Open Link button to access these resources., 19
become proficient in this program, 198
Before and After Toggle Button, 153
Begin by opening the Adobe Photoshop Element installer on your computer., 16
Behance, 24
Behance is a platform for displaying your creative work, 24
beta version of Elements for the web, 4
beta version of the Elements mobile app, 4
better the efficiency, 198
bevels, 62
Bicubic, 43
Bicubic is the default resampling method, 43
Bicubic technique, 43
Bilinear interpolation, 43
birthday cakes, 11
birthday cakes and balloons, 11
Bitmap, 34
bitmap graphics, 34
black backdrop, 9
blacks, 63
blue tag, 19
Blur Tool, 57
Blurring you Image, 156
BMP, 34, 38, 39
BMP (Bitmap) standard image format, 34
BMP files, 34
BMP picture, 34
both novice and seasoned photographers, 198
bottom of the page, 11, 173, 174
bottom panel, 8, 9
bottom-right toolbar, 7
brand-new instrument, 4
brief overview of the extra panels, 63
brightness, 3, 20, 21, 45, 65, 101, 125, 128, 143, 146, 147, 150, 154
brightness adjustments, 3, 20
Browsing Through an Album of Photos, 83
brush option that control the feathering, 12
Brush Tool, 58
built expressly for animated GIFs, 9

201

built-in photo applications, 6
Burn Tool, 57
Byte Order, 37

C

Cache section to your preference and then select "Ok.", 29
calculate the edges of the object, 12
calendars, 24, 49, 63, 74
Calibrating Your Monitor, 45
Calibration panel, 104
Calibration panel and boasts enhanced features, 104
Camera Calibration tab, 105
Camera Matching, 107
Camera or Card Reader, 69
Camera Raw files, 101
Camera Raw files can be saved in various formats, 101
Canon, 101
Canon (.CRW, 101
capabilities, 4, 8, 9, 11, 51, 174, 193, 194, 196, 197
capabilities to crop, 4
capacity to create, 9
capture all types of grayscales, 46
Carrying our Basic Edits, 22
cartoons, 71
case-sensitive file systems, 14
Catalog Manager, 87, 88
Cataloging a File, 87
causing any disruption to the backdrop, 7
CCIT, 39
CCIT is another lossless compression, 39
CD or DVD, 90
Centimeters, 41
certain features in the Photoshop Element application, 19
certain file-saving options, 33
certain parts of a picture, 13
Change the slideshow settings in the Slideshow dialog box, 197
change workspaces, 18
Changing Colors, 142, 148
Changing People's Skin Tone, 151
Changing the Color Temperature, 153
Changing the Ruler Unit of Measurement, 171
Check out the Magnificent Box feature, 52

choose "**Slideshow**" from the menu that appears under it., 197
Choose a country or region, 67
choose a Layout, 11
choose a matte color, 35
Choose a theme in the middle of the Photo Collage, 177
Choose a tool from the toolbox., 61
choose an effect,, 8
Choose Baseline ("standard"),, 35
Choose **Before & After-Horizontal** from the View drop-down menu., 23
choose between a GIF or an MP4, 11
choose colors and tones from preloaded options, 2
Choose **General** and uncheck the box, 61
choose Guided Mode, 2
Choose one of the options, 46
choose Photo Reel from the list of options, 11
Choose **Preference** from the **Edit menu**, 29
Choose the **Browse button** to locate the folder, 70
Choose the Byte Order option, 37
choose the crop tool, 8
Choose the directory, 32
Choose the **File Format option**, 32
Choose the **File option**, 32
Choose the folder, 35, 36, 37
Choose the image quality level by inputting a value, 35
Choose the image's thumbnail, 63
choose the Interlace option to select either None or Interlaced, 36
choose the **language and installation location**, 16
choose the method for compressing the image data, 37
choose the most flattering expression, 13
Choose the picture you want and click on the Open button., 51
choose to automatically update the Element application, 67
choose **Undo**, 26
choose **View all**, 19
Choose your previous version of Photoshop Element, 16
choosing a different Plug-Ins folder, 67
Choosing between Print and On Screen Resolutions, 44
choosing from the available options in the pop-up menu, 52

202

choosing from the Quality menu, 35
choosing the image you want to save as a file, 32
Choosing the Right Color Scheme for Your Workspace, 46
Choosing the right tools, 53
chromatic aberration correction, 9
Chrome, 15
chronological, 85, 86
clean lines without any restrictions, 60
Click "**Ok**" to confirm the deletion., 29
Click OK after you've made your choices., 178
click on Add Text, 2
click on **Create**, 3
Click on Photo Editor from the right-hand side of the Home Screen Interface, 21
Click on **Share** and choose an option from the Share drop-down menu., 25
Click on the **Download button**, 15
Click on the Try button to test out any, 19
Click on the **Zoom tool** in the Tool panels to zoom in on the image., 64
Clone Stamp Tool, 56
Close Button, 52
closing a document, 30
cloud and syncing functions, 7
cloud icon located in the upper right corner of the screen, 7
CMYK color space for the page, 47
collages, 4, 7, 19, 49, 74, 180
Collapse All Keyword Tags, 79
collect creative ideas, 18
color and texture selection, 55
Color Edit, 65
color enhancements, 20
color management, 46, 47
color number, 40, 47
Color Picker Tool, 59
Color Replacement Tool, 58
Color Settings, 46, 47
color space is perfect for viewing images, 46
Color Swatches, 63
Colored photographs, 71
colorize, 4, 161, 162
Colorizing a Photo, 160
colors displayed on the screen, 46
Combine or connect multiple images or photos, 65
combining search criteria, 6
comics, 71

commonly utilized compression techniques, 39
commonly utilized compression techniques or formats, 39
companion mobile app, 3
comparable alternative, 3
comparing photos, 80
compatible with smartphones., 11
compile multiple images, 24
Complete the collage, 179
Complexity, 194
Components, 198
composition, 7
compressing images, 39
Compressing the layers can help reduce the overall file size., 38
Compression, 4, 38, 39
Compression in this popular picture file format can result in distortions that are not realistic, 4
compromising the image's color information, 33
computer automatically creates based on the information you have uploaded., 5
computer screen, 45, 46
Computers with Pixar image files, 34
CONCLUSION, 198
connect the camera to your computer using a USB connection., 69
connecting with others through uploaded images, 24
Consider specific printing factors, 47
Consider using the complimentary Adobe Stock photo, 2
Constraint Proportions box, 44
contemporary collages, 3
Content-Aware, 61
Contiguous, 113, 120, 121
control how transparency is displayed in the Element, 67
converting the color of a pixel to transparent pixels, 58
Cookie Cutter tool, 118
Cookie Cutter Tool, 60
copyright, 87, 174
Copyright Warning, 174
Corel PaintShop Pro, 3, 5
correct resolution, 44
CORRECTING CONTRAST, 142
CORRECTING CONTRAST, COLOR, AND CLARITY, 142
corrects closed eyelids in your photos, 56

Country/Region, 67
crafting engaging image compositions, 1
Crafting rectangular and elliptical selections, 108
Create a New Group, 125
create a panorama, 13
Create a slideshow and export it as a movie file, 24
Create a Video Story, 184
create a wide range of shapes, 59
Create Clipping Mask, 127
Create menu, 9, 11, 173, 175, 184
Create Stylized Text, 2
create websites, 9
Create/Share Panel, 63
Creating a Catalog, 87
Creating albums, 24
Creating albums allows you to compile multiple images for easy sharing or uploading, 24
Creating an Album, 81, 82
CREATING AND ADJUSTING SELECTIONS, 108
Creating and Viewing Tag, 77
Creating Fin Pieces, 173
creating multiple pages, 34
creating precise, 60
Creating Profiles for Raw Images, 107
Creative Profiles for Raw and Non-Raw Photos, 107
Crop Tool, 22, 60, 118, 135
Crop Tool,, 22
Cropping Images, 135
cultivate a greater appreciation for the art of photography, 198
Current Tool, 52
Custom Shape Tool, 59
Custom Tags and their Uses, 78
Custom Workspace, 63
customize a program to match your unique working style, 66
customize gridline color, 67
Customize the collage, 179
customizing photos., 21
CyberLink PhotoDirector, 3, 12

D

Dark mode has been added, 3
data are included, 87
dates, 6, 68, 92, 99, 189
Decontaminate Colors, 9, 123
decrease file size, 33
decrease grayscale noise, 105
decrease the amount of specific colors in your photo, 58
default browser, 7
Defined Proportions, 118
Defined Size, 118
Defining Selections, 108
dehaze, 4
delete a photo from an album, 85
Deleting an Album, 84
deletion of all subsequent states, 30
delve into the new features driven, 2
depth of field,, 65
Design professional-looking text with the Add Text Guided Edit, 2
designated area of an image, 59
designed and manufactured for sophisticated graphics applications, 34
designs, 1, 24, 33, 62, 182
desired form size and location, 13
Despeckle, 155
detail adjustments are all accessible, 9
detailed guide, 25
detailed instructions, 36, 37, 38
Details, 92, 97
different locations using the Photo Bin., 63
different platforms and applications., 34
different subcommands, 48
different view of the same image, 64
directly attach tags to photographs, 6
Discover engaging editing projects, 18
Discover the latest features in the 2024 version, 2
Display and Cursor Preferences, 67
display profile, 46
Display resolution, 14, 15, 44
Display the Image Resolution and Dimensions, 42
Displaying Image Screen, 41
Displaying information about the size and resolution, 52
displaying the font name in English, 67
Displays the image in a browser once the download is complete, 37
distinct plug-in, 9
distinct subject, 11
distributing, 24
dividing the physical size by the resolution, 42
divisions, 67
do a variety of other editing tasks, 4

document default resolutions for precise control, 67
Document Dimension, 52
Document Profile, 52
Document Profiles, 47
Document Size, 42
Document Sizes, 52
Dodge Tool, 57
DotPhoto, 24
DotPhoto is an extra platform, 24
Download and Install Adobe Photoshop Element, 15
Download Images, 69
download on Adobe's official websites, 62
download photos from a media card, 70
downloaded Photoshop Element on your computer, 16
downloading and installing Adobe Photoshop, 14, 15
downloading and installing Adobe Photoshop Element 2024, 14
downloading and installing Photoshop Element 2024, 18
downloading and installing Photoshop Element 2024 on your PC, 18
downloading features, 14, 15
downsampling, 43
Draw, 53, 58, 118, 136
drawing a rectangle or shape, 12
DSLR camera, 9
duplicates the color of a section in an image, 59
during the current session, 27
Dust, 155

E

easily crop images into any shape you want, 60
easily make one-click edits to your images, 2
easily makes quick edits, 3
easily see how a picture is zoomed in or out., 52
easily select backgrounds for editing, 2
Edit Mode, 23, 48, 53
Edit mode includes buttons for File, 22
Edit modes, 22, 62
editing and creating images and videos, 1
Editing and making changes, 23
EDITING CAMERA IMAGES, 100
EDITING CAMERA IMAGES USING THE CAMERA EDITOR, 100

editing program, 9, 193
Editor, 7, 16, 75, 93, 100, 101, 102, 103, 104, 107, 164, 165, 177, 178, 182
edits made to the image, 27
effectively reduces the file size of photos., 39
Effects, 8, 12, 23, 62, 164, 182, 183, 185
Efficiency, 52
Efficiency is determined by the number of operations, 52
efficiently reduce file sizes, 34
effortlessly transform your photo into black and white, 65
Element has two Preference dialog boxes, 66
Element inherited this function, 63
Element Web,, 23
Elements and other Creative Cloud applications,, 4
Elements does not need a membership to continue using it, 3
Elements Effects seems to be a squared version of Instagram, 8
Elements feature, 12
Elements version of Adobe Creative Retouching, 9
Elements Web, 50
Elements Web option., 50
eliminate people from a landscape, 13
eliminate the need for additional applications, 6
eliminates color distortion, 9
Eliminating Color with Remove Color Command, 148
Eliminating Haze, 153
eliminating specific features, 39
Elimination Noise, 155
Elimination Noise, Artifacts, Dust, and Scratch, 155
ellipse, 59, 109
Elliptical Marquee Tool, 54, 109
email or social media, 198
enable users to share their modified photographs, 198
enables users to quickly share their photographs with others, 198
encountering unfamiliar words, 31
Engage the contextual menu, 52
Enhance navigation menu, 9
enhance photo sharpness, 2
enhance photographs, 198
enhance the appearance of an image, 9
enhance the appearance of your text., 2
Enhance the preservation of layers, 33

enhance your document by adding text,, 62
Enhanced Dehaze slider, 104
Ensure the camera or scanner title is connected, 87
ensure to set the color workspace to either sRGB or Adobe RGB., 46
Ensure you have at least 6 GB of hard-disc space available, 15
Ensure your display driver is compatible with Microsoft DirectX 12., 14
enter the URL link provided, 15
entry point, 5
Equalize, 154
Erasement Refinement Tool, 123
Eraser Tool, 58, 119, 120
Erasing and Deleting States from The History panel, 29
examine the file types, 33
examine the file types supported by Adobe Element for saving files, 33
excellent appearance, 13
except for a basketball, 11
EXIF, 87
Expand All Keyword Tags, 79
expanding your images on the internet, 24
Expert Edit, 22, 62
Expert mode,, 9
Explore, 19, 88
explore some of the commands in the Help menu, 31
Exploring all the Preference Panes thoroughly, 66
Exploring the Attributes of Raw File Formats, 101
Exploring the background of a media file., 87
Exploring the History panel, 27
Exploring the Home Screen, 18
exploring the images in the photo, 58
EXPLORING THE PHOTO EDITOR, 48
export your images using the Organizer program, 5
Exporting Images with your Mobile Devices, 72
exposure, 9, 13, 63, 65, 103, 194, 196
extra space needed for downloading online content, 14
Eye Tool, 56
Eyedropper Tool, 40

F

Facebook, 11, 23, 24, 182

FaceBook, 24
Facebook Messenger, 11
facilitate the creation of slideshows, 7
falling overlays, 11
familiarize yourself with all of Photoshop Elements' many features and functionalities, 198
familiarized yourself with the minimal and recommended system requirements, 15
fascinating features, 19
faster download times, 37
favorable version, 13
Feather, 110, 118, 123
Feathering a Selection, 122
feature displays the color profile of the file., 52
Feature Set, 194
feature that radically alters the colors of the picture, 8
Features Buttons, 74
features like B&W color pop, 65
features that are found in both Lightroom and Photoshop., 3
Feel free to use the scroll arrows, 52
fewer options available, 7
fifty greatest photographs, 7
file and type the name in the Save As text box., 37
file extensions commonly used by professional camera brands, 101
file format, 32, 33, 34, 35, 39, 40, 71, 87
File Format, 32, 33, 39
file format efficiently reduces data, 33
File Format Options for Saving Files, 33
file in Windows Explorer, 23
File information, 92
File Name, 52, 88, 92, 99
files contain layers, 38
fill an area with a color value that matches the pixels you select., 59
filling option, 13
fills in empty regions, 13
Filter, 22, 48, 62, 128, 153, 154, 155, 156, 191
filter material based on persons, 6
Find the file you want on your hard drive, 23
Finding files that have been lost or disconnected, 190
finding in the Organizer, 20
fine-tune the tone and color balance, 56
fine-tune the tone and color balance of specific areas in a picture, 56

fine-tuning the color and enhancing the details of the image, 58
finish a specific project., 63
Firefox, 15
first image displays the actual image, 40
Fixed Ratio, 110
Fixed Size, 110, 118
fixing photographs, 21
flags, 14
Flickr, 1, 6, 23, 24, 187
focus, 7, 30, 31, 52, 125, 141, 157, 176
focusing on soft edges, 57
folders, 6, 68, 70, 74
following screen, 16, 17, 91, 190
footsteps of the AI and machine, 6
format in the File format section, 37
format under File Format, 38
Forum, 31
four different options available, 8
four primary modes, 6
frame creator, 65
frames, 8, 9, 11, 177, 178, 180, 181
Frames, 23, 62, 165, 179
Free Access to Adobe Stock, 2
free account, 24
Frequently Asked Questions, 193
fresh skies are added to the Perfect Landscape feature, 4
From Center, 118
Full Back up, 90
fundamental components of all digital images, 41
fundamental editing features, 4
fundamental editing tools, 198
further exploration and use of its capabilities, 198

G

Gain access to thousands of free Adobe Stock photos, 2
galleries without any coding knowledge, 24
Gaussian Blur, 157
General Preference, 66
generate a style that you can then fine-tune using hue, 3
generate an ICC profile stored on the computer, 46
generate films from your photos of an event, 4
generating a design over an image, 56
generative artificial intelligence, 3

Geometry Options, 118
get a comprehensive grasp of the possibilities of Auto Creation, 80
get a nice 3D effect, 11
Get Photo and Videos option, 68
Get Photos from drop-down list inside the Adobe Photo Downloader, 70
get the most out of your digital photographs, 198
Getting a Helping Hand, 30
Getting Familiar and Proficient with the Use of Color, 44
Getting Started, 18, 31
Getting Started with Image Editing, 18
Getting Very Familiar with the Photo Bin, 64
GIF, 9, 10, 11, 32, 34, 37, 40, 165, 182
GIF animation, 10
GIF format, 34
GIF or MP4 format, 9
Google + is an online platform for sharing photos, 24
Google Photos, 6
Gradient Map, 128, 154
Gradient Tool, 59
gradually included more sophisticated enhancements and capabilities, 4
graphic designers, 1, 194
Graphics, 2, 33, 34, 50, 62, 63, 74, 165, 179, 180
Graphics Interchange Format, 34
Graphics options, 62
grasp the concept of pixels, 41
gray display., 22
grayscale and 24-bit RGB color, 34
grayscale and 24-bit RGB color palettes, 34
Grayscale Images, 70
Grayscale images or grayscale graphics, 70
grayscale picture, 70
great deal of control, 13, 191
Grid Overlay, 135
group photographs, 8, 13
Guided, 2, 4, 21, 48, 65, 185, 194, 195
Guided and Advanced, 21
Guided Edits and Content, 4
Guided Edits are one of Elements' defining characteristics, 4
Guides & Grid Preferences, 67

H

Halftone, 71

Halftones are types of images, 71
Hand Tool, 22, 40, 49, 54, 124, 161
Hand tool in the Tools pane, 52
Hasselblad, 101
Hasselblad (.3FR),, 101
Having a firm foundation from which to begin researching, 198
Having Access to Additional Dialog Box Options, 172
Haze Reduction, 153
Head to Edit in the **Menu bar**, 26
Head to the **Edit menu**, 46, 66
Head to the Edit menu and choose **Color Settings**, 46
Head to the **Edit Menu** and choose **Revert**., 28
Head to the Enhance Menu and choose **Adjust Lighting**., 44
Head to the **File Menu**, 37
Head to the **Image Menu**, 42, 43
Head to the Image Menu and select **Resize**., 42
Head to **Windows** and choose **History** to open, 27
Healing Brush Tools, 22
Healing Brush Tools,, 22
Here is where you can view a preview of the output., 40
Hidden Files, 92
Hide Panel, 75
hiding photos, 63
high-end image modification, 7
high-end image modification features, 7
high-end mirrorless camera, 9
highlights, 63, 101, 103, 140, 150, 159
highly special kind of animation, 9
Histogram, 63, 103
histograms, 9
history of an image, 27
History panel to adjust your work, 27
home screen, 18, 50, 184
Home Screen, 18, 19, 20, 21, 25, 26, 50, 68, 75, 121
Home Screen feature, 50
Home Screen under Recent Files., 20
horizontal bar, 92
Horizontal Mask Type, 59
Hover the cursor over an image or a panel item., 52
how images look, 45
How much does it cost to get Photoshop Elements?, 3
how to calibrate a monitor, 45

How to Create a Color Map, 154
How to Create a Greeting Card, 175
How to Create a Photo Book, 180
How to Create a Photo Calendar, 174
How to Create a Photo Collage, 177
How to Create a Photo Reel, 181
How to Create a Quote Prints, 182
How to Create a Video Story, 184
How to Download and Install Adobe Photoshop Element 2024, 15
How to make a collage of photos, 177
How to Resample an Image, 43
How to Save a File, 34, 36, 37, 38
How to use the Color Curves command, 150

I

ICC Profile, 33
icon with horizontal lines., 62
iconic location, 13
ideal format for showcasing images, 33
Identify the image compression and resolution, 35
Identifying Contextual Menus, 52
ideographs, 71
Image analysis, 8
Image Attributes, 40
image being a maximum of 3MB, 24
Image Compression, 37
image corrections, 20
image determine its resolution and dimensions, 41
image editors, 1
image file has transparency, 35
Image Format, 40
Image Pyramid option in Adobe Element, 38
Image Requirements, 70
Image Requirements for Scanning, 70
image resolution, 41, 42
Image resolution plays a crucial role, 41
Image Resolution When Printed, 42
Image Size, 42, 43, 44, 186, 196
images in 8-bit color are compatible, 34
images with size limitations, 24
images with transparent backgrounds, 34
Imagine spending hours perfecting an image, 45
Immediate feedback, 174
immediately share the modified photos, 198
Import, 70, 74, 78, 79, 86, 185
Import panel, 70

Importing Images Through the Use of the Scanner, 71
improve the quality of photos, 13
improved features designed to enhance user experience, 1
improved image quality, 33
improved performance compared to previous versions, 2
In addition to sharing individual photo files online, 23
Inches, 41
include any color, 70
include noise reduction, 9
include the layout, 197
include Vertical Type, 59
includes Adobe's raw profiles, 9
includes options for Instagram, 11
includes Smart Looks, 8
includes various tools like Photo Bin, 23
including Asian characters, 67
including backdrops, 9
including instructions on how to trim, 198
including lighting, 7
including the Zoom Tool, 22
increasing compression, 33
Incremental Backup, 90
Info, 6, 63, 191
information about Elements, 31
Information about new features in the Photoshop Element application, 19
Information Box, 52
information you want to display, 52
initial state of the photo, 30
innovative styles for landscapes, 8
Input Device Profile, 47
insert the media card, 69
insert the media card from the camera, 69
inside the program, 198
inside the software, 198
inspirational ideas, 19
Instagram Stories, 4
Installation Options screen, 16
installing the application, 15
Instant Fix, 75
Intel 6th Generation processor, 14
Interface update with dark mode, 3
Interlaced, 37
International Color Consortium, 45
Internet connection, 14, 15

INTRODUCTION, 1
invitations, 24
Involves using the Undo and Redo options found in the Edit Menu., 28
IPTC data, 87
Is it possible to immediately share the modified photos that I have created using Adobe Photoshop Elements?, 198
it is also available as a subscription for $54.99 a year, 3
It is possible to preview the slideshow, 197

J

Joint Photographic Expert Group, 33
JPEG, 2, 4, 32, 33, 34, 35, 39, 40, 101, 155, 179
JPEG artifact removal, 4
JPEG is a compression method, 39
JPEG is the ideal format for showcasing images on websites., 33

K

keep your image collection effective and well-organized, 20
Keeping more states in your History panel, 30
Keeping up with the most recent features and functionalities in Photoshop Elements, 198
Key Concepts, 31
key items that will be showcased, 51
Keynote/Information, 75
keyword tags, 6, 79

L

large areas of uniform color., 39
large number of creative and visual effects, 9
larger audience, 198
larger file sizes,, 33
Lasso, 49, 54, 55, 61, 110, 111, 112, 115, 116, 122
Lasso Tool, 49, 54, 61, 111
Launching and navigating preferences in the photo editor, 66
Layers are crucial and stand out, 62
layer's panel, 62
Layout, 50, 181, 182
layout accommodates grayscale, 34

layout accommodates grayscale and RGB., 34
learning trend, 6
Lemple-Zif-Welch, 39
lens distortion correction, 9
lens profile corrections, 9
Let's delve into the new features driven by Adobe Sensei., 2
level of complexity as Photoshop, 7
levels, 9, 58, 65, 120, 125, 128, 134, 144, 154, 155, 196
light several excellent photographs, 7
lighting, 13, 63, 75, 137, 142, 143, 144, 145
Line Art, 70
list of some highlights, 3
list of the web pages, 24
list of the web pages for Photoshop Element, 24
locate the desired image in the library, 2
locate the Help menu, 30
locate the Photo Bin below the Element window, 63
Located at the right-hand side of the Home Screen is The Organizer, 20
Lock Transparent Pixels, 125
lomo camera effect, 65
longer compatible, 34
Looking for Untagged Items, 95
Lossless compression, 39
lossless compression algorithm, 39
lossless compression technique, 39
lossy and lossless., 39
lossy compression, 39
Lower Case Extension, 33
lowercase or uppercase for the file extension, 33
LUTs, 8
LZW, 39

M

Mac, 14, 15, 23, 74, 90, 181, 183, 184, 186, 195
macOS 12, 14
macOS 13, 14
Magic Wand Tool, 55
Magnetic, 55, 61, 111, 112
Magnetic Lasso Tool, 55, 61, 112
Magnificent Box, 52
main types of file compression, 39
majority of my findings involved human subjects, 7
Make a selection by right-clicking and choosing a command from the menu, 52

make a slideshow, 197
make any required edits by clicking the "**Preview**" button, 197
Make sure to choose **Yes** from the menu bar that appears to confirm the deletion., 29
Make sure to input the serial number, 17
Make sure to open the Photo Editor, 16, 23
Make sure to sign in again with your Adobe ID and password., 16
Make sure you have a valid Adobe ID., 15
Make sure you have the latest version of Internet Explorer, 15
make the experience even more enjoyable, 198
make use of the command., 26
making a creation from photos chosen in the Photo Bin., 50
making color corrections, 7
making the animation, 11
manually insert location tags, 6
Many apps use contextual menus for standard commands, 52
many different types of line art, 71
many of the same functions that are available in Photoshop, 3
mapping photographs, 71
master sharing photos with the Photo Editor, 25
Mastering Eraser Tools, 119
Mastering Selections Using the Lasso Tools, 110
Mastering the Art of Pixels, 41
Mastering the Cookie Cutter Tools, 118
Mastering the Editing Environment, 66
Mastering the Magic Wand, 112
Match color, 3
Match Color and Tone, 2
means to share a film with your friends, 11
measuring and adjusting the colors, 45
Median, 155
Memories, 93
memory settings, 67
Menu Bar, 48, 73
menu option, 11
menu with the Preset option, 40
Merge and Flatten, 127
Metadata such as pixel sizes, 87
method for compressing data for pixels in layers, 38
Microsoft Corporation, 34
Microsoft Windows, 14
Microsoft Windows 10, 14

210

Midtone, 63
Millimeters, 41
minimize chroma noise, 105
minimizes the file size, 9
Minimizing Noise in Camera Raw Images, 105
mobile and web versions, 7
mobile and web versions of Elements, 7
mobile app just cannot compete with, 8
Mode Toolbox, 56, 60
Monitor Profiles, 47
Monitors and inkjet printers excel, 47
more complex ones, 198
more expedient and straightforward manner, 198
More panels, 63
most impressive photographs, 7
most impressive photographs of cats or mountains, 7
most recent features and functionalities, 198
most significant panel, 62
mostly unchanged for more than a decade, 3
Motion Blur, 157, 159
move photos, 11
Move Tool, 22, 49, 54, 61, 179
movement options, 10
MOVING ALONG WITH THE ORGANIZER, 68
Moving Elements, 9, 164, 165
moving from the Organizer to the full Editor software, 7
Moving Overlay, 9, 165
Moving overlays, 11
Moving Overlays, 165
Moving Photos, 4, 9, 164
Moving Pictures, 9, 10
MP4 video clip, 10
MS Windows and OS/2., 34
multi-photo text using the Fun Edit., 65
multiple layers is RLE, 39
multiple panes, 66
multiple photographs, 62
My preference for Quick over Auto, 13

N

navigate the picture within the window, 52
Navigate to **File** and select **Backup Catalog.**, 90
navigate to **Preferences**, 61
Navigate to the "**Create**" tab, 197
navigate to your photos, 2
Navigator, 63

Nearest Neighbor, 43
need some assistance, 30
new backgrounds are added, 4
New Category, 79
NEW FEATURES, 2
New features have been added to both the mobile and online versions, 4
NEW FEATURES IN ADOBE PHOTOSHOP ELEMENTS 2024, 2
new image shown on the Image window, 64
New one-click adjustments, 4
new patterns are added to the Pattern Brush Guided Edit feature, 4
New Sub Category, 78
new textures or overlays, 62
new version is available, 67
newer version, 14
newly added Photo Reel tool, 9
Next, simply click on Ok., 35, 97
Nikon (.NEF),, 101
No Color Management, 46
No Restriction, 135
Noise Reduction slider, 105
None, 36, 37, 135
number of pixels, 41, 43, 152, 192
number of pixels increases, 43

O

Object Removal, 4
offer access to information about new features, 19
offering 1TB of photo, 24
offering automatic color adjustments, 62
official website, 15
Oldest, 86
Olympus (.ORF),, 101
one hundred finest photographs, 7
One of the closest competitors, 3
One of the latest additions to Adobe Photoshop Element, 2
One such tool for improving photographs, 13
One-click photo selection, 3
one-click skin smoothing, 4
OneDrive, 6
one-time price of $149.99, 3
one-time pricing of $79.99, 3
one-time pricing of CyberLink PhotoDirector, 3
online galleries, 198
online photo management, 24

online viewing on various websites, 24
open any of your photos, 2
Open Closed Eyes, 4, 159
Open dialog box, 23, 51
open Photoshop Elements, 197
open the History panel, 27
Open the **Photo Editor application**, 26
open your images, 3
Opening a Catalog, 88
opening and closing photos, 63
opening Photoshop Element, 32
Opening the Photo Editor, 21
opportunity to further restrict your decision, 10
opt for the Flip Row Order, 39
optimal image resampling, 43
optimal location, 42
optimal web file saving, 40
option available, 13
options include printing selected images, 50
Organize your photos efficiently with tools for tagging, 20
organizer., 33, 37, 69, 75, 76, 81, 160
Organizer's Places mode, 6
organizing the photographs, 68, 76, 85
ORGANIZING YOUR PICTURES, 73
ORGANIZING YOUR PICTURES WITH ORGANIZER, 73
original dimensions, 40
original picture, 12
originally photographed, 11
Orton effect, 65
other applications, 12
other motion pictures, 11
other platforms, 11, 24
outlining a rectangular area, 54
Output Device Profile, 47
Output To, 123
ovals, 14
overexposed, 63, 142, 150
Overlay Edge, 157
overrun any significant elements of a picture, 9

P

package with Premiere Elements, 3
page layouts, 34
paid account, 24
Paint Bucket Tool, 59
paint over elements in your image, 56
paint over objects., 56
paint specific sections of a photo with adjustments., 56
painting tool, 56
Panasonic, 101
Panasonic (.RW2)., 101
Panel Bin, 21, 23, 50
Panel Bin., 50
Panel Options, 125, 127
panel uses the hard drive as an extension of the RAM., 67
Panelists, 66
paper type and ink, 47
particular area within an image, 57
Pastel, 11
pattern objects, 4
Pattern Stamp Tool, 56
Pattern Tool, 59
PDF, 24, 34, 36, 177, 179, 181, 198
PDFs display, 34
PEF, 101
Pencil Tool, 60
Pentax, 101
Pentax (.PEF),, 101
People module, 6
Percentages, 41
perfect landscape, 65
Perfect Landscapes Guided Edit,, 4
perform all tasks via a single user, 6
perform all tasks via a single user interface, 6
Performance Preference, 67
personalized gifts, 24
person's face, 13
person's face using another photo, 13
Photo Bin, 49, 50, 63, 64, 65, 135, 174, 175, 178, 180, 181, 183
Photo Bin Options Menu, 50
Photo Bin Options Menu button, 50
photo cards,, 24
Photo Collages, 74
Photo Creation Format, 34
Photo editing tools, 20
Photo editing tools are provided for creating and modifying images, 20
Photo Editor, 17, 21, 22, 25, 26, 30, 48, 49, 50, 52, 66, 75, 182, 183
Photo Editor for sharing photos, 25
Photo Editor from the right-hand, 21
Photo Editor that provides fewer options, 22

Photo Reels, 3, 4, 11, 74
Photo Reels are a powerful feature included with Element 2024., 3
Photo Sharing Providers, 24
Photo Tabs, 50
Photobucket, 24
Photobucket is a user-friendly and robust platform, 24
PhotoDirector also can brush the effect on and off, 12
photographs and stitching, 13
photographs and videos, 7
photographs for display on the internet, 9
photographs of people hugging each other, 7
photographs' quality decreases with each resample, 43
Photomerge faces, 65
Photomerge Group Shot tool, 13
Photomerge group., 65
Photomerge Panorama tool, 13
Photoshop and Lightroom versions, 9
Photoshop Element 2024 includes a web and mobile app, 3
Photoshop Element Help, 31
Photoshop Element is linked to certain photo-sharing websites, 24
Photoshop Element Software, 14
Photoshop Elements is an excellent tool, 198
Photoshop Elements is an excellent tool that is suitable for both novice and seasoned photographers simultaneously, 198
Photoshop Elements is compatible with Adobe's Creative Cloud services, 198
Photoshop Elements' many features, 198
physical dimensions of your photographs, 63
Physical size, 42
Physical size is determined by multiplying resolution by pixel dimensions., 42
Picas, 41
pick Refine Edge, 9
Picture dimension is related to the width and height of the image, 41
Picture dimensions can be displayed in various units including Pixels, 41
Picture element, 41
picture resolution, 41
picture subject, 11
Pixar, 34
pixel density on the printed image, 42

Pixel Dimension, 42
Pixel dimensions, 42
Pixel dimensions are calculated, 42
Pixel Order, 37
Pixels are the fundamental components, 41
pixels or percentages., 40
Pixels/ins Pixel/cm, 135
Places part of the Search page informed, 6
platform designed for sharing an endless number of photos, 24
platform for reading the file, 37
platform simplifies the process of showcasing, 24
platforms like Email, 1
Plug-Ins are third-party programs, 67
Plugins Preference, 67
PNG, 32, 33, 36, 40, 70, 71
PNG (Portable Network Graphics), 33
PNG image, 34
Points, 41
polished and efficient image collection, 50
polygon, 59, 110
Polygonal, 55, 61, 111, 112
Polygonal Lasso Tool, 55, 61, 112
popular picture file format, 4
pop-up menu with access to additional panels, 63
Portable Network Graphics, 33
Portrait, 9
possibilities include looping, 11
Posterize, 128, 154
Post-Impressionist, 12
powerful and simple to use, 198
powerful design tool, 7
powerful feature, 3
PPI, 41
predefined forms, 14
Preferences, 33, 67, 72, 80, 102, 173, 186, 187
Preferences dialog box,, 33
Premiere Elements, 5, 184
Presenting One-Step Auto Fixes, 137
preserve all image data, 34
preserve all image data and layer information in a multi-page file, 34
Preserve features, 155
preserve fonts,, 34
Preserve multiresolution information, 38
Preset, 40, 119, 135, 137, 154, 159, 167, 168
press Enter on your keyboard, 18
Preview area, 40, 149
Preview font sizes, 67

213

Preview Menu, 40
Previews, 40
previous version, 16
previously known as Expert, 21
primary editing program, 5
primary picture editing, 4
Print a Picture Package, 183
Print a Picture Package or Contact Sheet using your local printer, 183
Printing Bin Files, 65
Printing Images, 41
prints, 1, 65, 179
Problems with saving files, 189
Proceed by clicking on **Continue** when the next screen appears., 16
proceed by selecting **Continue**, 16
proceed to Save., 32, 36, 37, 39
Proceed to the next page and select **Activate Now** on the Welcome screen., 16
proceed with the installation, 16
Process Version 2, 105
Process Version 4, 104
Process Version 5, 104
Process Version 6, 104
Process Versions in the Calibration Panel, 104
produce a new image using the Photomerge Edit feature, 65
producing high-quality images, 43
professional assistance with Photoshop, 30
proficiently edit photos, 41
Progressive from the Quality Menu., 35
Project parameters., 87
Protect Subject check box, 11
Provide the name and location of any related audio files., 87
Provide the original file's location and name., 87
providing satisfactory results., 43
Providing the dimensions in pixels for each image and video file., 87
providing users with continuous access to its features, 1
providing users with new tools and techniques to express their creativity, 198
PSD, 9, 34
put in the effort to practice, 198

Q

quality of the photographs, 7

Quality Settings, 40
Quick Actions, 2, 4, 7, 23
Quick mode, 7, 21, 53, 137
Quick mode lacks sufficient controls, 21
Quick or Advanced mode, 13
Quick Selection tool, 12, 113, 115, 117
Quick tab is selected by default, 21
quickly add color to old photos, 2
quickly find Help documents, 18
quite some time, 14
Quote Graphics., 2

R

Radial Blur, 157
RAM usage reaches, 52
range of functions in the preference panes, 66
range of tools, 21, 102
rating, 20, 68, 74, 81, 194
Ratings/Auto Curator, 74
raw importer, 9
Reasement Refinement Tool, 123
reason to pick it over full-fledged Photoshop, 4
Recent Files, 20
Recently Edited File, 172
recently introduced Firefly image-creation features in Photoshop, 3
Recompose Tool, 60
Recomposing images, 137
Rectangular Marquee Tool, 54
Red Eye Removal Tool, 22
Red, Green, and Blue, 44
Red-eye removal and cropping are features, 9
Reduce Color Noise, 155
Reduce Noise, 155
reduce the results., 6
Reducing compression, 33
Reducing Shake, 163
reels, 7, 11, 49
Reels could be beneficial, 11
Refers to the physical dimensions of the image when printed., 42
Refers to the width and height of the image., 42
Refine Edge, 13, 110, 113, 116, 122, 123, 167, 168
Refine Radius Tool, 123
Refining the Edges of a Selection, 122
refining the selection of what moves, 11
regions of a photograph, 13
regularly generated by the software, 19

Remember to access the contextual menu from the Menu bar., 53
removable flash, 14, 15
removable flash storage, 14, 15
Removal option, 153
remove an item from its background., 58
remove any stored data online, 67
remove image imperfections, 56
remove imperfections from an image, 56
remove the red-eye effect and pet-eye appearance,, 56
Removing an Image from an Album, 85
Removing Colors Cast Automatically, 142, 145
removing JPEG fragments, 2
removing sections or objects, 7
removing the background, 7, 136
Replace Background feature, 4
replicas of great painters, 8
Requires 8 GB of available hard-disk space, 14
Requires an Intel 6th Generation processor or newer, 14
Resampling involves adjusting the size of a file, 43
Resampling Techniques, 43
reset all account information., 67
Resetting a Dialog Box without Closing It, 171
resize images while preserving all their original features, 60
resolution, 37, 38, 41, 42, 43, 44, 70, 71, 87, 133, 135, 192, 193
Resolution is determined by the physical size and pixel dimensions., 42
Resolution Problems, 192
Resolution selection, 135
Resolving Lighting Issues, 142
Resolving Lighting Issues through Shadows and Highlights, 142
Restoring a Catalog, 91
Restoring your catalog, 191
restricted selection of visuals available, 11
reverse any action, 28
reverse chronological, 85
Reversing the Selection, 121
revert an image, 27
Reverting To a Previous State of an Image, 27
Reverting to the Last Save, 28
Revisiting Your Actions, 26
RGB or sRGB, 47
Right-click on the action and choose the **Delete option**., 29

RLE, 39
Rotate, 23, 50, 75, 133, 179
rotating photos, 63
rough edges, 57, 110, 123, 124
rounded rectangle,, 59
ruler units, 67
Run Length Encoding, 39

S

Safari and administrative rights for your account, 15
saturation, 3, 57, 103, 125, 128, 138, 146, 147, 148
Save and Export, 173
Save as command, 31
Save As dialog box, 23
Save Bin As An Album, 65
save bitmap digital images, 34
Save command, 31, 32
Save for Web, 9, 39, 40
Save Image Pyramid, 38
Save In Version Set with Original, 33
Save Keyword Tags to a File, 79
Save Transparency, 38
Save your work, 34
Saving and Loading Selection, 122
saving files in Adobe Photoshop Element, 33
saving files in different formats, 39
Saving Files References, 66
saving files,, 32, 66
saving option for Image Preview, 33
saving photos,, 32
Saving your Selections with your Photos, 169
scale factor, 14, 15
Scan or create an image at a high resolution to avoid resampling., 43
scanning line art, 71
Scratch Disks, 67
Scratch Sizes, 52
scroll bar, 52
Scroll Bars, 52
seamlessly pick up, 20
Search Bar, 73
search based on faces, 6
search for new services, 67
Search on Adobe Stock option, 9
Searching by All Stacks, 99
Searching by All Version Set, 99
Searching by History, 97

Searching by Metadata, 97
Searching by Using Visual Searches, 99
Searching for all missing files, 99
Searching for Captions and Notes, 96
Searching for Photos, 94
second panel, 9, 183
section of a program, 6
seek help from the Adobe community, 18
select a color from an image, 40
select **Activate Now**, 16
Select Background buttons, 13
select Basic, 2
select conventional aspect ratios, 8
Select function of the menu, 9
select **Get Photo and Videos**, 69
select **Open**., 51
select **Performance**, 29
select Photo Reel, 3
select **Save As**., 32, 34, 36, 37, 38
select Search on Adobe Stock, 2
Select Sky, 13
select the Custom Shape tool, 59
select the images you want to include., 197
select the Quick Action panel in the Quick Mode, 2
Select the state from the History Panel., 27
selecting a photograph, 11
selecting a specific area of the picture, 56
selecting a state, 30
selecting Add media, 19
selecting an area that may be animated based on logic, 10
selecting the background, 7
Selection Brush Tool, 55, 114, 116, 117
selection of 27 different sorts of overlay objects, 11
Selection Tool, 55, 115, 116
selection tools, 9, 13, 108, 194
Selection Tools, 22
Sensitivity, 153, 164
separate Adobe Camera Raw, 9
Setting up Adobe Photoshop Element 2024, 16
settings menu, 11
Several panel objects, 53
Several panel objects are currently missing the context menu., 53
Shadows, 142, 143, 159
Share button, 7, 26, 188
share files, 34
share photographs via email, 198

share your images on a wide variety of photo-sharing platforms., 24
SHARE YOUR PHOTOS AND VIDEOS, 186
Share your Photos via email, 186
Sharing a Photo, 23
sharing and hosting images, 24
sharing application is among the top choices worldwide, 24
sharing images that require a club membership fee, 24
sharing options, 5, 198
Sharing photo files with the organizer, 25
sharing photographs, 198
Sharing Photos, 25
Sharpening for Better Focus, 157
Sharper, 43
sharpness, 21, 57, 63, 105, 156, 157, 162, 164
shortcut bar, 48
shortcuts bar, 48
shorter term for "**pixel**.", 41
Show Grid, 65
showcasing a range of tools for creating and editing photos., 21
Showing Different Views of the Same Image, 63
Showing Recent Searches, 95
shrink the preview image., 40
Shutterfly, 24, 177, 180, 181
Shutterfly focuses on creating photo books, 24
side profiles, 6
Sign in with your Adobe ID., 16
significance of cataloging and tagging photographs, 198
significant number, 7, 12
significant number of tools, 7
significant way, 7
SIMPLE IMAGE MAKEOVER, 135
simple process, 7, 175, 191
simply click on the **View button**, 19
Simply type the keyword into the search bar, 18
six categories in the Guide Edit mode,, 65
sketching, 13
sky or a river, 10
SlicPic, 24
slide presentations, 5
slide presentations and collages, 5
Slide shows, 74
slider is used to adjust the degree of transparency of the overlay, 11
Slideshow, 24, 75, 93, 173, 197

slideshow settings, 197
slideshows, 18, 19, 24, 49, 197
slideshows tailored by the software, 18
Small animations and pictures, 34
Smart Blur, 157
Smart Brush Tool, 56, 167, 168
Smart Brushes, 13
Smart Looks tool, 8
Smart Tags can automatically recognize what is included inside a photograph, 6
smooth out rough edges or areas by eliminating some of the edges, 57
smooth skin, 4
Smoother, 43
Smoothing Skin, 162
smoothing the skin, 7
Smudge Tool, 57
SmugMug, 24
SmugMug is a photo-sharing website, 24
social media, 4, 24, 182, 198
software begins in a different window, 9
software has expanded to include a wider range of digital capabilities, 1
some common elements often found in the carousel, 19
some extra features, 33
Some functions in the Menu bar are unavailable, 22
some of the most notable features, 4
Sony, 101
Sony (.ARW, SRF),, 101
sophisticated choices, 9
sophisticated enhancements, 4
Sort By, 73, 85
sorting, 20, 50, 68, 85
Sorting Images, 68
Sorting Photos in an Album, 85
special effects, 13, 62
specific areas of an image, 57
specific RGB, 47
Specify whether you want Elements to add your photos, 178
Specify your column guide, 67
spectrometer, 45, 46
Sponge Tool, 57
Spot Healing Brush, 53, 56
stage of the production process, 62
Status Bar, 49
steps to access the color workplace settings, 46

steps to calibrate your monitor, 45
stock content, 3
stored files is available in the Document Sizes option., 52
storing digital photos, 33
Straighten, 22, 53, 61, 136
Straighten Tool, 22, 61
strange angles, 6
Strength, 117, 155
strength attributes, 12
Style Transfer Effects, 12
Styles, 44, 62
Styles tab, 62
subdivisions, 67
subject of the picture, 10
Subject Select, 4
subsequent states, 30
suggested crops, 8
Support, 31
swap out your background image., 2
Swatches panels, 63
Switching from one view to another, 92
synchronize your photographs and videos with Adobe's online storage service, 7
System Menu Button, 48
System requirements, 14

T

Tagged Image File Format, 33
Tagging the media file with keywords., 87
tailor your job experience, 66
take a page from Photoshop, 4
tapping the **Play arrow**, 10
Target Audience, 194
target size in pixels using the crop tool, 8
targeting casual photographers, 1
Task-execution commands, 48
tasks, 6, 7, 19, 41, 64, 66, 67, 169, 174, 195
temporarily deactivated firewalls, 15
temporary files, 14, 15
temporary files during installation, 14, 15
ten is the minimum, 7
Text on Custom Path, 59
Text on Shape,, 59
text overlays, 197
text overlays., 197
Text Tools, 22, 194
Textures, 23, 62

thanks to the new Guided Edits feature, 4
the "**Newest**" option, 86
the 2024 update provide new creative tools, 3
The 3D option is likely more stunning, 11
The Adobe Photoshop Element 2024, 23
The album contains the media file., 87
the Auto Creation menu, 19
the Auto Creations thumbnail, 19
The Auto Curate check box, 7
The Basic Panel, 103
The Black Edit and White Edit, 65
The Camera Calibration Panel, 104
The Carousel of Cards, 19
the case with Photoshop, 9
The changes to the media file, 87
the character-styling possibilities, 9
The Create Button, 49, 74
The creative Effect tool also allows you to create new creative styles, 4
The Detail Panel, 104
The Dialog Box Links, 31
the drop-down menu, 40, 46, 65, 67, 70, 71, 77, 78, 82, 83, 85, 179
The Edit Buttons, 48
The Edit Panel, 103
The Elements Organizer is equipped, 7
the Enhance menu, 11, 137, 148, 158, 159, 161, 162, 163, 164, 165, 192
the File format., 36
The Fun Edit, 65
The Help Menu, 30
the highest resolution available in the file, 38
The History panel in Photoshop Element, 29
The Home Screen features automatically generated photos, 18
The Home Screen will display the pertinent results, 18
the Home Screen., 18, 25, 26, 121
the image file, 35, 41
The image resolution dictates the size, 41
The image window, 51
the incredible Open Closed Eyes capabilities, 4
the limited visuals, 11
the main colors used in Element, 44
the main icons on the Home Screen, 18
the Match Color and Tone feature, 2
The media file contains images, 87
The Menu Bar, 48

The menu bar contains various commands such as File, 48
The name of the tool or command, 30
the new Color Match, 8
the new Dark mode enhances the user interface, 7
the next screen to access the Adobe Photoshop Editor Workspace., 16
the number icon, 19
The Open Bar, 48
the Panel Bin and the tools available, 21
the panel Bin on the right side of the workspace, 21
The Panels, 103
the Performance tab's History, 29
The Photo Editor, 20, 21
the Photo Editor offers features, 21
The Photomerge edit, 65
The Photomerge Edit, 65
the physical size and pixel, 42
The PNG image can display a transparent background, 34
the process of creating, 9
The process of sharing edited or curated photographs with family, 198
the production of picture collages and slideshows, 4
the PSD format, 9
The resolution of an image is determined by the number of pixels per inch, 41
the same level of flexibility, 14
The Save As Command, 32
The Save Command, 32
The Search Bar, 18
The Select Subject button, 9
The Share, 49, 74
The Special Edits, 65
The Start Window and Organizer App, 4
the three "Moving" tools, 9
The Tool Box/Panel, 49
The Tool Options bar provides a variety of shape tools such as rectangle, 59
The Tools panel, 21
the top of the workspace, 21
the topic of the photograph, 11
The upper part of the Home Screen features a carousel of cards, 19
The Video Editor, 20
The Views Tabs, 75

218

The workspace is structured into three editing modes, 21
third-party security software, 15
three primary colors, 104
Threshold, 128, 137, 154, 155
Thumbnail, 33
thumbnails and hyperlinks, 18
thumbnails in the Photo Bin, 63
TIFF, 33, 37, 107, 179
TikTok, 11, 182
Timeline, 92, 181, 184
Timing, 52
Tint, 8, 104
TIPS AND TRICKS ON PHOTOSHOP ELEMENTS, 169
Tool Options, 23, 49, 50, 59, 61, 109, 113, 115, 116, 117, 118, 121, 135, 137
Tool Options menu, 49, 61
toolbox in Expert mode, 53
Toolbox's Quick Edit mode, 22
Tools panel, 21, 108, 111, 112, 113, 115, 116, 118, 119, 135, 140
Tools within the Enhanced Group, 56
Tooltips, 31
top of the History panel, 30
transfer multiple open photographs, 63
transforms still images, 4
transitions, 11, 93, 197
transparency preferences, 67
Transparency Preferences, 67
transparent regions of layers in an image, 39
trial version available for thirty days, 3
Troubleshooting Elements 2024, 188
Try This, 19
tutorials for different features., 18
twisted edges, 13
twists, 14, 174
Twitter, 1, 23, 24, 182
Two applications on the Home Screen, 25
two options for exporting, 11
Two utilities are connected to the primary picture editing application, 4
Type Preferences, 67
Type Tool, 59
types of media, 6, 7, 92
types of sports balls available, 11

U

Uncompressed files, 34
uncompressed raster image format, 33
Unconstrained, 118
underexposed, 63, 142
understand how to share photos, 25
Understanding Image Dimension, 41
Understanding Resolution, 41
Understanding RGB, 44
Understanding the functions of a profile, 47
Undo/Redo, 50
unique text patterns, 3
Units and Ruler Preferences, 67
unlimited storage. In addition, 24
unnecessary duplicate, 9
Unsharp Mask, 157, 158
untagged documents, 47
Untagged documents, 47
Update to Current Process button, 105
upgrading from an earlier version, 3
upload capacity with no restrictions., 24
uploading your videos, 11, 188
Upon selecting the Help menu, 31
upsampling, 43
use Auto Curate, 7
use different font types, 67
Use gradients, 2
Use Lowercase Extension, 33
Use of Replace Color, 148
use of Scene Cleaner, 13
use of stock pictures from Adobe's stock, 4
use of the Organizer search bar,, 6
use the Save As Command, 32
Use the search bar at the top of the Home Screen, 18
use the search box to find relevant topics, 31
user interface has been updated, 3
user-friendly assistance, 1
Users can build PDF slideshows, 198
Users can create dynamic picture slideshows, 197
users have the opportunity to enhance their picture editing skills, 198
Users of Adobe Creative Cloud's online storage service, 4
users who are familiar with the usage of these tools, 198
users with new tools and techniques, 198
using a case-sensitive file system, 15

Using a Slide Show, 93
Using a Slide Show (Memories) to browse through PAt, 93
using Adobe Photoshop Elements, 87, 197, 198
using Adobe RGB, 47
using captions and annotations, 96
Using Color Curves to Make Corrections, 150
Using Hue and Saturation, 146
using one of the brush tools, 59
Using preference options, 66
Using Selection Borders for Cropping, 136
Using Stars to Rate Images, 81
Using Tags to Sort Images into Groups, 76
Using the application, 11
Using the Catalog, 89
Using the Element Downloader, 69
Using the Element Downloader to Download Images from a Camera, 69
using the imported media in the Elements, 19
using the layer panel, 62
Using the Marquee Tool, 110
Using the Panels, 62
Using the Scanner, 70
using the Search Bar facility, 73
Using the Search Icon, 94
using the shape or rectangle, 12
using the Slideshow function, 197
using the Special Edits feature, 65
using the Text tool, 9
Using the Toolbox, 53
using two or more photographs, 13
usual organizing tools, 5
utilities are the Home screen and the Organizer, 4
Utilize the Save As Web feature, 34
utilizing comparable colors, 9

V

value indicating the image's size, 42
variety of profiles, 47
Various image file formats, 39
Various image file formats are used for compressing picture data, 39
various layers, 62
Various options in the Tool Options section, 61
varying shades, 70
varying shades of black, 70
Verifying the program's suggested pictures, 7
versatile graphic editing software, 1

versatile tool, 23
versatile tool for sharing media files, 23
Version 1(2003, 105
version 13.4 or newer, 14
Version 3(2012, 104
Vertical Type Mask, 59
vertically, 2, 61
video collages., 19
video editing companion, 3
video editing tools, 20
Video Editor, 20
Video Files, 24
Video files can be uploaded, 24
Video files can be uploaded using Adobe Element, 24
Video Tutorials, 31
videographers, 1
videos, 4, 11, 18, 23, 24, 25, 31, 87, 90, 174, 184, 185, 187, 188
View, 19, 22, 23, 48, 53, 54, 63, 70, 73, 75, 92, 93, 117, 123, 169, 171, 172
view recently opened files, 18
view the image, 42
View Windows, 22
Viewing Additional Files in the Recently Edited List, 172
Viewing an Image in Two Windows, 169
VIEWING AND LOCATING YOUR IMAGES, 87
viewing file metadata, 63
viewing photos, 46
Vimeo, 1, 25, 173, 187
Vimeo is a video-sharing platform, 25
Vintage, 8, 11, 107
visual tales, 198
vital role in Photoshop Element, 21
Vivid, 9

W

wall art, 24
We also investigated the sharing options that are available in Photoshop Elements, 198
we discussed the procedures for organizing items in Photoshop Elements,, 198
we have covered a wide range of topics that are essential to the use of Photoshop Elements, 198
Web and Mobile Companion Apps, 3
web app enables you to design a slideshow, 3

web browser-based beta versions of the software., 3
Web File Saving, 39
web pages, 31, 34, 62
well-known software,, 1
wet paint-smearing brush, 57
What's New, 19
What's New in the Version?, 3
Whiten Teeth, 22, 53
whites, 63
whole photograph, 11
whole shot zooms, 10
wide range of options for enhancing,, 21
wide variety of professional use cases, 8
Width (W) and Height, 110, 135
Width and Height, 137
Window, 4, 14, 50, 51, 52, 63, 69, 101, 127, 128, 169, 172, 177
window displays historical statistics, 67
window is opened whenever a raw file, 9
Windows 11, 14
Windows 7, 14
Windows 8.1, 14
Windows 8.1 not supported, 14
Windows and Mac, 14, 195
Windows and macOS, 6
Windows or Mac system meets the requirements, 14
With 200 pixels in a 1-inch horizontal line, 41
with hints on how to make use of new editing tools, 5
Within the New Size Area, 40
wmv, 24
work with the imported media., 18
Working Intelligently with the Smart Brush Tools, 167
working on a creative project, 62
Working Space choices set, 47
working space profile, 47
Working Tips, 176
WORKING WITH LAYERS, 125
Working with the Levels, 144
Working with the Photo Bin, 63

Y

You can adjust four aspects of the picture, 42
You can adjust the image size in the Image Size dialog box, 42
You can also access Adobe Stock, 2
You can change a picture either manually or automatically to a selection, 14
you can easily crop a specific section of an image., 60
You can efficiently retrace your steps using the Undo and Redo commands., 26
you can expedite the installation process., 15
You can find drop shadows, 62
you can import, browse, and organize photographs, 20
You can make the sky bluer or darken, 13
You can navigate through the carousel by clicking the arrows on the right and left sides., 19
You can now add compelling text to photographs, 4
you can now get stock photographs, 9
you can remarkably showcase your top photos, 3
you can search for and make use of stock pictures from Adobe's stock service., 4
you can see all the auto-created projects, 19
you can use this tool to apply a fill or pattern to your picture., 59
You can wrap text around a form, 9
you create an account, 24
You have administrative privileges for the account you are using., 15
You have disabled pop-up blockers, 15
you have the option to add audio files as well., 24
you have the option to browse through images uploaded by other users, 24
you have the option to choose a layout from the available size options., 3
You have the option to share a maximum of 2GB, 24
you may either use a preset or one of your photos before beginning the process., 3
You possess a legitimate serial number, 15
you want to save the file and type in the name in the Save As text box., 35
you will be able to locate certain photographs within a vast collection, 198
you will find a variety of tool buttons, 9
you will find the main interface of the Photo Editor, 21
your artistic expression., 4
your image library., 2
your Photo Editor will open., 17
Your use of actions and features in Photoshop, 19

your web browser, 15, 31, 181
YouTube, 1, 4, 11, 25, 173, 182, 188
YouTube is a popular video-sharing platform, 25
YouTube Reels., 4

Z

ZIP, 39
ZIP is a lossless compression method, 39
Zoom Tool, 40, 49, 54, 124, 161

Made in the USA
Columbia, SC
27 August 2024